Spirituality and Alternativity in Contemporary Japan

Bloomsbury Advances in Religious Studies

Series Editors: Bettina E. Schmidt, Steven Sutcliffe and Will Sweetman

Founding Editors: James Cox and Peggy Morgan

Bloomsbury Advances in Religious Studies publishes cutting-edge research in the Study of Religion/s. The series draws on anthropological, ethnographical, historical, sociological and textual methods amongst others. Topics are diverse, but each publication integrates theoretical analysis with empirical data. The series aims to refresh the interdisciplinary agenda in new evidence-based studies of 'religion'.

A Phenomenology of Indigenous Religions
James L. Cox

A Sense of Belonging
Stephen Friend

American Evangelicals
Ashlee Quosigk

Appropriation of Native American Spirituality
Suzanne Owen

Becoming Buddhist
Glenys Eddy

Community and Worldview among Paraiyars of South India
Anderson H. M. Jeremiah

Conceptions of the Afterlife in Early Civilizations
Gregory Shushan

Contemporary Western Ethnography and the Definition of Religion
Martin D. Stringer

Cultural Blending in Korean Death Rites
Chang-Won Park

Free Zone Scientology
Aled Thomas

Globalization of Hesychasm and the Jesus Prayer
Christopher D. L. Johnson

Individualized Religion
Claire Wanless

Innateness of Myth
Ritske Rensma

Levinas, Messianism and Parody
Terence Holden

New Paradigm of Spirituality and Religion
Mary Catherine Burgess

Orthodox Christianity, New Age Spirituality and Vernacular Religion
Eugenia Roussou

Post-Materialist Religion
Mika T. Lassander

Redefining Shamanisms
David Gordon Wilson

Reform, Identity and Narratives of Belonging
Arkotong Longkumer

Religion and the Discourse on Modernity
Paul-François Tremlett

Religion as a Conversation Starter
Ina Merdjanova and Patrice Brodeur

Religion, Material Culture and Archaeology
Julian Droogan

Secular Assemblages
Marek Sullivan

Spirits and Trance in Brazil
Bettina E. Schmidt

Spirit Possession and Trance
Edited by Bettina E. Schmidt and Lucy Huskinson

Spiritual Tourism
Alex Norman

Theology and Religious Studies in Higher Education
Edited by D. L. Bird and Simon G. Smith

The Critical Study of Non-Religion
Christopher R. Cotter

The Dynamic Cosmos
Edited by Diana Espírito Santo and Matan Shapiro

The Problem with Interreligious Dialogue
Muthuraj Swamy

Religion and the Inculturation of Human Rights in Ghana
Abamfo Ofori Atiemo

Rethinking 'Classical Yoga' and Buddhism
Karen O'Brien Kop

UFOs, Conspiracy Theories and the New Age
David G. Robertson

Spirituality and Alternativity in Contemporary Japan

Beyond Religion?

Ioannis Gaitanidis

BLOOMSBURY ACADEMIC
LONDON • NEW YORK • OXFORD • NEW DELHI • SYDNEY

BLOOMSBURY ACADEMIC
Bloomsbury Publishing Plc
50 Bedford Square, London, WC1B 3DP, UK
1385 Broadway, New York, NY 10018, USA
29 Earlsfort Terrace, Dublin 2, Ireland

BLOOMSBURY, BLOOMSBURY ACADEMIC and the Diana logo are trademarks of Bloomsbury Publishing Plc

First published in Great Britain 2023
Paperback edition published 2024

Copyright © Ioannis Gaitanidis, 2023

Ioannis Gaitanidis has asserted his right under the Copyright, Designs and Patents Act, 1988, to be identified as Author of this work.

For legal purposes the Acknowledgements on pp. x–xii constitute an extension of this copyright page.

All rights reserved. No part of this publication may be reproduced or transmitted in any form or by any means, electronic or mechanical, including photocopying, recording, or any information storage or retrieval system, without prior permission in writing from the publishers.

Bloomsbury Publishing Plc does not have any control over, or responsibility for, any third-party websites referred to or in this book. All internet addresses given in this book were correct at the time of going to press. The author and publisher regret any inconvenience caused if addresses have changed or sites have ceased to exist, but can accept no responsibility for any such changes.

A catalogue record for this book is available from the British Library.

Library of Congress Control Number: 2022936797

ISBN: HB: 978-1-3502-6261-4
PB: 978-1-3502-6265-2
ePDF: 978-1-3502-6262-1
eBook: 978-1-3502-6263-8

Series: Bloomsbury Advances in Religious Studies

Typeset by Newgen KnowledgeWorks Pvt. Ltd., Chennai, India

To find out more about our authors and books visit www.bloomsbury.com and sign up for our newsletters

Contents

List of figures	viii
List of graphs	ix
Acknowledgements	x
Note on naming conventions	xiii
Introduction	1
1 Spiritual therapists	22
2 Spiritual academia	44
3 Print spirituality	73
4 Alternative therapies in the age of attention	106
5 Precarities in the spiritual business	132
6 Spirituality on trial	155
Conclusion: Spirituality and the 'alternative'	181
List of Japanese terms and names	191
Notes	197
References	214
Index	239

Figures

0.1	The cover of the Japanese edition of *Newsweek*, 16 May 2007, featuring a photo of Ehara Hiroyuki and the title *Supirichuaru and the Japanese*	9
1.1	Example of a disclaimer found on the website of a typical spiritual therapy salon	31
1.2	Ms Koyama's salon	34
3.1	*Asahi* newspaper article on the translation of Shirley MacLaine's book by the Yamakawas	101
4.1	A booth at the Iyashi Fair in 2012, selling healing crystals, power stones and other objects used in spiritual therapy sessions	109
4.2	*Therapy All Guide* catalogues	119
5.1	Ms Seiko treating a client with reiki	151
6.1	A typical illustration found on posters and websites warning against spiritual sales	175

Graphs

3.1 Number of NDL entries of book-length publications in NDC categories 147, 148 and 159 since 1945 — 82

4.1 Categories and number of therapies listed in the *Therapy All Guide* catalogue between 1999 and 2013 — 120

6.1 Number of entries corresponding to the keywords *reinō*, *uranai* and *supirichuaru* in the LEX/DB database — 171

Acknowledgements

I always thought that my first monograph would reflect the kind of books I like to read. An introduction that explains enough about the topic without giving everything away. A narrative that, instead of repeating my arguments at every corner, unfolds progressively through each chapter to reach momentum only in the conclusion. A book that keeps zooming in and out of various phenomena that have never previously been considered together on the same pages. I think that I have managed to achieve this with this book, and it is all thanks to my friend and copyeditor, Jane Caple. I am not exaggerating by saying that without Jane's careful reading and editing, this book might never have come out. I would also like to thank the three anonymous reviewers who steered me in the right direction from the start of this project, the editors of Bloomsbury Advances in Religious Studies who welcomed me into their series, and Lalle Pursglove and Lily McMahon for their support in producing this volume.

More than a decade has passed since I submitted my doctoral thesis at the University of Leeds under the supervision of Victor T. King and Mark B. Williams. The present text is an entirely different monster, but as I was writing it, I kept recalling some of the comments offered during those years to which I have now tried to respond. My discussion, for example, of the problem of using statistical data to 'measure' spirituality in Japan goes back to a session I had with Terry and Mark in December 2009. Other advice I received during those years from Michael J. G. Parnwell, Martin Seeger and Jane Caple (especially during weekly meetings at our local pub, the Victoria Hotel, sometimes in the warm company of the White Rose East Asia Centre's administrator, Jenni Rauch) only really made sense much later. Anyone who has read some of my earliest papers on the topic will realize that I used to be much less objectively critical of the subject than I am now. Retrospectively, I owe this to discussions that started back then and continued to play on my mind as I met and became inspired by the work of the following scholars: Erica Baffelli, who since our first meeting at the EAJS PhD Workshop in 2008 has been a friend, pillar of scholarly support and voice of reason; Ikegami Yoshimasa, who supervised my doctoral fieldwork in Japan and exemplified how one can be empathetic towards *and* critical of one's subjects; Mark Mullins, who showed me what scholarly rigorousness is about; Eguchi Shigeyuki and Shimoji Akitomo (and later Yoshida Naofumi) who initiated me into the world of cultural psychiatry and medical anthropology through numerous (delicious) dinners; and Yoshinaga Shin'ichi, who taught me what scholarly generosity means and opened the doors to the vast, complicated and global history of the therapies I was observing.

As I look back into my files, I realize that the first draft plan of this monograph dates back to 2012, when I was still trying to make ends meet while working several adjunct lectureships in the Tokyo metropolitan area. Needless to say, the book would have never seen the light of day if it were not for the financial stability and intellectual stimuli that I eventually found at Chiba University, where I have worked since 2013. After my graduation, I remember spending my last £500 to buy a ticket to join my current life partner in Tokyo, hoping that my language abilities would allow me to find a job, even if temporarily. Again, if it were not for Inoue Nobutaka and Hirafuji Kikuko at Kokugakuin University who sponsored my visa and allowed me to make a start in Japan, my plans would have failed. The two years I spent with them allowed me to immerse myself in the local academic culture and forge professional relationships with lasting impact. Tsukada Hotaka, who has remained a critical friend since then, deserves special mention, but also the rest of the team at the Centre for Education in Religious Culture: Murakami Aki (with whom I later wrote a paper), Takahashi Norihito (who later introduced me to the Japanese publisher of my first edited volume), Imai Nobuharu, Carl Freire, Amada Akinori and many others. Some of the research I undertook at that time in order to understand scholarly trends in religious studies in Japan, as well as the materials shared during contemporaneous discussions of the regular SPIEM (Spirituality Information Exchange Meeting) organized by Horie Norichika were critical to the framing of the arguments I make in the introduction and Chapter 2. Many thanks, therefore, to SPIEM regulars Koike Yasushi, Hashisako Mizuho, Takahashi Naoko and Kawanishi Eriko.

Despite their early origins, many of the core arguments of this book developed in a more concrete fashion thanks to my entrance into the circle of collaborators of Professor Yoshinaga Shin'ichi, whose vast and ever-expanding network of researchers working in modern metaphysical and alternative religion introduced me to a more complex view of what I had, until 2012, considered typically 'contemporary'. Many, like Justin Stein, Hirano Naoko, Hidehiko Kurita, Philp Deslippe, Orion Klautau and Avery Morrow have since become friends as we continue to cooperate through the East Asian Network for the Academic Study of Esotericism that Yoshinaga-sensei created in 2020. Key incentives for rearranging my arguments were also spurred by other colleagues with whom I have conversed over the years, including Jørn Borup, Aike P. Rots, Levi McLaughlin, Elisabetta Porcu, Jolyon B. Thomas, Christopher Harding, Fabio Rambelli and many others.

Much of the literature used in framing Chapters 1, 3 and 4 was acquired thanks to funds made available by Yoshinaga-sensei's projects (Japan Society for the Promotion of Science [JSPS] Grants-in-Aid 17K02244 and 20K00090). A considerable amount of my ethnographic data was gathered during my doctoral fieldwork. This was supported by a fourteen-month Japan Foundation fellowship, an ESRC postgraduate studentship and a University of Leeds Research Scholarship. Updates of that original data and further research into the 'ditching spirituality' phenomenon and the legal disputes which appear in Chapter 6 were made possible thanks to the JSPS Grant-in-Aid for Early-Career Scientists 18K12205. The same grant and the JSPS Grant-in-Aid for Scientific Research 22K00070 were used to fund the copyediting of the book. It goes without saying that without the cooperation of the therapists whose lives I discuss in this monograph, especially those with whom I have managed to keep in contact for more than ten years now, nothing could have really been written, no matter how much funding I had at my disposal.

Finally, this book is a Covid-19 'baby'. It came out of two six-month sabbaticals that I was granted by my employer, Chiba University, in the autumns of 2020 and 2021. During that same period, we also welcomed a real baby, our second son, Zenon, who we named after the founder of the Stoic school of philosophy. Both babies were miracles, although my family, who had to listen to my constant complaints about the slow progress of my manuscript in the midst of a global health crisis, probably hates the first as much as they love the second. This monograph is un-stoically dedicated to them.

Note on naming conventions

All Japanese names are given in the order of surname first, followed by forename(s), with a few exceptions where a scholar's primary language of publication is English and they have adopted the Anglophone naming convention of forename(s) first, followed by surname. These conventions are followed throughout the main text, notes and references section of this book.

Introduction

On a Sunday morning in late March 2008, I found myself riding a lift in a high-rise building in the business district of the popular touristic area of Asakusa, in eastern Tokyo. As soon as the elevator doors opened, I could hear loud voices from the other side of the floor, which seemed to be mostly composed of vast and empty conference rooms ready to be rented out for events. As I walked through the corridors following the voices, I passed in front of a hushed room fronted by a reception desk and two men in suits holding a list of names. A sign hinted that this was some kind of meeting of a scholarly association. As I passed by again at the end of the day, I thought how interesting it would be if religious studies researchers were to hold a meeting here, just a few doors away from the mind-body-spirit fair I had just visited. Located in the room at the very end of the floor, the fair was set out as a labyrinth of narrow passages running between rows of small, classroom-type desks, each showcasing a different kind of service. From hand-reading or tarot divination to 'energetic' massage treatments and machines that purported to be able to photograph human auras, the bulk of what was on offer was described using the adjective *supirichuaru* (spiritual). The people offering those services, mostly clad in colourful casual clothing, distributed business cards and invited visitors to have a look at their websites and book a session at their salons or to read their newly published books. They used different professional labels – *kaunserā* (counsellor), *serapisuto* (therapist), *hīrā* (healer) – and claimed to be offering short ten- to twenty-minute tasters of what could be more thoroughly experienced during a visit to their salons. Although these trial sessions cost no more than 3,000 yen (approximately US$26), it would be easy to spend 20,000 or 30,000 yen in a day given that there were more than eighty booths to pick from. 'Business is booming', a reiki massage therapist explained as she rubbed my left arm with aromatic oil.

That fair was the second day of the monthly Tokyo SUPICON, an abbreviation for 'spiritual convention', a mind-body-spirit fair that I had been told was the quintessential proof of the popularity of the spiritual in Japan. SUPICON's predecessor had been a showcasing fair organized by the New Age magazine *Fili* in 1996. From 2002, SUPICON started opening several times per year in Tokyo and increasing its locations on a nationwide level, with about 1,300 visitors each paying 1,500 yen to try out dozens of healing services and products (Isomura 2007: 58). In 2009, approximately 100,000 people visited SUPICON in its sixty locations across the country (Sakurai 2009a: 139). Another key indicator that spirituality was in vogue was the popularity of the television personality and self-proclaimed spiritual counsellor Ehara Hiroyuki. In addition to his prolific magazine columns and books, Ehara's flagship television program me, *Ora no izumi* (The Fountain of Aura), had become a weekly fixture by April 2005 and was attracting audience ratings of over 10 per cent, which was very high for its late-night timeslot (23:15 to 00:10) (Kayama 2006: 74). But Ehara was only the tip of the iceberg. At the time of my visit to the fair, nearly 1,000 websites of individuals offering spiritual services were listed on the web portal of Koizumi Yoshihito (d.2016), a tech entrepreneur and the first manager of SUPICON, who was a key actor in Japan's 'spiritual boom' in the first decade of this century. Even if it was only a fad, there were a lot of people who were engaged in this business of the spiritual.

 The scholars whose work I was reading – and who had launched a new academic subfield of '*supirichuariti* (spirituality) studies' – seemed convinced that this fascination with spirituality was a novel phenomenon, a contemporary alternative for religion. So too did the practitioners I was meeting, who I found through Koizumi's now deleted online listings; many had turned their lives around within the preceding few years, quitting their jobs to enter the spiritual business after having experienced spiritual therapies themselves. To a doctoral candidate looking for original research material, the subject asked for immediate scrutiny. However, it soon became apparent that my fieldwork had, in fact, caught the tail end of what both the media and scholars had dubbed the 'spiritual boom', a relatively short period between 2005 and 2009 when the interest in spirituality seems to have been at its peak. Things were happening so fast that by the time I submitted my thesis in September 2010, Ehara Hiroyuki had all but faded away from television screens, SUPICON had changed management *and* name to become SUPIMA or Spiritual Market (and would eventually be discontinued in 2018), and some of the therapists I had talked to had already disappeared. Six months later, the tragedy of the earthquake of 11 March 2011 seemed to have put a final stop to the spiritual boom, encouraging scholar-specialists of the phenomenon to announce its fragmentation into various sections of

Japanese sub-culture (Gaitanidis 2012a: 379). Had I been studying something so ephemeral that I would have to frame my future writing around its death rather than the significance of its novelty?

Scholars who had been writing about spirituality in Japan soon started differentiating between what had subsided and what had transformed into other things (e.g. Shimazono 2012). But looking at the end of or what came after spirituality would not tell us why people had thought that the popularity of the words *supirichuaru* and *supirichuariti* was an expression of something new and significant. What had encouraged scholars to talk of the 'rise of spirituality' (Shimazono 2007) and of a 'spiritual revolution' (Kashio 2010), and more specifically to consider it a form of religiosity arising from the contemporary search for an alternative for religion? Did the booth owners and visitors to SUPICON agree with this kind of prognosis or did they frame the alternativity of spirituality against another mainstream? What hopes and concerns led individuals to enter the spiritual business in the first decade of the twenty-first century – and then in some cases to leave?

It is these and related questions that this book explores, with two main objectives. As the first part of this introduction discusses, a major limitation of existing studies of spirituality – the representative form of alternative religiosity – is that 'religion' has to be placed in a separate realm before arguments can be developed regarding its contemporary 'forms'. This book sets out to reconnect spirituality in the Tokyo metropolitan area of the last forty years to key contexts in which it was made, namely the complementary and alternative therapy business, academia and the publishing industry. It does so in order to unfold how spirituality (and religion more generally) is co-constituted by other 'realms' or domains, in this case therapy and precarity. The second objective is to highlight the reasons why the most quintessential representatives of spirituality, the spiritual therapists, have espoused it, imagining in it an 'alternative' for themselves and others. What are the moral imperatives and associated responsibilities that have driven the practices of these therapists? Are they any different from those of the imagined 'non-spiritual' mainstream, or are spiritual therapists essentially acting within the same normative regimes?

Spirituality and the study of religion

In the religious studies literature, spirituality is constituted by its relation, complementary or alternative, to religion (Woodhead 2010: 38). As such, the term has been used as a means of estimating the size and value of religion. It has, for example, been employed to indicate what is not organizationally religious (Fuller 2001). In this context, spirituality has been either a gauge of secularization as the decline of institutional religion or a gauge of the metamorphosis of religion in a secular environment. From a second, recently more common perspective, spirituality, especially in its casual appearance, has been associated with qualitative descriptions attached to religious vocabulary, such as the notion of 'fuzzy fidelity' (Voas 2008). Here, the use of spirituality as a category not only underscores existing methodological problems of naming and quantifying religious identities, but it also works as a descriptor for the indescribable. De-traditionalized, de-institutionalized religion, detached from whatever we thought it had been anchored to, is now liquid, floating, implicit, generic or light.[1] The past seems at least relatively clear, while the present is unstable, blurry and relative.

To make this blurry novelty of phenomena contemporaneous to their time more legible, scholars often use one or more strategies to argue for a certain formativeness comparable to that of 'religion'. Replying to Matthew Wood's (2007) critique of the non-formativeness of the New Age movement, for example, Ann Taves and Michael Kinsella (2013) point to the existence of organizational forms, such as the Theosophical Movement or Alcoholics Anonymous, that are distinct from conventional religious institutions and that have had a significant impact on the global religious landscape. We find a similar use of formative-based arguments among sociologists of religion writing on the rise of spirituality in Japan. The first appearance of *reisei*, the Japanese translation of spirituality,[2] as a significant notion to describe contemporaneous religious change is in the work of Shimazono Susumu, the foremost scholar in this field.

In his early work Shimazono (1992: 23–50) distinguishes what he calls 'new spirituality movements' (*shin-reisei undō*) from two other developments in the post-1970s 'religious boom'. The first was the appearance of 'post-modern' new religious movements, which responded to feelings of emptiness and employed newly popularized psychological and person-centred techniques to preach self-development and benefits related to a holistically conceptualized universe. The second was 'the rise of a magico-religious popular culture', by which Shimazono was referring to a popular fascination with occult-themed media products (such as horror movies and televised performances by psychics such as Uri Geller). He positioned 'new spirituality movements' as a third alternative, something less organized than new religions, but expressing a more unified worldview than the popular *okaruto* (occult) cultural phenomenon (54).[3] In his later, more detailed studies of spirituality movements, Shimazono (1996, 2007) employed the category *seishin sekai* (lit: spiritual world), which came to be understood as the Japanese equivalent of the New Age, to foreground his argument for the existence of a 'wide range of individualistic spiritual quests developing in many parts of the world, especially in advanced industrial societies' (Shimazono 2004: 276).[4] As both *resei* and *seishin sekai*, Shimazono's spirituality remained constructed against established religions, which he called salvation religions, and echoed contemporaneous trends that saw holistic spirituality as the next step in the decline of the authority of religious institutions or as their replacement (Heelas and Woodhead 2005).

If the construction of spirituality through its relation to religion has called for arguments that prove how formative – how like religion – it is, it has also called for similar tools of measurement. American and British research, for example, has built its arguments regarding the rise of spirituality based on surveys in which people were asked if they were spiritual or religious (but often replied both; see Zinnbauer et al. 1997). Quantitative data on beliefs in ghosts or the afterlife have also been drawn upon to show that approximately three quarters of Americans are believers in the paranormal (Josephson Storm 2017: 23–33). Such statistical data, used to 'prove' the existence of a new category, are, however, difficult to interpret. What are we to make of the finding that at the end of the twentieth century, 59 per cent of the American population was found to be both 'religious' and 'spiritual' (Roof 2003: 146), other than to conclude that people do not make much of a distinction between those two terms? Statistical analysis often also assumes certain tendencies depending on whichever pre-determined category the analyst has put in place to develop their argument. Is, for example, belief in the paranormal a sign of being 'spiritual but not religious'?[5]

In Japan too, religious statistics are difficult to rely upon. Even introductory books on Japanese society, which deal with religion only in passing, include a note on the apparent contradiction between the high number of religious memberships, which have surpassed the total Japanese population since the government started collecting statistics in 1948 (Roemer 2009: 301), and the equally high number of people self-identifying as *mushūkyō* (lit. 'non-religious') (Sugimoto 2021: 265).[6] Through its nationwide surveys, the national newspaper *Yomiuri* found that the percentage of people who hold no faith (*nanika shūkyō o shinjite inai*) remained at around 71 per cent during the 1990s and the first decade of the 2000s (Kinoshita 2008). It should be noted that the Japanese public has been told they are *mushūkyō* since at least the 1950s.[7] The problems with trying to quantify religion or spirituality based on questions of belief are exemplified in the results of an NHK Broadcasting Culture Research Institute survey of religious behaviour and belief, which was held from 1973 to 2018 (Aramaki 2019: 28). Among the sample of 5,400 Japanese older than sixteen, the percentage of respondents who had *used* fortune-telling services rose a modest 5 per cent from 19.2 to 24.4 between 1973 and 2017, while the number of people who professed to *believe* in fortune telling had decreased from 6 to 4.6 per cent during the same period. There have been more targeted surveys of particular sectors of the population (Ishii 2008; Kokugakuin University and Inoue 2017), but these are usually short-term projects that do not contradict the general tendencies illustrated by more wide-ranging polls.

With regard to spirituality specifically, there has been one large-scale survey on the spiritual market in Japan, which relies on two different (hence not entirely comparable) online questionnaires, each administered during a single day in May and September 2008, respectively. The survey was conducted by a business consulting company associated with the Mitsubishi Financial Group, the owner of the largest bank in Japan. An analyst of the survey, Arimoto Yumiko (2011: 52–3), claims that the size of the spiritual market in Japan is equal to the size of the pet market, namely approximately a trillion yen. The only hard data that exists to back up this claim, however, are the estimated sizes of the online fortune-telling market (20 billion yen) and yoga market (160 billion yen). The rest is really unknown and probably varies significantly depending on what the adjective 'spiritual' is taken to include. Consider a question asked by *Yomiuri* in its 2008 nationwide survey of 3,000 adults (aged twenty years and above) (Kinoshita 2008: 25): 'The *supirichuaru*, which is the gaining of peace of mind by connecting oneself to invisible, spiritual (*rei-teki*) elements, such as one's past-life, guardian spirit(s) or aura(s), is recently attracting attention. Do you feel drawn to this or not?' The survey results seem to mirror older statistical findings on the proportion of self-professed 'non-religious': 75 per cent replied negatively, while 21 per cent said that they were drawn to the spiritual. Since the survey was conducted at the near peak of the so-called spiritual boom, we might have expected it to have shown the 'real' impact of the so-called new spirituality culture in Japan. It is entirely possible that people responded to the survey's explanation and examples of *supirichuaru* rather than to the adjective itself and whatever that meant to them personally. The same survey found that 26.1 per cent of its respondents claimed to believe in 'something religious' (*nanika shūkyō*); it is impossible to know whether these respondents include some or even all of the 21 per cent who professed an attraction to spirituality or whether the latter are 'spiritual but not religious'.

Some scholars have argued that Japan, like Western nations, has seen a steady post-war public withdrawal from engagement with the religious sphere (Reader 2012: 10), and that there is no evidence to consider *supirichuaru* as anything more than 'an *alternative* label' for religion used to overcome the decline of religion and stem the tide of secularization (31; emphasis mine). Helen Hardacre (2017: 519) also argues that, in broad statistical terms, Japan is similar to Western European nations, with only one area that seems exceptional: a low confidence in religious organizations, which may stem from the 1995 Aum incident, when members of Aum Shinrikyō perpetrated a sarin gas attack on the Tokyo subway. Horie Norichika, one of the foremost scholars still working on spirituality in Japan, seems to have implied early on in his work that the use of 'the spiritual' could therefore be interpreted as a tool of discursive secularization (Horie 2009–11). Discursive secularization is defined by Aike Rots (2017b: 190) as 'processes by which beliefs, practices, and institutions previously classified as "religion" are redefined and reconfigured (by many of the leading actors involved) as "culture", "tradition", "heritage", "science", or even "nature"; in sum, as non-religion'. However, as Rots argues, this does not necessarily imply any decline of faith in supernatural beings, ritual activities or places of worship – only the disentanglement of these activities from the category of religion.

In other words, the *supirichuaru* is not constructed against religion, but is an extraction out of religion of something that some people may not want to associate with 'religion' anymore. As such, the study of 'spirituality' in contemporary society, whether quantitative or qualitative, needs to be built on schematics that tell us *how* changes in religiosity/religiousness[8] relate to other changes in society. One scholar to have taken that direction, Fujiwara Satoko argues that what some scholars have associated with the rise of spirituality may only be one aspect of a much larger shift in human relationships in Japan, in which the youth seek to express the uneasiness of human relationships by consuming opportunities of over-connectedness with others (Fujiwara 2019: 143). Fujiwara's argument echoes Judith Butler's (2004) exploration of ontological precariousness and the vulnerability that stems from the social nature of human existence. More significantly for this book, it also points to how the discourse on spirituality has tended to construct a discursive bubble around the idea that this phenomenon is first and foremost 'religious' through definitions of spirituality that emphasize the non-empirical nature of the beliefs of its adherents.

Perhaps, as Courtney Bender observes, 'we might understand spirituality as religion that is produced in secular institutions' (Bender 2010: 19). But to this I would add that it is produced in secular institutions in which self and therapy are at the apex of human expression. Even the phrase 'spiritual but not religious' originates in how the cofounder of Alcoholics Anonymous described the group as early as 1940, based on a sense of 'spirituality that is at once deeply personal, optimistic, and progressivist and is couched in the essentially therapeutic language of self-actualization' (Fuller and Parsons 2018: 17). Studies of the therapy culture abound (see Nehring et al. 2020 for recent global perspectives) and have increasingly complicated – and often negated – the 'rational' and apolitical assumptions with which it has been associated (Aubry and Travis 2015). In a similar vein, my discussion of spiritual therapies shows how the actions of individuals associated with spirituality have been driven by moral imperatives no different to those shaping the lives and practices of their contemporaries beyond the so-called spirituality culture. But this still leaves us with the question of why people thought that *supirichuaru* was something new and different.

Media, precarity and the problem of looping effects

Given the difficulties of employing statistical surveys about beliefs to ascertain the existence of a new spirituality culture, the vast majority of the literature in Japan has relied on the visibility argument: mass media presence of and a booming market in the spiritual is employed as proof of its popularity and, moreover, its significance for understanding contemporary religiosity. The term *seishin sekai* (the spiritual world), which entered scholarly discourse through Shimazono Susumu's works and formed the stepping stone for his argument of the rise of 'spirituality', is a book category in the publishing market. It was used in the name of a fair of 'Books about India and Nepal's Spiritual World (*seishin sekai*)' held in the Shinjuku branch of the bookseller Kinokuniya in June 1978, after which many other book fairs used the same appellation (Shimazono 1996: 221–2; see also Chapter 3), establishing it as a category.[9] More recently, Ehara Hiroyuki, the television personality and self-proclaimed spiritual counsellor, has been a convenient point of reference to explain what the spiritual refers to in popular, twenty-first-century terms. In 2007 (later identified as the peak of the 'spiritual boom'), Isomura Kentarō's solidly researched journalistic account of spirituality in Japan talks of an Ehara 'phenomenon' (*genshō*) and locates the 7 million copies of Ehara's books within the contemporaneous therapy culture (Isomura 2007: 133). The abovementioned surveys often referred to Ehara Hiroyuki when they asked respondents about their beliefs in psychics appearing on television

(Figure 0.1). Moreover, Horie's earlier works were solely concerned with Ehara (Horie 2006, 2008, 2010).

Underpinning such visibility arguments is, I argue, an assumption or imagination of what can be called an invisible majority that exists under the surface of what is made visible through the media or popular culture. Authors who rely on mediatic or popular expressions to claim the rise of a new spirituality culture basically imagine that what was originally a blurry phenomenon arises out of a pool of relatively unknown, fringe or rejected ideas and spreads through society, creating a new religiosity or culture that is self-aware. A representative example is Wouter Hanegraaff's (1998: 17) argument that 'the New Age is synonymous with the cultic milieu having become conscious of itself as constituting a more or less unified "movement"'. Echoing Hanegraaff, Shimazono calls the *seishin sekai* 'a cultural space of people who, through their spiritual quests, gain comfort and are conscious that they are part of such new contemporary culture' (Shimazono 2000: 545). The problem, of course, is that the only evidence of this new

Figure 0.1 The cover of the Japanese edition of *Newsweek*, 16 May 2007, featuring a photo of Ehara Hiroyuki and the title *Supirichuaru and the Japanese*. Reproduced with permission.

phenomenon is its current popularized or mediatized form (which is often then criticized as somehow corrupted). Behind popularization and mediatization theories of spirituality, therefore, lurks an implicit assumption of the existence of an 'authentic', yet invisible and inaccessible source or essence (=spirituality) which rises to the surface. This is a point that I delve into in more detail in Chapter 2.

A larger issue associated with the visibility argument, however, is its lack of recognition, even effacement of the iterative relationship between media and scholarly discourse. How can spirituality simultaneously be both a media phenomenon and the concept that is employed to understand that phenomenon? This problem can be illustrated with reference to Horie's (2019b) influential thesis on *supirichuariti*. Based on a combined quantitative and thematic analysis of the *published* books that come up in the results when searching for *supirichuaru* and *supirichuariti* in Japan's National Diet Library catalogue, Horie claims that there are in fact two understandings of spirituality. His argument can be summarized as follows.

At the start of the twenty-first century, these concepts written in the katakana script (the Japanese syllabary for loanwords) were essentially scholarly terms. They had been adopted by transpersonal psychologists, hospice ('spiritual') care specialists and sociologists of religion who, in a post-Aum environment of general negativity towards religion (*shūkyō*), wished to talk about transcendental matters without referring to the compound *reisei*, which was the common Japanese translation of 'spirituality' (Horie 2019b: 27–30).[10] *Reisei* remained too close to 'religion', since the character *rei* is also found in *reikon* (spirit, soul) and *shinrei* (spirit of the dead). By then *rei* had also taken on ominous undertones through its use in the writings of Asahara Shōko, founder of Aum Shinrikyō. In addition, the use of katakana script 'gifted' *supirichuariti* with the image of a foreign concept employed by leading scholars in foreign countries.[11] However, the use of *supirichuaru* and *supirichuariti* as scholars had been employing them was never popularized, Horie continues. It was instead Ehara's *supirichuaru*, which Horie calls 'pop spirituality', that became the norm (31–5). While scholars do not specifically concern themselves with belief in spirits (*reishinkō*), Horie argues, Ehara's *supirichuariti* (a term that he started using in 2001) is premised on the existence of such belief, to which he added the novel approach of counselling and vocabulary borrowed from trauma-oriented psychology. Horie sees Ehara's blend of British spiritualism with Shinto theology as detraditionalizing popular beliefs in spirits and bringing them closer to contemporary psychological 'healing' (*iyashi*), enhanced by the narrative qualities of the mass media. Therein lay his success (35).

But how can *supirichuariti* come out of the field of psychology and yet have no influence on the psychological counselling techniques that Ehara employed several years later? How can Ehara's case be used to argue for the popularization of a second, non-scholarly understanding of spirituality when both academic and popular uses of the term belong to the very same context of general negativity towards religion and ensuing discursive secularization?

Such arguments, I argue, demonstrate a 'looping effect' between media and scholarly discourse. Ian Hacking's notion of 'looping effect' was most famously used to explain the development of the idea of multiple personality as a feedback process between the people who are known as multiples, how they are known and who knows about them:

> The doctors' vision was different because the patients were different; but the patients were different because the doctors' expectations were different. That is an example of a very general phenomenon: the looping effect of human kinds. People classified in a certain way tend to conform to or grow into the ways that they are described; but they also evolve in their own ways, so that the classifications and descriptions have to be constantly revised. (Hacking 1995: 21)

In the second half of this book, I borrow this concept to consider the looping effects that produced spirituality, questioning the idea that the scholarly vision of spirituality was somehow separate or distinct from 'popular' spirituality, and also the notion that spirituality is the distinct religiousness of a post-Aum era. To do this, I try to show the looping effects between, on the one hand, the conditions created by the therapy culture and precarious business environment within which spiritual therapists operate and, on the other, the spirituality of these therapists – a spirituality that scholars have so far evaluated as a response to those conditions. Sakurai Yoshihide has, for example, characteristically linked the growth of the spiritual business to the growing social disparities of the 'lost decades' of the Heisei era (1989–2019) (Itō, Kashio and Yumiyama 2004). During this period, economic stagnation has been associated with every single issue the country has faced, from the more 'obvious' demographic collapse and a diminished post-Cold War global role (Funabashi and Kushner 2015), to the immediate and tragic circumstances of homelessness and social collapse (Allison 2013) and increased public consciousness about such inequalities (Hommerich, Sudo and Kikkawa 2021).

I am not arguing that spirituality has answered (effectively or not) to the needs of a precarious public (Aupers and Houtman 2010), as do Sakurai and his peers. Nor am I saying that it has duped a precarious public into thinking that there is an alternative (Martin 2014). Rather than judging the value of spirituality, I am interested in taking a step back to consider how spirituality inspires such debates about its function. I see these debates as, essentially, discourses of alternativity. Whether it is imagined as an alternative expression for 'religion' and transcendental matters, as an alternative solution for the alleviation of social disparity or as an alternative means of therapy, spirituality has been instrumental in the construction of alternative imaginaries in both academia and in everyday life.

Contemporary usages of spirituality in academia share a lot with those of 'precarity'. Since the 1980s, both terms have attracted the interest of scholars who want to talk about phenomena considered quintessentially new, even if they are historically not (Quinlan 2012). They have also both been associated at times with what commentators originally saw as a potentially dangerous (because anomic and disorganized) class or social group. Similar to how sociologist Guy Standing (2011) has talked of the 'precariat' in pejorative terms, popular and scholarly critics of spirituality have tended to 'incriminate' the users of spiritual therapies in Japan as 'losers' (see Chapter 6). Over the last forty years, both concepts have developed from labels marking specific conditions, socio-economic for precarity and religious for spirituality, to signifiers of ontological experiences. While Judith Butler (2009) talks of precariousness as a common human vulnerability, spirituality studies scholars in Japan talk of spirituality as a new type of human-to-human connection, a civic ideal. As extrapolations from observations originally thought unique to their place and time, both concepts are therefore inevitably riven with hidden politics. Precarity idealizes a stability that, if not imaginary, is in some raw form the privilege of the very few. It is a third, alternative reality that promises the best of both worlds – a stable income *and* prospects for greater wealth – but is (for most of us) essentially impossible in the current capitalist system. This monograph aims to describe what this third reality is in the case of 'spirituality'.

Spirituality and alternativity

It is not difficult to see how spirituality fuels imaginaries of an 'alternative' for people who like neither religion nor science, for clients who do not care about their bodies or their minds in isolation but seek holistic care, and for the creators of books that neither inform nor entertain but instead offer opportunities for self-transformation. Taking a step back, the appearance of such triads simply means that we are in a constant act of comparison between things that we believe are different from one another. As Jonathan Z. Smith (1990: 51) has shown, such comparison 'is never dyadic but always triadic; there is always an implicit "more than", and there is always a "with respect to"'. It is not X that is compared to Y. Rather, X is compared to Y with respect to Z. According to Kocku von Stuckrad (2015: 19), 'thinking in triads, in which the third is not the synthesis of one of the opposites, is a red thread that runs through many disciplinary contexts, from philosophy to anthropology to sociology to the study of religion, and even to economy and law'.

The rise of 'spirituality' as a 'Z' hides the varying agendas – the interests, concerns, hopes and fears – behind the comparisons that have constituted it. The alternativity of spirituality meant different things for the various actors involved in its making. As I will unfold, while scholars looked for what they believed to be alternative ways that popular religion may withstand and even possibly solve national crises, publishers, editors and translators of the widely read spiritual literature considered it an alternative within the frame of self-development ideals. The spiritual therapists on whom this monograph focuses in large part, employed the 'spiritual' as an adjective to denote other kinds of alternatives often conceived in a purely therapeutic setting. In other words, the 'Z' of therapists who employ the adjective 'spiritual' to describe their work (Chapter 1) is different from the 'Z' of scholars (Chapter 2) and different again from the 'Z' of the publishing industry (Chapter 3).

At the same time, I argue that in its opening of alternatives, the 'Z' of spirituality also exhibits our precariousness. Research on precarity has recently concentrated on its relational character; 'it aims to capture the relationship between precarious labor and precarious life' (Millar 2017). But what does this mean for those who follow the alternative, third paths opened by spirituality? What does the search for, and the study and practice of, spirituality reveal about what we are really holding onto in life? If our concern with precarity demonstrates how much we value waged work (Weeks 2011), what is the valuable thing that our concern with spirituality conceals?

As this book shows, analysing the practice of 'spirituality' reveals its proximity if not sameness to the 'mainstream' from which it discursively seeks to distinguish itself. But stopping here provides no answers to the perennial question: 'Why do people still say it is new or different (=alternative)?' As I have described elsewhere (Gaitanidis and Rots 2021), it sometimes seems that in answering to this 'scholars consider people as only capable of lying', whether to themselves or to others. The question then is how we account for the 'apparent honesty and sincerity' with which individuals engage with 'alternative' religious practices, without either romanticizing them as 'seekers' or reducing them to villains or victims of the corporate system. This is fundamentally a question of agency. By way of answering to it, this book considers the moral imperatives that alternative imaginations rely upon, and which drive our ideas and actions. These imperatives complicate simplistic explanations in which the agent is conceived as only able to react to a certain set of conditions, either by being subdued or by being absorbed.

What, for example, are we to make of Ms Kayama, an angel therapist who I met in a central Tokyo park in June 2009? Sitting under a tree, I was about to start asking my usual questions when I heard a scream of joy. As I lifted my head from my notebook, I heard Ms Kayama exclaim: 'Can you see them? Those fairies under the tree. Can you see them? They are smiling at you!' Taken by surprise, I remained momentarily motionless, but soon managed to whisper while looking towards the tree: 'I am sorry Ms Kayama. I do not have your abilities, but I'm glad there are fairies to accompany our discussion.' We were in Shinjuku-gyoen, a beautiful park near Shinjuku station, and one of the very rare public green spaces that require an entrance fee. The location had been chosen by Ms Kayama, who had just opened her salon the previous year. As for many involved in the spiritual therapy business, she described her life as one that had been full of challenges: a very difficult childhood with problems of domestic violence, followed by a young adulthood occupied with business initiatives and travel abroad, which did not seem to fulfil her. When we met, she was recently divorced and sustaining herself and her young daughter on her savings until her business of oracle card readings and hypnotherapy sessions picked up to the level of a comfortable income. The spiritual boom may have subsequently subsided, but as of spring 2021 Ms Kayama was still going strong, her salon having just turned thirteen years old.

When one visits Shinjuku-gyoen, the way that most park visitors dress and talk, especially those who seem to be regulars, gives the impression of a certain financial security. Given the abundance of parks in Tokyo, there seems little reason to pay to enter such a place just for an hour-long interview. For someone in Ms Kayama's line of work, however, everything from clothing to location was important. Salons of the type that Ms Kayama runs rely heavily on a regular clientele to survive. But even today, her cheapest one-hour session costs 15,000 yen, roughly 4.5 per cent of the average monthly wage in Japan in 2020, which stood at 330,000 yen, although this varies significantly even within Tokyo.

Using Ms Kayama's thirteen-year-old business to argue for the rise of a new spirituality culture in Japan would require significant generalization. This book aims to do the opposite. It instead asks further questions. If spirituality arises out of precarity, what was Ms Kayama doing in that park? What does the presence of Ms Kayama tell us about contemporary religion in a city where only a non-precarious minority would be able to access her hypnotherapy sessions on a regular basis? It was obvious that Ms Kayama was neither just coping nor a victim of the 'system', but she was nevertheless in a precarious position. Where does spirituality fit into this?

Note on methodology

As Peter van der Veer (2014: 117) illustrates, 'spirituality' is a Euro-American, modern term, intimately related to the imperial expansion of Christianity, to the emergence of new varieties of religious experience in conjunction with that expansion ('at home' and 'abroad'), and to the ensuing development of the comparative study of religion in academia. A book like this, which has both 'spirituality' and 'Japan' in the title, risks reifying the problems present in explicit and implicit comparisons of Japan and the Other through the use of academic concepts falsely presumed neutral. Parallels can be found between the way New Agers have been 'accused' of an ethos bricolage (van Hove 1999: 166) and how 'Japanese non-religious religiousness' (Horie 2019b: 35–6) has been described. In both cases the moral superiority of a lifetime of dedicated faith to what is assumed to be a single religious tradition seems to be implicitly extolled. Classic examples include Ama Toshimaro's association of 'Japanese' non-religiousness with 'natural religion' (Ama 2004) and the expression *kurushii toki no kamidanomi* (one seeks out the deities in times of trouble), which has for decades played the role of a 'key' to understanding 'eclectic' Japanese religious behaviour (from Swyngedouw 1976 to Lewis 2017). Ama (2004: 8–9) argues that 'the majority of Japanese dislike revealed religion [e.g. Christianity, Buddhism], not because they are uncomfortable with the teachings themselves, but because they lack the courage to find true meaning in life through such religions'. In a seminal textbook on religion in Japan, Jan Swyngedouw (1993: 52) notes that 'the expression *kurushii toki no kamidanomi* ("turn to the gods in time of distress") is indeed a living reality in Japan. Present-day youths in particular are not ashamed to acknowledge their "use" of the divine for concrete, immediate problems'. Utilitarianism, nonchalant consumerism and individualism at the expense of the collective are characteristics that could thus be assigned to both New Agers and to the Japanese practice of religion.

Essentialist arguments about 'alternative' religion thus bear a cunning resemblance to essentialist arguments about 'Japanese' religion, both having perhaps been compared to the same standard. Within the academy in Japan, many of the arguments regarding Japan, from its spirituality to its ageing society, continue to be made in comparison with an increasingly blurry 'West'. The nation, in a world made of other nations, remains the ultimate scale of conceptualization from Shimazono Susumu's work, which started in the 1970s in the midst of Weberian debates about non-Western patterns of modernization, to Horie Norichika's (2013) more recent comparisons between spirituality in Japan, the United States and the UK. This monograph draws on data from a variety of Japanese language sources, including scholarly works, autobiographies, magazines and periodicals, websites and blogs, statistical surveys and court rulings, which can provide something of a 'national' picture of academia, the publishing industry, the media, the economy and the legal system as contexts within which spirituality in Japan has been made and experienced. But the nuances of my explorations into 'the spiritual' itself rest heavily on ethnographic research in Central-West Tokyo. In contrast to the abovementioned scholars, I do not claim that my findings are characteristic of a 'Japanese' religiosity or spirituality. I do not think that there is or has ever been such a thing.

In 2008 and 2009, I spent fourteen months interviewing and investigating the business activities of about sixty-eight practitioners of holistic-religious therapies who, at the time, identified themselves or were categorized on websites as *supirichuaru* ('spiritual'). I refer to them as 'spiritual therapists' to emphasize their strong association with the term 'spiritual', which lay at the core of how they attempted to explain their work to me at the time (Gaitanidis 2010, 2011, 2012a, 2012b), but I am aware that this appellation remains vague and is bound by the time during which our conversations occurred. Since this initial fieldwork, I have met some of these individuals again, as well as more than twenty-five other self-ascribed members of the spirituality culture. I have also interviewed other key players such as translators and book editors. My attempts to meet as many therapists as possible to grasp something of the larger picture has perhaps placed some limits on the depth of the relationships that I built with individuals. Many have stopped their businesses since I interviewed them, while some who I met through chance encounters I never managed to meet again. I can consider two or three as 'friends' (McLaughlin 2019: xi) who I have met regularly over the years. Their advice has been precious. I have always made my identity as a researcher known. To my knowledge, no one has ever doubted that my purpose has been anything other than purely academic. When I meet a new therapist,

I usually give them or point them towards my first publication (Gaitanidis 2010). This was published in a Japanese scholarly journal, is freely downloadable, and, although written in English, is headed by a summary in Japanese. Reflective research starts, I believe, at the start of an interview.

Structure of the book

This is a book composed of two parts. Chapters 1 to 3 describe the rise and fall of an interest in spirituality – the representative format of 'alternative religion' – as Japan became engulfed with therapeutic and welfare ideas at the turn of the twenty-first century. Here, I follow a historical constructionist approach to the study of religion, analysing the making of 'spirituality' in Japan against developments in three, often mutually informed, fields: the complementary and alternative therapy business (Chapter 1), academia (Chapter 2) and the publishing industry (Chapter 3). Taking inspiration from Russell T. McCutcheon (2016: 163), I examine spirituality not as the expression of some 'ineffable sentiment', but as the product 'of wider procedures and rules that we invented and which continually reinvent us … processes whereby we collectively manage what it is that we focus on and who we think ourselves to be, all within the otherwise hectic domain that is social life'. My analysis necessarily reflects the usual (but, of course, important) relativism that accompanies the placement of new fads inside longer processes of change. But beyond this I offer alternative, perhaps more accurate interpretations of spirituality and, most significantly, of the contexts in which the *supirichuaru* ought to be considered by homing in on the interests, concerns and hopes of some of the individuals involved in spirituality-making.

More specifically, Chapter 1 delves straight into the practices of spiritual therapists, but rather than presuming that the therapies they provide are first and foremost spiritual, I sketch out the therapeutic settings in which the term *supirichuaru* is used and explore what it *does*. By situating these practices within the twentieth century's long history of *minkan ryōhō* (lit. 'popular therapies'), I argue against the prevailing interpretation to show that the adjective 'spiritual' does not announce that these therapies are not religion; it actually distinguishes them from medicine. In the second part of the chapter, I explain how the strategic usage of this adjective in the early twenty-first century also sought to harness the increased popularity of counselling services in various domains of Japanese social life. Noting, however, the strong Rogerian pedigree of psychological counselling practice in Japan, which presented many affinities with what are today considered 'spiritual but not religious' beliefs, I suggest that counselling has not psychologized spirituality – it is what makes therapies spiritual.

Following the same argumentative thread, which does not take a particular understanding of 'spirituality' as given, Chapter 2 engages with scholarly debates within the field of the sociology of religion in Japan, and more specifically with discussions in the late 1990s and early 2000s among the first generation of researchers who later came to be associated with a new subfield, *supirichuariti kenyū* (spirituality studies). In a nutshell, I claim that these early engagements were a missed opportunity to go beyond an institutional or tradition-based idea of 'religion' by exploring the broader contexts and relational dynamics of what they identified as 'spiritual' and how the 'spiritual' connected to other concerns. Despite their own recognition of the need for a new, post-Aum study of contemporary religion, I show how many of those scholars assigned to the notion of spirituality a panacean function of religion-making, equating it with a timeless and dormant ability that people exert to fight the status quo. This meant that nothing had really changed from earlier post-Second World War academic engagements with the study of new religious groups through a *minshū shūkyō* (popular religion) approach. Scholars were still looking for positive salvific and therapeutic potential in contemporary religion.

Having examined how therapists employ the 'spiritual' and how scholars came to espouse 'spirituality' in their study of contemporary religion, Chapter 3 deals with the elephant in the room, namely the media, and more specifically the publishing industry. Books, magazines, television programmes, internet websites and SNS platforms often form the basis of scholarly arguments about an alleged 'rise of spirituality'. They also remain the main sources of information on the latest trends in the world of spiritual therapy and the fora for debates about what the spiritual is or should be. It is no coincidence that the 'spiritual boom' in the first decade of this century was often synonymous with the 'Ehara boom' and now, more than ever, digital media are playing a central role in the dissemination of 'the spiritual' and the advertisement of spiritual therapy salons. But while it is common for therapists to deploy (and consume) spiritual narratives across several forms of media, most of the spiritual therapists whom I interviewed had 'entered the spiritual' through the reading of books. Even if internet blogs and online forums were, at that time, already important tools for sustaining both their interest and their businesses, the narratives that circulated through these sites constantly referred to key texts published in book format. Even Ehara Hiroyuki was and continues to be first and foremost an author of magazine articles and books; his television and radio personality status are secondary. Chapter 3, therefore, analyses the role that the publishing industry played in the 'rise of spirituality' by discussing the role of translators, editors and publishers of *seishin sekai* literature at the end of the twentieth century.[12] Arguing that this literature can be situated within a longer history of Japanese self-cultivation (*shūyo*) books, I focus on how the structure of the book market in the late twentieth century may have facilitated the excessive concentration of certain publishers on what they considered to be the didactic and therapeutic potential of the biographies of successful personalities. I then shed light on the equally important role played by Akiko and Kōya Yamakawa, prolific translators of New Age literature who have, since the late 1980s, helped to configure alternative religious discourse in Japan around therapeutic messages of hope.

As critics of the constructionist approach have pointed out, phenomena like spirituality are not just processes of construction; regardless of their history, they have a real effect on the people they touch. It is important, therefore, to also investigate 'how those things themselves go out and do things in the world' (Fong 2014: 1131).[13] I take this up in the second half of the book, where I examine what the *supirichuaru* does by telling the stories of specific individuals in conjunction with materials that seem to have informed their lives and actions. I explore the developments in the understanding of healthcare that the spiritual highlights (Chapter 4), the aspects of social precarity that it conceals (Chapter 5) and how it illustrates larger ethical concerns in daily capitalist endeavours (Chapter 6). I do not make any psychological arguments. I show how these individuals' actions were in dialogue with larger developments with the purpose of contextualizing their lives, rather than explaining them out through an artificially pre-determined 'spiritual'. My argument, in a nutshell, is that the aspirational character of the concept of spirituality has fuelled an alternative imaginary populated by the hopes, interests and concerns of a precarious public.

More specifically, Chapter 4 illustrates the various types of spiritual therapy and shows how their association with an alleged healthist boom in late-twentieth-century Japan was more of a marketing strategy than a reflection of a wish for therapeutic experiences that were alternative to the biomedical model. In fact, the spiritual therapists I interviewed shared the same 'mainstream' biomedical narratives of depression and other contemporaneous social malaises, enhanced by an increased focus on our ability to pay attention to ourselves among mental health professionals *and* spiritual therapists. Taking 'hypnotherapy' as an example, I show that self-attention was understood in spiritual therapy salons just as it was in other therapeutic settings: as an expression of freedom, a therapeutic means and a harbour of valuable secrets. For some individuals, these 'new' secrets were experienced as a new professional skill that could be monetized through the establishment of a spiritual therapy salon.

By entering the spiritual business, however, therapists faced the precarities that are ubiquitous in the service industry, as well as issues more specific to the nature of their work. Chapter 5 employs the cases of several salons opened in the first decade of the twenty-first century to illustrate how, as small companies, they remained at the mercy of the economy and struggled to appeal to their clientele while also abiding by the professional ethics required of all welfare professionals. Spiritual therapists, the majority of whom are women, also fell victim to the gendered economy of spirituality. Although many had sought this profession to escape discrimination, they found themselves dealing with and reproducing gender assumptions that linked 'femininity' with therapeutic work and client issues with 'women's life cycles'. If spiritual therapy presented itself as a coping mechanism for working and living within the neoliberal capitalist system, it also reflected some of the neoliberal ideals that therapists had been trying to escape from.

This connection to capitalism is even more apparent when we turn to consider situations in which the spiritual business has come under criticism and been subject to legal scrutiny. Chapter 6 addresses the rhetoric of disillusionment expressed by former clients and spiritual therapists who, in the 2010s, employed the hashtag *datsu-supi* ('ditching the spiritual') to launch online attacks on what they considered predatory marketing practices and exorbitant prices. It couples its discussion of this phenomenon with an analysis of court proceedings related to the category of 'spiritual sales' (*reikan shōhō*) to argue that spirituality, therapy and the market are engaged in a constant battle to attribute a material and moral value to our fictitious selves. Spirituality ditchers and spiritual sales lawyers seem to espouse the ideals of sincerity and integrity often associated with consumer protection laws, all the while hoping that a 'good' spirituality will continue to help us find our 'true' selves.

Like scholars who debate the consumerization or marketization of spirituality, critics of spiritual business imagine religion and the economy as distinct fields of activity, but the values they espouse in their complaints demonstrate the exact opposite. In the conclusion, I explain this apparent contradiction, as well as the other discourses espoused by therapists, publishers, translators and scholars of spirituality, by returning to the concept of alternativity. I argue that therapists, scholars, and publishing professionals and translators all imagine religion and its alternative (=spirituality) to have a 'therapeutic' function, but the way they understand the alternativity of 'spirituality' is distinct. Yet, they all exist in a common epistemic field, explained and explainable by the existence of its homonymous media 'boom' and what came to be considered the new spiritual needs and wants of the (Japanese) people. By means of this looping effect, the rider of alternativity seems to acquire value by erasing the concerns, hopes and interests that originally connected the alternative to its context and building a new cross-contextual frame.

If the first half of the book is full of 'spirituality' and tries to untangle how its alternativity is imagined by different actors, the second half is full of everything else that supported its alleged rise, from healthcare concerns and economic precarities to neoliberal ideals.

1

Spiritual therapists

Mr Suzuki, a casually dressed middle-aged man, lit one cigarette after another as he sat across the table from me in a lavish coffee shop five minutes on foot from Shinjuku station in central Tokyo. His business card read *supirichuaru adobaizaa* (spiritual advisor) written in katakana, the Japanese syllabary employed for loan words. I had already guessed that Mr Suzuki had not been doing this work on a regular basis, since his email address, provided by the wife of a friend, was from a generic rather than custom domain. Unlike the dozens of therapists I would subsequently meet, Mr Suzuki had no presence on the internet. I had been told, however, that he was the 'real thing'. After two months and a couple of suddenly cancelled appointments, here I was, early in the afternoon on an autumn day, talking to Mr Suzuki about his counselling business and, unavoidably, receiving his advice about my future professional life and wedding prospects. Over the next hour, Mr Suzuki occasionally passed his hand over my name (which he had asked me to write on the back of his business card) and had visions of the three ancestor-guardian spirits floating above my head, of my past life as a primary school teacher and of my future career in Japanese academia. He would make some right and wrong guesses about my personal life based on the writing of my name. He would also give me some general advice on how to lead a healthy life, prompted by a look at my face and what he called my 'Western' body posture, and encourage me to visit the graves of my grandparents to show gratitude. When the time was up, I handed Mr Suzuki the fee of 5,000 yen and parted with him at the exit of the building.

Like the majority of the sixty-eight therapists whom I interviewed in 2008 and 2009, Mr Suzuki was very aware of the fashionable character of the adjective 'spiritual'. The name Ehara Hiroyuki was at the tip of the lips of those who, by the end of the first decade of this century, had adopted this adjective to describe their services and attract clients. In return, by their very existence, these counsellors, healers, masseurs and other therapists seemed to mirror the popularity of

Ehara and were, as a consequence, treated as the representatives of the so-called spiritual boom. But, as I argue in this chapter, they only represented one small portion of a larger market of services centred around the experience of 'healing' (*iyashi*). Scholars had already identified the growing *iyashi* market in the 1990s (Haga and Yumiyama 1994). As early as 2006, Hirano Naoko (2006) was suggesting that the popularity of the term *supirichuaru* had simply been a fad of the past three years, in which Ehara Hiroyuki was only the most visible factor. But as I examine in the second part of this book, *supirichuaru* and *supirichuariti* are employed as words with certain meanings and effects on people's actions. As such, neither they nor their use by practitioners like Mr Suzuki can simply be dismissed as a passing fad.

In 2008, when I first met Mr Suzuki, his main source of income was the salary he received as a mobile phone salesman. New clients heard about his services through word of mouth. I later realized that the apparent secrecy of Mr Suzuki's side business was not necessarily purposeful. Many of the spiritual therapists who I met had started off like Mr Suzuki by trying out their craft with friends and a wider circle of acquaintances who, if satisfied with their sessions, would introduce the therapist to third parties. Some gained enough confidence to quit their jobs and open a salon (Gaitanidis 2011, 2012b), while others preferred to keep their practice to themselves and their circle of friends. As I argue elsewhere (Gaitanidis 2010), the circumstances under which individuals chose to consider spiritual therapy as a livelihood, even temporarily, reflected a certain generational gap. The older the therapists were when they became interested in this profession, the quicker they seemed to be in deciding to open a salon. This suggests that there were factors other than the temporary popularity of the word *supirichuaru* in spiritual therapy becoming a 'legitimate' business.

As I discuss in the first section of this chapter, if we take Ehara Hiroyuki's counselling and his version of the *supirichuaru* as the model for what contemporaries looked for in the services of spiritual therapists, it is easy to read 'spirituality' as representative of a new, detraditionalized and psychologized post-Aum religious landscape. However, I argue that this tells us more about how figures such as Ehara have constructed the spirituality discourse than about why and how they have espoused that term. As we shall see, using spirituality as a descriptor for their services has for many therapists been more of a business strategy than the adoption or acceptance of an authoritative framework. Rather than turning to the narratives of spiritual therapists like Mr Suzuki to try to describe or define what spirituality *is*, I therefore sketch out the therapeutic setting in which this term is used to explore what it *does*. What kind of shared understanding does the use of the term *supirichuaru* achieve for a therapist and a client meeting for a spiritual therapy session in twenty-first-century Tokyo? What work does it do? I approach these questions first from a historical perspective, contextualizing therapists' contemporary use of the spiritual in the history of *minkan ryōhō* (lit. 'popular therapies') before *supirichuaru* entered Japanese vocabulary. Viewed from this angle, we find that the spiritual in the spiritual therapeutic setting is not *not religion*; it is *not medicine*. I then delineate spiritual therapists' usage of spirituality during and after the Ehara boom, within what we must assume is a broader field of alternative and complementary therapies, highlighting its constant need for qualification. I argue that, far from 'sacralizing the self', spiritual therapists make careful use of the spiritual in their daily practice in an attempt to achieve the shared understanding that they are, first and foremost, *therapists*.

Ehara's shadow: The -ization of spiritual narratives

Ehara Hiroyuki's 'spiritual counselling' seemed to confirm at least two scholarly assumptions about religious change in contemporary societies. The first is that religion becomes detraditionalized, with a subsequent spiritual turn to the self, as identified by scholars discussing 'post-Christian spirituality' (Houtman and Aupers 2007). By the time I started my fieldwork, Ben Dorman (2007) had already noted how the fortune teller Hosoki Kazuko framed her ancestor worship-based advice as 'non-religious' in order to appeal to a post-Aum population suspicious of organized religion. The second assumption that Ehara seemed to confirm concerned the psychologization of religion, since he appeared to employ familiar psychotherapeutic techniques, such as building a rapport, relating issues to past traumas, reframing the client's perspectives by pointing out the good aspects of their life and empowering clients through words of encouragement and references to the protection of guardian spirits (Horie 2006: 245). The same could be said about the activities of the majority of spiritual therapists I met during my fieldwork (Gaitanidis 2012a: 376). However, as McLaughlin et al. (2020) argue, both the 'detraditionalization' and 'psychologization' of religion theses reduce 'religion' to its *-ization*s. If religion has been decoupled from 'tradition' and absorbed into therapy culture, so what? What does this mean in practice and, more importantly, what does this perspective conceal?

Established argumentative lenses help to connect a subject to what the reader *already* knows. Arguments regarding the detraditionalization of religion, for example, can be thought of as attempts to make sense of the so-called superficiality that representatives of the 'new' spirituality culture have been accused of by scholars.[1] This idea of superficiality stems from the common, double assumption that 'authentic' practices should be traceable to a unique and identifiable lineage *and* that 'cross-pollinations' ought to occur over (preferably) long periods of time and be authorized by 'legitimate' members of each lineage. Mr Suzuki does not seem to be (or to be claiming to be) part of any kind of lineage. His combination of techniques to diagnose me did not seem to follow a specific pattern, although they undoubtedly followed an order that he deemed appropriate at that moment. Using a detraditionalization lens to analyse Mr Suzuki's practice would require breaking up his counselling techniques into fragments and tracing them (probably intuitively and with no concrete proof) to a religious lineage deemed traditional.

This kind of approach has led scholars of New Religious Movements, of the New Age and even more generally of the privatization or individualization of religion to describe what looks like a selective combination, amalgamation or collage of scientific, religious and popular beliefs and practices. This 'bricolage' is then often positioned in implicit contrast to the assumed uniformity and rigidness of established traditions (Roof 1999). But, as Véronique Altglas (2014a) demonstrates in her study of yoga and Kabbalah centres in Europe, the concept of bricolage 'fails to understand the social significance of individualism and overlooks the ways in which, in contemporary society, social norms and power may be expressed through culture' (475). In other words, tracing the lineage of Mr Suzuki's techniques would not tell us anything about why Mr Suzuki performed his counselling with me in the way that he did on that day, nor about his knowledge regarding the techniques that he used.

The same can be said about use of the psychologization framework. Most studies of contemporary spirituality have pointed to 'the sacralization of the self' in explaining the emergence of spiritual practices (Heelas 1996). Much of this research is based on the analysis of biographical or hagiographical accounts. As Courtney Bender (2010: 65) has shown in her study of mystics in Cambridge, Massachusetts, the way that these narratives tend to be built means that they say very little about long-standing social ties or about the communities and 'cultures' that have bolstered and shaped spiritual experiences. This helps to explain why most scholarly definitions of 'spirituality' refer to individualistic ideologies that relate to a sense of connection to a transcendental power, coupled with varying degrees of counter-cultural tendencies (see Chapter 2). In other words, when mystical accounts are taken at face value as a means of convincing the listener of their verity and authenticity, they all sound the same, creating the illusion of a uniform phenomenon. They also project the narrator as the sole protagonist of a transformative experience that simply and directly explains *out* their present self.

Arguments about detraditionalization and psychologization perhaps tell us more about how spiritual therapists such as Ehara Hiroyuki *build* their narratives than what these narratives reflect. As anthropologist Tanya Luhrmann (1989: 312) notes in her study of magicians in 1980s England, individuals change their ways, language and performance to fit a certain religious frame by experiencing an interpretive drift. Their manners shift slowly as they become more and more involved and encouraged in pursuing a certain activity. In Mr Suzuki's case, his grandmother encouraged his sightings of supernatural beings when he was a child. This might have contributed to the legitimization of his abilities. In many other cases, practitioners were drawn in by individuals who already practiced some type of spiritual therapy, or were encouraged by friends and colleagues who were impressed by their ability to explain how an other-worldly experience could lead to all sorts of individual benefits. Returning to Bender's (2010) argument: 'Mystical texts do not (always) hark back to a claim to an original meaning ready to be interpreted and reiterated but rather build on practices in which meaning irrupts in the moment of retelling, thus capturing speaker and listener, text and interpretation, experiencer and divine in a new moment filled with transformative power' (89). In the remainder of this chapter, I take a similar approach to exploring the meaning of *supirichuaru*, taking therapists' words as texts that are constantly open to interpretation and reiteration.

The discursive use of *supirichuaru* in historical context

In the early stages of my fieldwork, I heard through a friend of a friend about a woman based in the outskirts of a small town in Chiba prefecture (east of Tokyo), who was locally known for her 'spiritual powers' (*reinōryoku*). After arranging an appointment by phone, I reached an old farmhouse with a large garden designed to resemble the compound of a Shinto shrine, with a narrow path going through a small *torii* (gate) and across a couple of ponds before reaching what looked like the back of the house. There, I was greeted by an older woman, clad in the white upper garment worn throughout Japan by people engaged in activities endowed with religious meaning, such as ascetic training, mountain climbing and pilgrimage. I was told that Ms Minami would see me soon. As I handed the woman a small box of edible snacks which custom requires on such visits, I slipped in an envelope containing 5,000 yen. My contact had previously informed me that this sum was the token of appreciation expected by every client of Ms Minami.

Sitting behind a table, Ms Minami, also dressed in white, greeted me in a lively fashion and asked for a cup of tea to be served. After I had explained the purpose of my visit, Ms Minami inquired whether I knew where the graves of my ancestors were located and if I was regularly paying a visit to them to show gratitude. The conversation then veered into the importance of hard work, humility and family relations. As a few more visits allowed me to learn, Ms Minami remained constantly aware of her family's legacy within a local community of followers who had formed a semi-official group around her, called Tenmyōdō Shinkyōkai. She explained that her parents had both offered the same services for more than fifty years, and that it was her father who had founded this community in 1978. When I accompanied Ms Minami and her group for their official New Year's visit to the Yasukuni shrine a few months later, it became clear that this community of mostly old clients, who felt that the Minamis had helped them with a variety of issues from financial bankruptcies to domestic violence, possessed multiple identities. The visit to Yasukuni shrine was scheduled under the auspices of Shintō Taikyō, an umbrella association of Shinto-derived groups that since the end of the nineteenth century had sought to bring together communities, such as that of the Minamis, which had not managed (or did not want) to become independent religious groups.[2] Minami's group is also registered as an association of worshippers of Mount Fuji (Fuji-kō), and perhaps under other such umbrella organizations, which have tended to link local informal groupings with national religious and political symbols.

Many of the spiritual therapists I met built their identities on a negative comparison with people like Ms Minami, who they criticized as being too authoritative and 'old-school' in seeking 'believers' rather than clients. This boundary-work, however, was not based on the apparent 'detraditionalization' or 'anti-authoritarianism' usually associated with the New Age movement in scholarly exegeses. When self-ascribed spiritual advisor Mr Suzuki offered me advice, he relied as much on the spirits of my ancestors as on my aura.[3] Many spiritual therapists become fervent followers of their favourite channelling or hypnotherapy teachers to the point of pursuing them in their speaking tours around the world or becoming their official partners in Japan. Rather, their insistence that the 'spiritual' was something new and different from what *reinōsha* like Ms Minami were offering was most frequently expressed in claims of dilettantism and disinterest in the seriousness of what they were doing.

They sought to do no more than their clients were willing to take in, framing their services as responses to specific issues, not as advice on how one ought to live one's life. Such claims might seem to contradict the sustained efforts (and financial investments) often made by therapists to study and acquire a license to practice this or that therapy. But I argue that their disinterested stance and pursuit of legitimacy as a 'therapist' simply relate to two different planes of action on which they operate. The first is that of a professional who seeks to offer a service that satisfies a certain need without infringing on the client's privacy any more than is necessary. The second is that of a person who wants to learn how to perform well on the first plane.

Like the Spiritual But Not Religious (SBNR) in North America and Europe, the 'religion' that post-Aum New Agers in Japan appeared to increasingly reject was more than the media-inspired image of the 'cult'. In their concerns for professionalization and privacy rights, therapists and their clients were rejecting any requirement to commit to anything beyond what was advertised on the therapist's website. This caution was not necessarily related to the therapists' fears of being mistaken for seeking 'religious' followers. It had to do with the reality that, to this day, people interested in practicing (or seeking help from) spiritual therapies continue to become involved in communities and organizations, not necessarily religious, that exploit them through means such as pyramid schemes – sometimes with disastrous results (see Chapter 6). Even if they would probably reject each other's approach to therapy, practitioners like Ms Minami and spiritual therapists share the same historical context. Ms Minami's association was officially founded in 1978, the year that the term *seishin sekai* was established as an all-encompassing term for the New Age in Japan. Antagonism towards 'religion' has been a familiar trope throughout the twentieth-century history of *minkan ryōhō* (lit. 'popular therapies'). It does not constitute a characteristic peculiar to a 'new spirituality culture'.

The term *minkan ryōhō* is today employed to refer to therapies with no scientifically proven effects. As such, it is sometimes synonymous with complementary and alternative medicine (CAM), although it covers a much wider group of techniques including many that, for various reasons, would not be considered 'medicine'. Within religious studies, the topic of *minkan ryōhō* was for a long time overshadowed by the study of shamanism, which in Japan, as elsewhere in the world, was significantly influenced by Mircea Eliade and the search for 'patterns' demonstrating the fitness or unfitness of local cases to a 'universal' phenomenon.[4] Until recently scholars in this field therefore went no further than identifying 'shamanistic elements' in the practice of New

Age or spiritual therapy (Sasaki 1995; Blacker 1999; Satō 1999; Katō 2000; Shiotsuki 2012). But in the late 1980s and increasingly in the 1990s (before the popularization of *supirichuariti*), some researchers sought to situate 'alternative' healing techniques within the Japanese history of popular therapies, in and across the modern categories of biomedicine, religion and tradition. In particular, the work of sociologist Tanabe Shintarō was of pioneering value.

Over the span of four books that he wrote and co-edited between 1989 and 2002 (Tanabe 1989; Araya et al. 1995; Tanabe, Shimazono and Yumiyama 1999; Tanabe and Shimazono 2002), Tanabe employed the word *iyashi* (lit. 'healing') to focus on how individuals sought to cure themselves and others, physically, psychologically and socially, from the late nineteenth century until the start of the twenty-first century. The originality of Tanabe's *iyashi* lens was that it allowed him to ignore ready-made shamanistic frameworks, and to focus on how personal experiences became entangled with medical advances, the legality of therapeutic practices, social shifts in urban daily lives and the complex intermingling of 'new' and 'old' religious symbolism. This is no clearer than in Tanabe's first book-length study which details the practice of a therapist based on a year of fieldwork (1987–8) in a newly built residential area of Kanagawa prefecture, south of Tokyo. Written at a time when the 'spiritual' had not entered Japanese vocabulary, Tanabe manages to situate this practitioner of *minkan ryōhō* in a modern history of experiential and empirical therapies that, at the start of the twentieth century, had come to be defined as everything that was *not* performed by medical doctors (Tanabe 1989: 69).

Tanabe's informant, Ms S, was officially a practitioner of shiatsu, but she and (based on Tanabe's count) her approximately seventy monthly clients, clearly believed that her technique functioned and affected the body in ways that went beyond regular massage. Ms S's clients, the majority in their forties, suffered from a great variety of ailments, from irregular headaches, backaches and other physical pains to more serious and sometimes chronic conditions affecting their internal organs or nervous system. The one commonality that Tanabe sees in the, on average, seventy-eight visitors who sought Ms S's assistance every month, is that they had all tried biomedical treatments that had failed (or that they remained dissatisfied with). Ms S offered them two- to two-and-a-half-hour sessions, during which they were 'touched' as they lay or sometimes sat on a futon, clad in their pyjamas, in silence or conversing about their daily lives. In practice, being touched meant that Ms S moved her hand(s) over their bodies, either in direct contact or at a distance of 5 to 10 cm, starting from the head and moving first to the right, then to the left, and then to the legs and to the back of the now-seated client, in a practice that might today sound like reiki (Stein, 2023).

Although they found it impossible to visualize what was happening, the clients nevertheless reported that it had felt like something had come out of Ms S's hands and that they had experienced a 'lightness' at the end of their session, relieving them from pain and bringing them back to Ms S on a regular basis. Although Ms S had graduated from a shiatsu massage school in 1969, she was not practicing shiatsu when Tanabe met her twenty years later. She explained to him that when she concentrated on her client's feelings, she started experiencing pain and uneasiness in her own body in the exact same spots that her client was experiencing them. Her body having become the 'mirror' of that of her client, she then proceeded to release 'energy' (*uchū no ki*) through her hands towards her client, with the purpose of unblocking or untightening those painful spots. Despite obvious similarities with the great variety of hand-healing techniques found in Japan and around the world,[5] Tanabe makes a point of reporting that, for Ms S, this treatment was not of a religious or spiritual (*rei-teki*) character but was 'based on experiential (*keiken-teki*) and physiological (*seiri-teki*) evidence' (Tanabe 1989: 37).

As Tanabe points out, today's conceptualization of popular therapies as 'alternative medicine' originates with the popularization of such techniques in Japan in the 1920s (69; see also Hirano 2019: 224–5). Stricter laws regulating the practice of medicine had been implemented a decade earlier, leading the general populace to become better informed about medical knowledge thanks to a growing publishing market. Tuberculosis, the Spanish flu and other conditions that killed many Japanese per year at the time, and which modern medicine could not completely alleviate, led, however, to a surge in *seishin ryōhō* (mind cures; lit. psycho-spiritual therapies). These therapies blended scientific, religious and esoteric concepts and methods from all over the world with experiential 'evidence' to promote treatments only defined by their 'alternativeness' to the newly established medical system (see also Kurita, Tsukada and Yoshinaga 2019; Yoshinaga 2021). This alternativeness can still be seen today in the disclaimers of the websites of spiritual therapy salons that warn visitors that they are not offering 'medical care' (*iryō*). Figure 1.1 is a typical example. Its last section reads as follows: 'Readings and healings are for support only. They are not a substitute for medical treatment, nor can they replace or take the place of any decisions you may make by yourself.' Yet, even if spiritual therapists are not offering medical care, they do offer *some kind* of care and are therefore not seeking (in the majority of cases) anything more than a therapist-patient type of relationship.

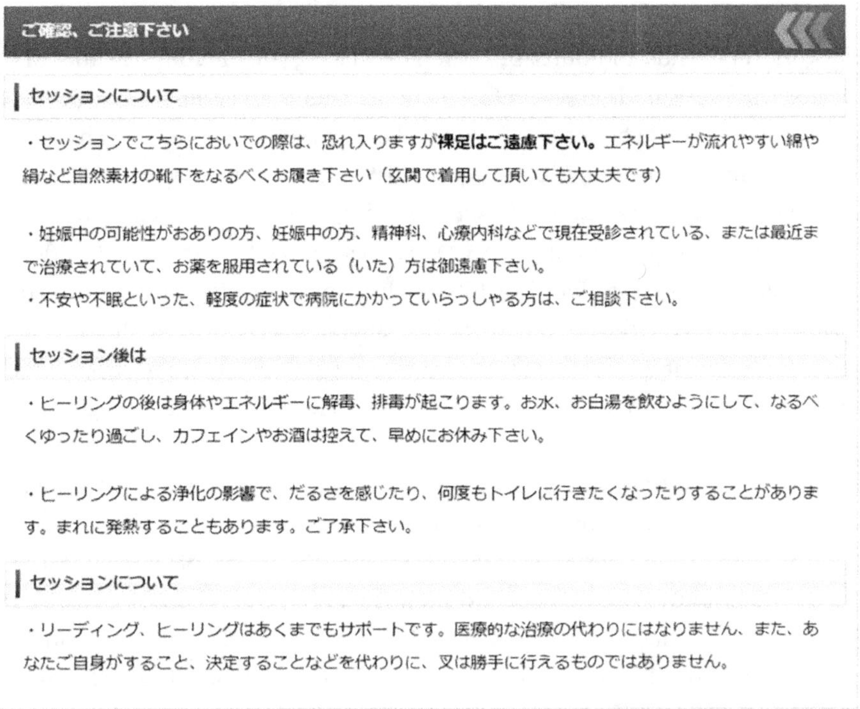

ご確認、ご注意下さい

セッションについて

・セッションでこちらにおいでの際は、恐れ入りますが**裸足はご遠慮下さい。**エネルギーが流れやすい綿や絹など自然素材の靴下をなるべくお履き下さい（玄関で着用して頂いても大丈夫です）

・妊娠中の可能性がおありの方、妊娠中の方、精神科、心療内科などで現在受診されている、または最近まで治療されていて、お薬を服用されている（いた）方は御遠慮下さい。

・不安や不眠といった、軽度の症状で病院にかかっていらっしゃる方は、ご相談下さい。

セッション後は

・ヒーリングの後は身体やエネルギーに解毒、排毒が起こります。お水、お白湯を飲むようにして、なるべくゆったり過ごし、カフェインやお酒は控えて、早めにお休み下さい。

・ヒーリングによる浄化の影響で、だるさを感じたり、何度もトイレに行きたくなったりすることがあります。まれに発熱することもあります。ご了承下さい。

セッションについて

・リーディング、ヒーリングはあくまでもサポートです。医療的な治療の代わりにはなりません、また、あなたご自身がすること、決定することなどを代わりに、又は勝手に行えるものではありません。

Figure 1.1 Example of a disclaimer found on the website of a typical spiritual therapy salon.

Not much has changed in the last hundred years. Spiritual therapists frame themselves as first and foremost 'therapists' and only secondarily as 'spiritual', 'religious' or any other adjective that distinguishes them from medical doctors. Disclaimers on the websites of my informants may also now contain references to the absence of connections with religion or religious organizations. Yet, 'tradition' and the authority of certain texts and individuals who have encouraged spiritual therapists to choose this profession remain an important element in both their lives and in the legitimization of spiritual therapy. The 'spiritual' is not *not religion*; it is *not medicine*.

Tanabe's Ms S refers to at least two persons and two texts instrumental in framing her experiences and sustaining her practice on a regular basis. The first person was a woman with 'spiritual powers' (*reinōryoku*) who lived in Aoyama (Tokyo) and who once blew on Ms S's hands, an act that Ms S later interpreted as having awakened in her the ability of feeling people's pain through her palms. The second person was a practitioner of *seitai* (bone manipulation),[6] who claimed to possess extraordinary powers (*chōnōryoku*) and who taught her and four to five of her closest friends his own healing technique. It was through her networks of friends and other practitioners sharing similar concerns that Ms S started reading esoteric and occultist literature after graduating from the shiatsu school. She cites two books that convinced her of the changes that she had been experiencing: the metaphysical and occultist author Miura Sekizō's (1929) *The Experience and Awareness of Spirituality: From Japan to All of Humanity*;[7] and the *Hotsuma Tsutaye*, a parahistory of Japan written in the form of a 10,000-line epic poem allegedly produced in 100 CE, but only surfacing in 1775 (Morrow 2014). Ms S was clearly looking for authoritative sources to ground her practice, even if these did not belong to those recognized religious traditions that scholars and commentators have contrasted with the 'eclecticism' or 'bricolage' of the New Age.

The *supirichuaru* therapists' rejection of the familiar, whether that be religion in general or more specifically the *reinōsha*, could therefore be conceived as 'grounding', a process through which interlocutors 'try to establish that what had been said is understood' (Clark and Brennan 1991), albeit here in a primarily non-biomedical therapeutic context. This is not 'detraditionalization' within a religious context. We often tend to imagine that non-biomedical settings are much more ideologically driven than our visits to the family doctor. But one way to understand the anti-authority/tradition/religion discourse among popular therapists is to consider it in relation to a wish to be treated *only* as therapists. If probed, spiritual therapists will effortlessly reveal their sources but they will also reject the authority that these sources have on the client being cured. After all, the client has come to see *them*, not those who have inspired them. This tendency to both look to and reject authoritative sources may sound paradoxical, but it is not. The therapists are neither effectively lying to others and to themselves, nor genuinely denying tradition, authority and religion. Many of the spiritual therapists who I met were not particularly well-versed in New Age literature, although they knew of all the classics. Like a doctor who had learned the tropes of diagnosis and drug prescription at medical school without necessarily remembering or remaining informed about the latest debates regarding specific methodologies to trace or treat a particular disease, many spiritual therapists put into practice what they had learned at a school of hypnotherapy or channelling and nothing more.

In other words, the counter-cultural tone of spiritual therapists could be viewed as an attempt to establish a common ground for their claims to be nothing more than practitioners of a technique that they think could help their clients improve their condition. This does not mean that they reject ideology.

If prompted, they will bring up a teacher that inspired them or a text that they keep going back to. According to Tanabe, Ms S sometimes used to intone parts of the *Hotsuma Tsutaye* during her sessions because she felt it revived her strengths (Tanabe 1989: 55). Ms S does not fit the frames usually applied to New Agers; she is neither someone who believes only in her own experiences nor a pure counter-culturalist. Defining the spiritual as a discursive strategy to talk about religious experience in a post-Aum climate of negativity towards religious organizations is clearly only part of the picture. It has perhaps contributed to the reduction of the *supirichuaru* to a fad as much as it has explained it. I suggest that we can move beyond the view of spirituality as a descriptor of some kind of new cultural phenomenon by disconnecting the use of the word 'spiritual' from what the popular therapists do, and instead focusing on how it functions as a grounding tool that therapists use to achieve a shared understanding with their clients.

Therapists, first and foremost

The meanings and nuances attached to the 'spiritual' constantly change as they are filtered through societal shifts and each therapist's personal challenges. As a general grounding tool, I have suggested that spirituality works to distinguish the therapies it is attached to from the legalized practice of medicine. It is not a counter to religion, but rather announces that these are *only* therapies and therefore do not require the type of commitment a 'religious' or other institutional setting does. At the same time, it can be a term that therapists – even those who explicitly call themselves 'spiritual' – can be dismissive of or feel that they need to qualify. This was encapsulated in my interactions with Ms Koyama.

The first time I met Ms Koyama was an afternoon of a weekday in June 2009. She had left her eight-year-old daughter with her mother and was in between two reiki sessions. Although she later changed her title to 'spiritual therapist', she was at the time calling herself a 'reiki master' and mainly focusing on what in this business is called 'energy work', namely therapies like that practised by Ms S, which are based on the manipulation of some type of invisible energy. As I found out during that first conversation, Ms Koyama was starting to generate a decent income from the spiritual salon she had opened in 2007 and was thinking of putting into use her recently acquired hypnotherapist certificate to expand her menu of therapies (Figure 1.2). In an interview conducted five years later, in April 2014, she would describe how, just a year after she first met me, she had become so busy that she ended up hiring three staff. This, however, did not last.

Figure 1.2 Ms Koyama's salon. Photo by the author.

In 2011, right about the time she discovered that she would have to undergo surgery for breast cancer, she had to close her salon temporarily and rethink her services. She resumed her practice in 2012 and, when I met her again in 2014 and then in 2019, I witnessed how she had learned to manage her clientele and increase her visibility through the publication of two books and a meditation-lessons DVD. Through our decade-long acquaintance, I came to understand that Ms Koyama was particularly good at the use of appropriate words to express what a spiritual therapist does and where they stand in relation to others in this business.

At our first meeting, Ms Koyama was clear that the Ehara boom had ended with the final airing of his regular television programme in 2009. But 'the spiritual boom continues on the internet', she explained, hence her presence (to this day) on all SNS platforms popular in Japan. She and many of the other spiritual therapists I interviewed had been involved in this kind of business for a while, first as fans in the 1980s, then as (semi)amateurs in the 1990s and later as professionals in the 2000s (Gaitanidis 2010). For them, 'spiritual' was merely a catchy term to attract people who were only starting to get to know this world of healing and counselling in the mid-2000s. In Ms Koyama's words, *supirichuaru* was the 'fancy', 'superficial' side of things that helped her and others raise their profile, but it was not what they were doing:

> What everyone does is healing plus counselling … that's it … but these are too broad concepts … [That is why] I have added 'reiki master' on my profile …

for business reasons; for people who don't know what healing refers to … I am not a *reinōsha*, simply because I do not usually see spirits … [and] I do not do channelling, because that sounds 'dubious' (*ayashii*) … I prefer counselling … I think people should not be told what to do but find it by themselves.

Contrary to appearances then, Ms Koyama preferred to distance herself from the catchy but superficial keyword 'spiritual', as well as from anything that could be interpreted as her conveying the advice of some other entity. She did not reject these entities; she told me that 'many members of my family thought they had spiritual powers and my grandfather was an ascetic (*shugenja*)'. But she considered that people needed concrete names for the therapies they were offered (some of her clients favoured her aromatherapy massage sessions) and that they needed to know that they were talking to her and no one or nothing else.

When I met Ms Koyama for the second time, in 2014, she repeated what she had written in her book, which starts with her experience as a cancer patient. 'Spiritual is not the keyword anymore' she said. 'People are interested in the "law of attraction" (*hikiyose no hōsoku*),[8] "letting go" (*tebanasu*) and so on … When they do not have time or money, people need realistic advice, not the *supirichuaru*.' To this day, nevertheless, Ms Koyama describes herself as a spiritual therapist in her business profile, and the section on her webpage targeting first-time visitors indicates that her motto is 'realistic spiritual (*genjitsuteki supirichuaru*)', reflecting her belief that people need to 'balance between the spiritual world and the real world'. When I met her again in 2019, she even exclaimed: 'The spiritual is not popular anymore. [*pause*] It has become *ayashii* [*pause*]. People want solutions here and now.'

One could easily connect Ms Koyama's emphasis on realism with her own life struggles, which she often mentions in her blog posts: being a single mother, having breast cancer and finding solutions through the concrete advice of other therapists early on in her career. She employs the word 'spiritual' to express what she thinks others will understand to be the 'other' world, not to provide a counter-religious discourse. The fact that she feels she must qualify her spirituality with the adjective 'realistic' clearly demonstrates that her main concern is to convey the effectiveness of her therapeutic services. The spiritual therapists who remain in business for many years are 'therapists' before all else. For Ms Koyama and others, the 'spiritual' has been an entry-level, grounding concept to distinguish themselves from medical doctors and to allow them to explain how their therapies work *despite* the popular image of the 'spiritual'. After all, theirs are not the only types of therapies positioned contrastively to biomedicine.

Spiritual therapies: A needle in the haystack of alternative and complementary medicine in Japan

In a policy speech delivered on 29 January 2010, then prime minster Hatoyama Yukio (b.1947) called for consideration of furthering the implementation of integrative medicine (*tōgō iryō*) (Hatoyama 2010). This launched Japan's Ministry of Health, Labour and Welfare (MHLW) into an investigation of the state of complementary and alternative medicine (CAM) in the country, resulting in a forty-eight-page report published on 26 April 2010. Although Hatoyama resigned from his position six weeks later, on 8 June, a review committee (*kentōkai*) on integrative medicine met five times between March 2012 and February 2013, its final report recommending continued investigation into the scientific basis of CAM (MHLW 2013: 13). Subsequent surveys indicated that approximately 80 per cent of the Japanese population were familiar with and had used at least one type of CAM (Ishihashi et al. 2016). Religious studies scholars have taken the growing market in alternative therapies as a sign of increased interest in the spiritual, seldom considering that the interest in non-biomedical treatments might be something else (i.e. not spiritual). The popularity of integrative medicine in Japan, however, suggests that the 'spiritual' came to be used as a label attached *post-hoc* by therapists, clients and other stakeholders to a range of CAM already in usage in Japan, and did not necessarily espouse the transcendental character assigned to spirituality by the scholars whom I go on to discuss in Chapter 2.

Acupuncture, moxibustion and massage treatments are covered by the national health insurance in Japan. Along with herbal medicine (*kanpō*), they are therefore the most frequently used CAM: at least once per year for approximately 12 per cent of the population (Yoshiharu et al. 2019). In a national survey of 3,208 participants, 1,757 were found to have visited a physician during the preceding twelve months, 184 had visited a massage/shiatsu practitioner and only 7 said they had consulted a spiritual therapist during the same period (40).[9] Even if consulted by a very small number, the inclusion of spiritual therapists in a national survey about CAM indicates that some clients consider them as part of that category. In fact, several of the therapists I interviewed were originally *seitai* practitioners or had graduated from one of the officially recognized schools of massage. They used *supirichuaru* explanations, such as references to past lives or the Higher Self, to frame the effects of their massage techniques for those clients who they thought might want such explanations or would be willing to accept them. Mr Nakai, for example, an osteopath and chiropractor specializing in various types of bone, muscle and inner organ manipulation, was clear about the use of the 'spiritual' in his salon. 'For clients who have never been to a spiritual therapist before, I ask them how they feel when I work on their body and sometimes employ some spiritual vocabulary to explain what is happening ... and if they keep coming, I might then use more [spiritual] words.'

This shows how the 'spiritual' could be grafted onto the practice of CAM by therapists who were interested in it. It became part of the semantic pool from which a therapist could borrow in order to adjust their and their client's understanding during a time when spiritual explanations seemed in demand. Yet, as was the case for Ms Koyama, their use of the spiritual always seemed to need qualification. To cite Mr Nakai:

> Most clients come here for muscular issues. Then, perhaps three sessions later, deeper problems start to come out like a childhood trauma ... I try to explain these issues by using words like 'energy blockage' ... but I do not like telling people that their worries are due to their past lives [or other things they cannot control] ... I want people to believe in themselves and choose what they think is best for their future.

The conflict that spiritual therapists seemed to feel in using the word 'spiritual' had perhaps to do with some of the *seishin sekai* and *supirichuariti* literature popular at the time, which focused more on searching for the causes of problems in spiritual realms than on how to solve those problems in the here and now. This was inherent in many of the theories and narratives of self-development and typical of their didactic tone, which always left room for answer-seeking. While this might have been perfect for participants of a personal-development seminar, clients with joint pain would have stopped visiting Mr Nakai if their pain persisted, no matter how many spiritual scenarios he may have employed to justify that pain. Scholars of religion and science have often used the concept of 'scientification' to explain how religious practices (often with therapeutic targets) legitimize their effects by imitating or borrowing scientific vocabulary, thus managing to remain relevant in a secularist setting (von Stuckrad 2015; for Japanese cases, see Schrimpf 2018). In the case of 'spiritual therapies', we find a similar process of legitimization but in a different form: the use of religious vocabulary to legitimize the alternativeness of therapy in a CAM setting in which therapies are built in opposition to biomedicine (science), while their usage remains essentially complementary to it. Too much *supirichuariti* would reduce the complementarity of spiritual therapies, so therapists were careful in how they used that framing in their daily practice.

None of the reports produced by the integrative medicine committees of the MHLW mention the word 'spiritual' or acknowledge any 'religious' dimension to these therapies. Given the strict constitutional separation of religion from the Japanese state, reports with possible policy impact associated with the MHLW could not take into account any factor remotely related to 'religion'. As such, they illustrate how healthcare policy needs to be based on evidence garnered from randomized trials. Even though committee members acknowledged the difficulty of assessing the effectiveness of CAM therapies by such scientific methods, their conclusions were clearly and entirely framed around biomedical discourse. To explain why 'spirituality' needs constant qualification in the spiritual therapeutic setting, it might therefore seem obvious to turn to arguments about the secularization or commercialization of CAM such as yoga (Jain 2014), which figures prominently in the MLHW reports. But that would again lead us to reductive *-izations*. Without undermining the possibility that therapists have internalized the secularism of public policies and the media, I would like to offer another explanation – one that provides an alternative reading of yet another *-ization*: the psychologization of the spiritual.

The spirituality of counselling

If healing essentially aims to relieve a client from worry or pain, what do spiritual therapists mean by 'counselling'? Most claim to have some type of training in counselling, whether certified or experience-based, and provide some sort of counselling, either in eponymous sessions (as in the 'spiritual counselling' of Ehara) or as the starting point of a session. Mr Nakai's massage, for example, always started with fifteen to thirty minutes of 'counselling'. If spiritual therapy is basically 'healing plus counselling' as Ms Koyama observed, perhaps clients seek it for the 'counselling' rather than the 'spiritual' part. Horie (2007) notes the close relationship between the development of transpersonal psychology and the spread of the concept of 'spirituality' among Japanese intellectuals in the 1990s, but also argues that Ehara's televised sessions have a distinctive psychotherapeutic tone, thus illustrating what appears to be the psychologization of the spiritual. But what if Ehara was just trying to set himself apart from the surge in counsellors in Japan in the late 1990s and early 2000s by emphasizing through his 'spiritual' vocabulary the religious and ethical underpinnings of existing understandings of counselling?

Until the first 27,876 public psychologists (*kōnin shinrishi*) passed the MHLW exam in September 2018, Japan had no national scheme for certifying counsellors. This did not mean that such services did not exist. The Japanese Union of Psychological Associations lists fifty-six member associations,[10] with some of the most prestigious, such as the Japanese Association of Counselling Science (JACS), dating back to the 1960s. Before the MHLW certification, the most authoritative credential for professional counsellors was the certified clinical psychologist license issued by the Japanese Board for Clinical Psychologists, which was approved as a requirement for Japan's first formal school counsellor programme implemented by the Ministry of Education, Culture, Science and Technology in 1995 (Kudo-Grabosky, Ishii and Mase 2012).[11] In the first decade of that programme, the number of school counsellors in Japan increased from 154 to 9,547 (School Pupils Section 2007). During the same period, the membership of the Japan Industrial Counsellors Organization (established in 1960) multiplied nearly four times, from 3,000 to nearly 12,000 (Maruyama 2008: 3). Overall, there were more than forty counselling- and psychology-related certificates available to practitioners (Kudo-Grabosky, Ishii and Mase 2012: 223). This does not include the counselling diplomas offered by a multitude of private schools and even individuals based on a few hours of lectures, which were the most popular avenues for spiritual therapists to legitimize their counselling skills.

This situation, which the national certification programme was undoubtedly meant to counter,[12] attracted attention at precisely the time when the *supirichuaru* was gaining popularity. In 2002, worried by the variety of meanings attached to the concept of 'counselling', the president of JACS commissioned a special committee to produce a 'scientific' definition. Watanabe-Muraoka Mieko, a professor at Tsukuba University, the cradle of research on post-war counselling psychology, had already raised the alarm earlier that year (Watanabe 2002), sounding a warning that she would repeat five years later, suggesting that it had not been heeded: 'the profession of counselling psychology in Japan faces a critical turning point regarding whether counselling will survive and be appreciated as a unique profession in Japan or will be forgotten and disappear in the next decade' (Watanabe-Muraoka 2007: 98). Watanabe-Muraoka's warning rested on two factors: the absence of professionalization[13] and the misinterpretation of counselling, which was sometimes equalled to psychotherapy and frequently used synonymously with 'one-to-one communication' or the practice of listening and accepting what the other person says while not giving advice or information (99). This is exactly how spiritual therapists understood their practice of counselling.

Instead of meeting me for an interview, Mr Masayuki answered some questions by email in the spring of 2009. Thirty-eight years old at the time, he had, according to his website, trained in hypnotherapy, channelling and alternative counselling:

> I do not think that I possess any ability or that I have contributed to helping people ... My objective is to be able to simply explain to people the mechanism of worrying, but there is no academic or medical basis to what I am doing ... I just tell people what I felt from listening to their story ... It is not the type of counselling in which I suggest what the client should do ... I think people should be left to decide about their own future and that endeavour needs training and cycles of failure and success ... There are different ways to achieve psychological relief and it all depends on what the individual chooses.

Such an interpretation of counselling echoes the earlier explanations given by Ms Koyama, Mr Nakai and other therapists, who wanted their clients to consider them as therapists rather than as advisors on spiritual matters. It also echoes Watanabe-Muraoka's critique of the state of counselling in Japan:

> [Carl] Rogers' early conception of a non-directive approach introduced to Japanese psychology in the 1960s has remained the dominant influence in constructing the image of counselling in Japanese society. This situation promulgates the view that counsellors are good listeners who never initiate problem-solving but rather wait for clients to make decisions when they are ready. Counsellors who are trained in this model tend to confine themselves to listening to and accepting students or employees or clients but not engaging actively in other interventions such as psychological assessment, information dissemination, advising, career planning, and other techniques. Because of the expense of such a practice and the perceived lack of substance in the approach, administrators in business sectors and in educational institutes, as well as schoolteachers and career centre workers, have tended to evaluate counsellors as unnecessary or useless. Currently, in various settings counselling is being replaced with the newer technique entitled coaching.[14] The Japan Ministry of Welfare and Labour decided to introduce a new title 'career consultant' as a substitute for the title 'career counsellor' for professionals who help clients with difficulties in career choice, planning, and adjustment. This transpired because the majority of policy makers viewed counsellors as merely non-directive listeners. (Watanabe-Muraoka 2007: 100–1)

New Age scholars describe the open-ended, constant answer-seeking that is encouraged by spiritual therapists in Japan as 'sacralising the self'. Meanwhile critics of these practitioners accuse them of avoiding taking any responsibility for their deeds and for generating addicts to lost causes (Kayama 2006). But Watanabe's observation points to the possibility that their counselling practices may originate from the application of (perhaps now outdated) psychological theories rather than their 'misuse'. Some practitioners might disagree with the emphasis that Watanabe-Muraoka places on Carl Roger's influence in Japan. After all, Kawai Hayao introduced the Jungian school into Japanese academia in the 1960s and local counselling and psychotherapeutic techniques such as Naikan therapy also developed during the same period (Ozawa-de Silva 2006). But Rogers certainly had a special history with Japan, which he visited twice (in 1961 and 1983), as did some of his influential students. These included Eugene T. Gendlin (1926–2017), who came to Japan in 1978 and again in 1987 to celebrate the establishment of a research association dedicated to 'focusing', Gendlin's famous psychotherapeutic technique.

One of the persons credited with introducing counselling in post-war Japan is another of Rogers's students, Logan J. Fox, born and raised in Japan in an American missionary family. During the Second World War, Fox went to the University of Chicago and studied under Rogers, before returning to Japan and contributing to the founding of Ibaraki Christian University. In 1948, Tomoda Fujio (1917–2005), a teacher with a degree in psychology who was working at Tokyo University of Education (now Tsukuba University), met Fox and asked him about the recent state of psychology in the United States. Fox, in response, lent him his copy of Rogers's *Counselling and Psychotherapy* (1942), which Tomoda reportedly became completely enchanted with (Sugitani 1989: 75). Tomoda spent the next thirty years translating Roger's works into Japanese and propagating Roger's person-centred counselling in Japan together with Itō Hiroshi (1919–2000), who studied counselling at the University of Missouri in 1950.[15] These Japanese versions were the first translations of Rogers's books. Sakanaka Masayoshi, a leading authority on humanistic psychology in Japan, estimates that since Rogers was introduced to the Japanese public in 1951 through Tomoda's translation of *Counselling and Psychotherapy*, 7,130 publications and translations related to the person-centred approach, basic encounter group, focusing and other Rogers-ian theories and techniques had been published in Japan as of 2013 (Sakanaka 2015: 169).

Koyano Kuniko (1995: 210) links the particular ease with which Carl Rogers's theories were introduced to Japan to the conditions of Japanese academia, where the field of clinical psychology was unknown until the late 1940s, and, perhaps more importantly, to a post-war social climate in which Japanese psychologists aspired to new political changes and were looking for 'foreign' models. American humanistic thought, as it manifested through Rogers's empathetic position towards his clients, felt 'democratizing'. Robert Fuller (1982: 24) argues that it was in tune with American melioristic concerns of the 1950s and 1960s, which were very much Protestant in the sense that they rejected external oppressive religious authority and emphasized autonomy, freedom and self-discovery. But it was not just that. Client-centred therapy required less rigorous instruction and could be more easily adopted by paraprofessionals. It was also more accessible to the public because it had a less technical vocabulary than Freud's psychoanalysis. This practical aspect reinforced the individualizing rhetoric that is today conspicuous in 'spiritual but not religious' mottos (Fuller 2001), suggesting that counselling has not psychologized spirituality – it is what makes therapies spiritual.

At the same time, however, the mainstreaming of counselling had the potential to collapse the alternativity of spiritual therapies in a way that worked positively for practitioners seeking to authorize their practices, but not always for clients who were seeking 'something else'. For some therapists, counselling was undoubtedly a way to legitimize their practice during the sudden surge of counsellors in Japan from the second half of the 1990s. Ms Kinoshita, for example, reported that she usually introduced herself as an aromatherapist even though her aromatherapy session figured at the bottom of her list of therapies, which centred on healing and hypnotherapy. 'For people whom I meet for the first time and for my eight-year-old daughter, I am an *esute* [cosmetic] masseuse', explained Ms Kinoshita, before adding: 'I also don't like calling my counselling sessions "channelling" because it sounds suspicious; I call them *esute* counselling.' There were times, however, when too close an association with 'mainstream' counselling could alienate some clients. Nearly one year after I met Mr Suzuki for the first time, I met the partner of the friend who had introduced us. She just happened to have sought Mr Suzuki's advice again the previous week, but this time she was disappointed: 'He has lost his powers. It just feels like counselling now', she exclaimed. In the past she had valued Mr Suzuki's support in allowing her to come to terms with her husband's wish to have a second child. Now, however, she had completely lost interest in him; his latest attempt to 'read' her issues had been unsuccessful.

Conclusion

In this chapter I have argued that the adjective 'spiritual' does not necessarily denote a new post-Aum phenomenon of detraditionalization and psychologization of religion or spirituality. Rather, it has played a grounding function. It distinguishes the therapies it is attached to from the legalized practice of medicine, while simultaneously signalling that these are only therapies and do not require any kind of 'religious' belief or commitment. Since the early 2000s, the adjective 'spiritual' has often been strategically employed by practitioners to place the therapies they offer within the discursive bubble constructed by the Ehara boom, but, at the same time, some of them have used the concept reluctantly, feeling that they have to qualify it if they want people to find solutions for their problems by themselves. In fact, a spiritual vocabulary seems to be most commonly used in the variety of counselling methods that spiritual therapists employ to get their clients to talk about and relate their worries or pains to their deeds. In this, however, they do not 'sacralize the self', as New Age scholars have claimed. Rather, they position themselves closer to the psychological counselling tradition that developed in Japan and attracted significant attention with the surge of counselling services from the late 1990s onwards. First and foremost, therefore, spiritual therapists define themselves in relation to contemporary therapeutic settings. This has had significant repercussions for both themselves and their clients, which I explore in the second half of this book.

Yet, even if spiritual therapists have been placed at the centre of phenomena described as *supirichuaru*, they do not have the monopoly over its meaning, as my references to scholarly and media usages of the term have alluded to in this chapter. In the following two chapters I show how scholars had already imagined a new type of 'spirituality culture' to explain the post-Aum religious landscape before therapists came to prominence in the first decade of this century, while the publishing industry had already familiarized the public with messages of therapeutic self-transformation in the 1980s and 1990s. The coinage of a new popular term – *supirichuaru* – had therefore lain just around the corner.

2

Spiritual academia

In a critical reflection on *supirichuariti* studies presented at the 2014 annual conference of the Japanese Association for the Study of Religion and Society (JASRS), scholar of new religions Terada Yoshirō remarked that, back in 2000 (when he was a doctoral student), he had written on the progressive turn away from organized religions and networks towards individuals in new religious studies research.[1] He had had in mind the study of spirituality, which, he now noted, had greatly influenced the JASRS during the first half of its existence since its foundation in 1993. The edited volume *A Sociology of Spirituality* (Itō, Kashio and Yumiyama 2004), Terada argued, could be considered as the apogee of this field and a manifesto for a post-new-religions research. As he pointed out, the book's editors had themselves made this claim, writing that the Aum affair had proved that objective, neutral and empathetic research was ineffective; *supirichuariti* studies would open up new possibilities for religious studies by taking a relational and linguistic turn, looking into individual and everyday self-understandings of religiousness and how these are relationally constructed, rather than viewing individual beliefs in the mirror of social trends (Kashio 2004a: 115–17). But, Terada asked, why had those scholars thought like that? What had been bad about religious studies research before theirs? In response, Yumiyama Tatsuya, the co-editor of *A Sociology of Spirituality* and author of many other papers using this concept since, stated that he had been motivated by a feeling that he needed 'to do something alternative (*sore ni kawaru*)'[2] after the publication of the *Encyclopaedia of New Religions* or *Shinshūkyō jiten* (Inoue et al. 1990), now the standard reference book on that topic. He had looked for that alternative in non-organized religiosity, in other words, 'spirituality' (Yumiyama 2015: 146).

While Terada's critique was primarily aimed at the tendency of JASRS scholars to rush to jump on the bandwagon of new contemporary topics at the expense of scholarly depth,[3] the questions he raised were valid, particularly as studies of *supirichuariti* had significantly decreased in number by 2014. There is no doubt that, as scholars, we engage in our work with certain personal messages about its value, especially as we are increasingly encouraged to define, calculate and promote that value to wider audiences. However, when scholars argue that there are good alternatives to the religion that they imagine their readers to have in mind, this begs the question of why such arguments need to be made in the first place. The classic response to this question is: 'because of the Aum affair'. This has become almost a gateway expression to explain everything that has happened to the study of contemporary religion in Japan since 1995 (and one which I have used in my own writing). In Horie Norichika's (2009–11) oft-cited paper,[4] which to my knowledge is the only attempt by a scholar of religious studies to analyse the discursive use of *supirichuariti*, the argument goes like this: in their popular usage, '"spiritual/spirituality" function as signs of security in a social climate that considers that religion is dangerous and should be excluded to maintain the social order. Thus, the use of the terms spiritual and spirituality enable people to hide and keep their intrinsic religiosity by positioning themselves closer to secularism' (11). Within academia, Horie claims, there were seldom any new 'new religions' to study after the Aum affair. Moreover, religious studies scholars, whether sympathetic to or critical of spirituality, 'agree that religion is dangerous and that priority should be given to this-worldly everyday life' (5).

There is no doubt that the question of what was considered appropriate scholarly engagement with religious communities, and how this came to be debated after the Aum affair, were major factors contributing to the conceptualization of *supirichuariti* within Japanese academia. This was a time when academic work on religion was, in a sense, forced to be proactive in pointing the finger at what an enraged and scared public considered bad religion. In 2012, Ben Dorman (2012: 171) suggested that 'the study of spirituality has become a "safety device" for scholars not wishing to deal with the complex issues that new religions can sometimes raise'. Yet, more recently, there has been an increase in (mostly historical) research on new religions (Nagaoka 2015; Kumamoto 2018), while *supirichuariti*-related publications have substantially declined. By examining the concerns and aims of scholars who espoused spirituality as a concept and contextualizing their arguments in the intellectual history out of which this subfield emerged, this chapter shows that the Aum affair ultimately had no effect on how scholars approached the study of religion, even if it prompted some methodological reflection. The academic concept of spirituality was constructed within an evolutionary framework and seen as a continuation (not a split) from the religiosity of new religious movements. Just as post-war scholars had looked to those movements in their efforts to reform Japanese society, spirituality was positively interpreted for its therapeutic and hence salvific promise – a uniquely contemporary 'alternative' that was simultaneously the (timeless) essence of religion, and had the potential to ameliorate the perceived loss of moral-social order in contemporary Japan.

Some of the authors whose work I discuss in this chapter have been prolific and have produced a respected record of arguments both within and beyond academia, the influence of which has spread beyond the very narrow field of spirituality studies. My critical engagement with their work is not intended to undermine it, but rather to account, as Jason Josephson-Storm (2017) suggests, for the reflexive aspects of scholarly work by examining how spirituality began to function as a concept and tracing 'the continuities and disruptions that this category produces in older conceptual orders' (12–13). My aim is to provide a much-needed alternative perspective and an impetus to build upon these scholars' valuable arguments in future studies of contemporary religion, as well as to deepen our understanding of how and why scholars contributed to the rise of spirituality in early twenty-first-century Japan.

Supirichuariti as everything and anything contemporary?

In summer 2009, the magazine *Star People*, 'a spiritual magazine for consciousness awakening' (*ishiki no mezame no tame no supirichuaru magajin*), included a thirty-five-page long special feature titled 'New Age vs Spiritual: Towards Integration' (*Nyūeiji vs Supirichuaru: Tōgō o mezashite*). Its aim was to compare the New Age with the spiritual in order to find 'a more holistic, integrated spiritual way of life'. Contributors included many authoritative figures, such as Harukawa Seisen, president of the Japanese Association of Spiritualists;[5] Kinjo Hiroshi, president of the International Institute for Spiritualism; Matsunaga Taro, translator of Ken Wilber's books; Anaguchi Keiko, a self-proclaimed 'spiritual entrepreneur' behind many alternative therapy schools, seminars and workshops, and Akiyama Makoto, a writer of more than a hundred books on (and practitioner of) everything occultist and alternative, who has intermittently appeared on television since 1974, when he claimed to have supernatural powers like those of Uri Geller. It also featured introductions to the thought of American personalities whose books had been or were about to be published by *Star People*'s publisher, Natural Spirit. But the special feature opened with two articles, each written by a leading scholar in the spirituality studies field: Shimazono Susumu, then Professor of Religious Studies at the University of Tokyo, whose proposal for the existence of a new spirituality culture or *shin-reiseibunka* (Shimazono 1996) can be said to have kickstarted the field; and Kashio Naoki, then Associate Professor at Keio University, and co-editor with Yumiyama and Itō Masayuki of *A Sociology of Spirituality*.

The way these scholars chose to engage with their field of study, or more specifically to provide their expert opinion to a group of people that is simultaneously an audience *and* the subject of their research, offers a first glimpse into how the academic discipline of spirituality studies in Japan has been reflexively produced. What researchers choose to emphasize in such instances undoubtedly reflects not only the result of their analysis (put in terms that they think appropriate for an interested general public), but also, perhaps more importantly, their fears and hopes about how that audience develops in the future. In their articles for *Star People*, Shimazono and Kashio are not just making scholarly arguments. As I go on to discuss, their respective exegeses on what distinguishes the New Age from Aum (Shimazono) and on the commercialization of spirituality (Kashio) can also be read as warnings. In other words, there is always a message in such scholarly opinions, a message coming from those who have been in the unique position of having built their professional identity on how 'objectively' well they know the receivers of that message.

Shimazono's (2009) feature basically consists of the argument that the New Age was the forerunner to the rise of spirituality. The text starts with the observation that there are more and more people today who have lost hope in modern rationalism, but who also cannot go back to traditional religions. These are people, he continues, who live in developed nations and who try meditation, therapies or pilgrimages; are drawn by animism, mysticism and the belief in reincarnation; feel familiar with the concepts of aura, qigong or near-death experience; and consider the fantastic worlds depicted in film and animations as desirable. This 'rise of spirituality', explains Shimazono, started with the millennial optimistic utopianism of the 1960s in America and the 1970s in Japan and manifested through the New Age and the *seishin sekai* movements, respectively. In the 1980s, in both regions, such marginal culture started becoming mainstream and exerted substantial influence in hospital and welfare institutions, in university lectures and in authoritative magazines. In the 1990s, Shimazono goes on, it eventually became impossible to distinguish between such culture and youth culture in general, since the younger generations were unable to find an optimistic utopianism elsewhere. Eventually, this spirituality became rooted in daily life and spread across society, as can be seen in the significant increase in self-help groups for all kinds of issues, from alcoholism to discrimination. 'Today's spirituality is spreading based on its strengths in attending to life's fundamental needs', Shimazono concludes (16).

For Shimazono spirituality seems to be something of a unifying concept that is employed to explain multiple phenomena, from anonymous gatherings of parents of children with disabilities to the popularity of Miyazaki Hayao's animated film, *Spirited Away*. Panacean powers are attributed to spirituality to explain nearly every contemporary social trend. Yet, one fifth of the piece is dedicated to the Aum affair. Shimazono admits that without an understanding of the New Age or *seishin sekai*, it would be impossible to comprehend not only the Aum affair but also other controversial new religious movements such as Lifespace and Pana Wave.[6] He stresses, however, what he considers a fundamental difference: the New Age consists of free individual networks, whereas Aum was a group formed by the students of a guru, Asahara Shōkō, who sought to bring about apocalyptic changes based on spiritual self-awareness. Those students, Shimazono argues, had originally joined Aum as youth looking for the same optimistic utopianism as the New Agers, but became dissatisfied with New Age spirituality, leading to the Tokyo subway sarin gas attack in 1995.[7] He clearly locates Aum as a sort of fake spirituality, at the opposite end of what readers of *Star People* are supposed to espouse. For Shimazono, spirituality does not include gurus, organized groups or violence. Spirituality is good, personal and private. As I will demonstrate, this message and its normative undertone characterizes *supirichuariti* literature more generally.

In his contribution to the *Star People* special feature, Kashio (2009) reinforces the idea that spirituality is essentially positive but subject to misunderstandings when he launches a critique of what he sees as its corruption by the media, which, he argues, focuses only on spirituality's superficial, commercial aspects. He defines spirituality as 'the [quality of the] sensation of being connected to something beyond the self, but which operates within the self and between the self and others' (18). This significantly broad conceptualization of the term renders spirituality opaque to scholarly scrutiny and, in this sense, occult. The author argues that spirituality is universal (*fuhenteki*), but also characteristically invisible (*fukashisei*), impossible to manipulate (*hisōsasei*) and transcendental (*chōetsusei*). For Kashio, the *seishin sekai* is basically a Japanese version of the New Age; a movement that arose out of specific socio-political circumstances. While it cannot be equated with spirituality, it was a movement that was essentially supported by the belief that various physical experiences could operationalize the invisible, impossible to manipulate and transcendental force inside each individual to transform that individual's consciousness and bring about a better world. In the subsequent rise of a new spirituality culture, this belief in the transformative potential of spirituality has weakened. Spirituality has been privatized and taken over by a market mentality, as seen in the booming healing business. This, Kashio concludes, as if warning *Star People*'s readers, is a serious problem.

These two accounts by scholars who have been significantly involved in the study of spirituality in Japan encapsulate how this concept has been approached by Japanese academics, presented as an 'alternative' to something else and associated with the experience of therapy. The first obvious issue is that scholars often commit an equivocation fallacy.[8] They use the term 'spirituality' in the same text to talk about what they consider to be some kind of timeless human essence, force or sensation *and* to refer to a cultural phenomenon characterizing 'postmodern' societies at the turn of the twenty-first century. Spirituality is a sensation, a force, the essence of religion, a contemporary mood, a way of looking at the world, a market trend, a media boom. In the first decade of the twenty-first century, spirituality in Japan was behind everything and anything – an all-encompassing word that sought to simultaneously shed light on a 'new' phenomenon and bring about the broader positive changes that scholars associated with that phenomenon.

There is also a clearly evolutionary understanding of spirituality in this scholarship, which resembles less an effort to critically analyse how those who espouse spirituality understand it than an attempt to take their empirical usages of the term as the basis for building scholarly arguments. Both Shimazono and Kashio present the New Age movement in the United States and the *seishin sekai*, its equivalent in Japan, as trigger events that awoke spirituality inside individuals and freed it from the grip of organized religion. In April and May 2012, I audited an undergraduate course titled *An Introduction to Spirituality* (*supirichuariti nyūmon*) at Rikkyō University in Tokyo, co-organized by Koike Yasushi, a frequent collaborator on spirituality studies projects (Koike 2007). One of the lectures was given by Yumiyama Tatsuya, the co-editor of *A Sociology of Spirituality* who we met at the start of this chapter. As he was explaining to over a hundred students how spirituality was found in all religions but had recently escaped them and spread throughout society, Yumiyama engaged in a theatrical move, violently shaking an uncapped bottle of water and spraying the first row of students who giggled loudly. Taken metaphorically, the comparison between spirituality and water seemed perfect: a basic human need was now available to everyone. We no longer needed to join religions to satisfy our thirst for answers and healing.

Finally, Shimazono, Kashio, Yumiyama and other *supirichuariti* studies scholars identify 'new' therapeutic experiences as the proof *par excellence* to support their arguments about the rise of spirituality and the potential hope for change that it upholds. This is exactly where they see a continuity between new religious groups and the 'new spirituality culture' they describe. As I will go on to examine in more detail, the study of spirituality therefore did not replace the study of new religions, as it may have seemed when Dorman (2012) was writing. Rather, spirituality was taken as the natural next step on from new religions (assumed to be in demise), a perspective that continues to form the prism through which these scholars approach contemporary religion. In his latest treatise on new religions in Japan, Shimazono (2020) lays this out very clearly in a discussion on the self-help groups that rose to prominence in 1990s Japan, which were taken as evidence that spirituality had become mainstream. There was a structural discontinuity between new religions and these groups, which were based on the Alcoholics Anonymous model and offered temporary human-to-human relations focused on a single issue. But Shimazono argues that they nevertheless functioned along the same ideological lines, since self-help groups, like new religions, were concerned with healing, self-change and, increasingly from the 2000s, with 'pain' (*itami*) (287).

To summarize: these scholars consider spirituality to be fundamental to human beings. It can be harnessed to bring about healing but has also fallen victim to the market and to the media. But why, as Terada asked, did scholars of religion start using *supirichuariti* as a concept in the first place – what did they seek to achieve? How was the academic study of *supirichuariti* originally thought to contribute to the discipline of religious studies?[9]

Supirichuariti as a manifesto for post-new-religions research?

Spirituality studies flourished in Japan during the first decade of the twenty-first century, beginning with *A Sociology of Spirituality* (Itō, Kashio and Yumiyama 2004) – the work that Terada considered an apogee of the field – and two other key texts (Kashio 2002; Itō 2003). The field peaked with Shimazono Susumu's second book, explicitly titled *The Rise of Spirituality*, which was published in 2007 (also the peak year of Ehara Hiroyuki's media popularity), before settling down with a special issue on spirituality published in 2010 by the journal of the Japanese

Association for Religious Studies. The diversity of case studies in that special issue, from Nishida Kitarō to contemporary school curricula, demonstrated the diffuse use of the term and, to a large extent, its loss of contextual value, even if key figures in the field continued to produce new publications on the *supirichuaru* (e.g. Horie 2019a, 2019b; Shimazono 2020; Itō 2021).

Many of the arguments found in the three key texts, authored mainly by sociologists, can be traced back to conversations that occurred during the annual meetings of the Japanese Association for the Study of Religion and Society (JASRS) in the late 1990s. Most of the authors took part in a series of workshops, the first two of which, held in 1997 and 1998, were dedicated to the 'composition of the *seishin sekai*'. These were followed by workshops on 'contemporary religiosity/spirituality (*reisei*)' (1999) and on 'the challenges and prospects of research on new religions' (2001).[10] Already apparent in the titles of these workshops is a widening of scholarly interest speared by research on the *seishin sekai* phenomenon, which had been the subject of Shimazono's (1996) seminal work and had also framed discussions about the self-development seminars prominent in the late 1980s and early 1990s (Haga and Yumiyama 1994).

The original objective seems to have been close to Shimazono's proposal: the *seishin sekai* would be analysed to reveal the characteristics of contemporary religious culture in advanced capitalist nations (Kasai 1998: 7). But this new generation of scholars disagreed with the simple comparative basis of Shimazono's argument, namely that the new spirituality culture was distinct simply because it was less organized than new religious groups. The initial discussions among the soon-to-be *supirichuariti* scholars first aimed at better defining the contours of *seishin sekai*, but there were already disagreements as to how widespread and counter-cultural that phenomenon was. At the end of the first workshop, for example, Yoshinaga Shin'ichi pointed out that the core participants of *seishin sekai* may have been the same generation of 1970s occulture fans who had simply continued exploring their interest in the paranormal (Yoshinaga 1998: 37).[11] In a footnote to an article on self-development seminars that appeared in the same journal that year, Koike Yasushi points out that despite *seishin sekai*'s origins in print culture as a specific category of books, scholars had tended to use the term for 'every small group or movement that is non-traditional' (Koike 1998: 73).

The adoption of the concept of *supirichuariti* was, therefore, an attempt to widen the scope and stress commonalities between the *seishin sekai* and other 'contemporary' cultural expressions, such as self-development seminars, that were popular in the 1990s. The presenters at the first workshop also seemed interested in discussing what they saw as a generational shift, by describing the concerns and needs of those fascinated by *supirichuariti*, whom they called the 'mind generation', something that Yumiyama would go on to emphasize further in his later contribution to the *Sociology of Spirituality* collection (Yumiyama 2004). In the second workshop, presentations were confined again to New Age phenomena but the roundtable discussion revealed a push by other participants to consider the connection of the *seishin sekai* to wider social and religious developments. This is when an interesting twist occurs. In reaction to a senior scholar's criticism regarding a lack of quantitative data, the *seishin sekai* starts being referred to as a twenty-year-old trend firmly established in Japanese society (and not just a topic appearing in recent magazines) (Itō 1999: 34), and as a possible window onto 'discovering' social malaise stemming from the capitalist market economy or the limits of healthcare. This legitimization of the study of *seishin sekai*, not for its own sake, but as essential to understanding contemporary social trends, malaise and instability, led scholars to consider in the next workshop, held in 1999, what they saw as the influence of the New Age on new religious groups and the connections that some New Agers may have to established religions. The post-workshop discussion reveals that participants such as Yumiyama and Haga were by then using the terms 'religiosity' and 'spirituality' almost interchangeably, in the sense that 'spirituality=contemporary religiosity' (Kashio 2000: 163–4).

In fact, in Haga and Yumiyama's first collaboration, a monograph on self-development seminars and New Age workshops in Japan published a year before the Aum affair (Haga and Yumiyama 1994), Yumiyama had already made the argument that the concept of 'religion' could be widened to accommodate these kinds of practices (Yumiyama 1994: 19). Religion, he had argued, is not just about religious organizations or 'timeless' folk traditions; it is a concept that should also be applied to forms of experience that lie outside normative scholarly frames of 'religion'. After the Aum affair, however, this was no longer a viable possibility. Given the negative connotations that became attached to 'religion', a new conceptual toolkit was needed. In other words, the Aum affair and its effects on religious studies confronted scholars with the limitations of previous scholarly approaches, while simultaneously preventing them from using 'religion' as their framework of analysis. This, I argue, explains why, during the heyday of spirituality studies, scholars reflected on how *supirichuariti* studies might forge a new methodological path. As the editors of *A Sociology of Spirituality* put it, there was a need to move on from the interpretive turn to 'the ontological turn which considers values to be intersubjectively formed out of the relationship between individuals, and to the linguistic turn by which words uttered by individuals are not simply carriers of thoughts and principles but come to bear meaning as they are used in specific contexts' (Kashio 2004a: 117).

What had been the problem with the interpretive approach? In an unfortunately little known review and conceptualization of scholarly reactions to the Aum affair published only a year after the incident, Fujiwara Satoko (1996) categorizes academic criticism of Aum into three types: 'authenticity-seeking' arguments which presented Aum as 'false religion'; 'enlightenment'-type sociological and psychological analyses that framed Aum as a manifestation of deeper social issues; and 'cultural critique'-type exegeses characteristic of religious studies scholars, which focused on the specificities of Aum and how these put into question larger social norms. A defining feature of the latter was recognition of the agency of religious individuals and groups and a concurrent belief that 'getting rid' of those groups would not solve the problems associated with Aum's actions (Fujiwara 1996: 19). Among both enlightenment- and cultural-critical type analyses, Fujiwara notes, Aum served as a 'mirror' for the problems of (Japanese) society, a metaphor that has since become common rhetoric and has also been used in critical analyses of *supirichuariti*. Scholars of religious studies in particular employed deprivation theories of religion as tools to understand the motives of Aum members' actions. Aum was described as fulfilling various kinds of 'lacks' (of social bonds, stable futures, psychological health, non-material aims to live for and so on) and as offering 'alternative' solutions to those issues (22). Fujiwara's most important insight is that the approach cherished by those scholars who had before the Aum affair stressed in a positive way the counter-cultural nature of new religious groups, could now be employed to critique these same groups (23). This highlighted a fundamental methodological flaw: the interpretation of individual beliefs in the mirror of social trends that were normatively assessed as positive or negative did not make scholars objective onlookers of religious communities.

I argue that this underlying normative lens on religion is what spirituality scholars at the turn of the twenty-first century wished to escape from – why we find the editors of *A Sociology of Spirituality* explicitly declaring the need to move beyond the interpretive turn towards a more constructionist approach. However, this opportunity was lost. The substantive contents of that volume show that the Aum affair did not ultimately change the way that these scholars approached the study of religion. They and the other contributors fail to keep to the editorial promises of attending to the relational and contextual meaning of 'spirituality' in the cases they examine, since their arguments share a common premise. All of the case studies are treated as expressions of a new world order, with 'spirituality' as the interpretive lens through which various post-1970s socio-religious changes are positively explicated. If Aum expressed everything that had gone bad with society, spirituality illustrated the changes that were good. As the subtitle of the book informs us, it is 'an exploration of religiosity in the contemporary world'.

Chapter 1, for example, provides a definition of global spirituality as 'a contemporary religious phenomenon that is formed of a loose network of individuals holding a holistic worldview, who value independence and aim for the transformation of consciousness' (Itō 2004a: 27). The following three chapters, we are told, will examine the special qualities of this spirituality. Chapter 2 proceeds to argue that the popularity of self-development seminars illustrates the contemporary shift away from social groups based on intimate relationships towards a situation where self-confirmation is sought in self-images reflected by an anonymous public (Haga 2004: 54). Chapter 3 uses the case of Alcoholics Anonymous groups to characterize 'spirituality' as the paradoxical stance of contemporary individuals who share their weaknesses to gain strength (Kasai 2004: 76), while Chapter 4 identifies the tendency among Japanese followers of the Rajneesh movement to 're-discover their Japanese traditional religiosity' as a global contemporary trend (Itō 2004b: 102). In each case the authors define spirituality as a contemporary phenomenon characterized by thoughts or behaviours designated as 'contemporary', which are then employed as evidence of the relevance of 'spirituality' as a concept to understand contemporary social trends. This strategic loop continues through the rest of the book, albeit with more specifically normative messages.

To be fair to the editors, their emphasis on the need to look into individual and everyday self-understandings of religiousness and how these are relationally constructed (Kashio 2004a: 111) fitted well with contemporaneous worldwide calls for the study of 'lived' or 'everyday' religion. But they and the other contributors then use the concept of spirituality to limit these constructions to a vaguely 'contemporary' realm and, moreover, to salvage from constructionist critique the 'essence of religion'. This seems to negate the original objective espoused in this volume of opening up a new path for religious studies. In Chapter 5, 'spirituality' is defined as 'the core of religious community that separates religiosity from other realms and which consists of a sense and stance of life that are peculiar to individuals whose reference point to understand and feel the world is a relation with something "outside" [that world]' (Kashio 2004a: 115). This essentialist association of spirituality with what the author clearly thinks of as the ethically good aspects of religiosity becomes even more apparent in Chapters 6–8 of the volume: the sharing of 'spirituality' in a Buddhist community in England is interpreted as meaning three values, 'think of others', 'accept others' and 'a calm mind' (Inaba 2004b: 139); 'spirituality' during an event for the youth division of the Buddhist lay group Shinnyoen is observed as originating from the sharing of individual experiences framed within the group's teachings (Kikuchi 2004: 152–3) and 'spirituality' in the French branch of the Japanese religious group Sukyo Mahikari is framed as the discrete community bonds that are typical of our fragmented pluralistic societies (Kashio 2004b: 183).

In retrospect, these studies do not differ in any substantive way from the approach that the editors of this collection claim to critique. Instead of moving away from an interpretive approach, the authors continued to seek to positively interpret thoughts and behaviours that they saw as peculiar to contemporary religion(=spirituality) in relation to some kind of human essence(=spirituality). For example, Inaba Keishin's contribution (Inaba 2004b) was based on three years' fieldwork (1997–2000) among the Friends of the Western Buddhist Order (renamed Triratna Buddhist Community in 2010). His fieldwork overlapped with the first public allegations of sexual misconduct in the group, published in the *Guardian* (Bunting 1997); an internal report produced two decades later found that one in ten members claimed to have experienced or observed sexual misconduct while in the order (Doward 2019). Yet, Inaba does not mention the issue, let alone examine members' reactions to it in relation to the altruism-fostering framework that he describes in his characterization of the group (Inaba 2004a). Analyses of religious forms that could not be interpreted in a positive light only serve to reinforce the message that spirituality is in (and as an) essence good. The rest of the book's chapters, which treat incidents involving members of the Unification Church (Chapter 10), Lifespace (Chapter 11) and Aum (Chapter 12), present the so-called cult problem as a violation (*shingai*) of spirituality.

As such, *supirichuariti* scholars eventually became embroiled in a rhetoric that conflated what they identified as contemporary privatized religion with essentialist hopes for the revival of a fuzzy 'traditional' religiosity. This is exemplified in the concluding remarks of Chapter 9, titled 'Cults and Spirituality Crisis', which is characteristic of the *supirichuariti* field in how it links social issues associated with religious groups to a perceived loss of spirituality:

That individuals who seek spiritual salvation do not knock on the gates of temples and shrines but get caught up in 'cults' is probably the biggest tragedy of the religious world. And considering that the meaning of life and death is not well conveyed in schools, hospitals or at home, a framework for fulfilling spiritual aspirations is absent from education, welfare and society. Hence, the danger of spirituality being turned into a business, of being used and infringed upon, will not disappear in the future. In that sense, we could probably say that the contemporary age is the age of 'spirituality's crisis'. (Yumiyama 2004: 204)

How did we come to this? If Aum did not effectively change the approach to the study of contemporary religion, besides making scholars aware (but not necessarily wary) of methodological flaws, how was it that the study of spirituality came to bear such salvific undertones? One possible answer is that *supirichuariti* allowed certain scholars of religion in Japan to leave behind the heavily criticized *minshū shūkyō* (popular religions) approach while still espousing its central message: that religion was and could be salvific and hence 'therapeutic'.

The *minshū shūkyō* approach

The *minshū shūkyō* approach characterized the study of (new) religions in Japan in the second half of the twentieth century. Although *minshū shūkyō* could literally be translated as 'popular religion', the term does not exactly correspond to the Euro-American concept, which has been criticized for its vagueness and the artificial division it creates between 'official' and 'popular' religion (which mirrors the high/low culture binary; see Hall 1997: ix). There were eventually overlaps between the Japanese and English terms, but the study of *minshū shūkyō* originated with 1950s and 1960s historical studies of nineteenth-century religious movements, such as Tenrikyō, Konkōkyō and Ōmoto. Scholars depicted these as 'persecuted resistance movements that were antagonistic toward the state's power' and 'gave sympathetic portrayals of the ways in which founders of new religions deviated from the ideology of the emperor system' (Hayashi 2006: 213). In the 1970s and 1980s, Shimazono and his fellow sociologist of religion Nishiyama Shigeru expanded the scope of their predecessors, drawing from those movements common characteristics that they associated uniquely with the modern period and Japanese culture.

In an interview with Itō Masayuki, Shimazono explains that the *minshū shūkyō* approach had been his starting point when he became a scholar in the mid-1970s:

I followed the trends of the time, which emphasized that religious movements were invested with a creative and revolutionary role rather than having bad effects on society ... I was interested in bringing to the contemporary period the type of research that had by then looked only at popular religions from the Edo period to the mid-Meiji or even up to Ōmoto [founded in 1899], and which it had considered as alternative (*orutanatibu*) to State Shinto. (Itō 2004c: 261)

In a chapter explicitly titled 'Popular Religions or New Religions?', Shimazono (1995: 162) questions why the concept of 'popular religion', used by scholars of history and folklore such as Murakami Shigeyoshi (1957), had only been employed to talk of religious movements founded in the nineteenth century that opposed and sought alternatives to existing political systems of control. Anticipating the criticism that categorizations like 'popular religion' rehash pre-Second World War attempts to valorize anti-establishment religions, Shimazono (1995) pre-emptively argues that the concept ought to be adopted across historical periods (164), since it was out of a lay or popular 'syncretic religion' (*shūgō shūkyō*) that the first new religious groups in the modern period emerged as a result of modern historical shifts (166).

This essentialist view of an unchanging 'popular' religious core was something that Shimazono himself used in his study of new religious movements and would re-emphasize in his developmental analysis of the shift to a new spirituality culture, which he interprets as a shift from a popular concern with salvation towards a popular concern with self-transformation, spurred by the rise of individualism (Shimazono 2004: 299–303). It is possible to trace whose perspective on *minshū shūkyō* inspired Shimazono to stress the popular salvific role of religion. In a footnote in his first monograph, Shimazono refers readers to Araki Michio's (1938–2008) use of the concept, although he disagrees with Araki's translation of *minshū shūkyō* as 'folk religion' (Shimazono 1992: 180).[12] Araki (1987) argues that the religiosity at the centre of new religions is essentially the same as that of the traditional religions that have existed in Japan since ancient times, which are the anthesis of the religiosity of the Jewish and Christian West (215). In his Eliadean analysis of 'folk religion'[13] he positions it as the universal basis for all human religion, a yet to be understood 'invisible' foundation that sits in contrast to the elite religions of nations and organizations (182). For Araki, 'new religions' are the perfect manifestation of this folk religion and share eight characteristics with all Japanese folk religion (184–7). In summary:

1. New religions arise in times of crisis out of the margins and depths of society, expressing the ethics and thought of the people and standing in contrast to established religions.

2. They are led by charismatic, shamanistic figures, who through their particular religious experiences give structure to the marginal and hidden elements of popular religion.
3. These leaders often become living gods.
4. They seek to renew the world (*yonaoshi*) by connecting their believers with an archaic religious essence.
5. New religions are monotheistic, reflecting their origins in social crises.
6. They are dynamically embedded in the lives of their followers through salvationist technologies that respond directly to people's needs in times of crisis.
7. They preach that all human beings are equal under their respective gods.
8. They are inspired by a Japanese traditional religious ethos whose existence precedes the birth of Japanese culture.

The 1970s witnessed a burst of literature in translation that sought to conceptualize religion during and after the 1960s counter-cultural movements: an abridged translation of Eric Hobshawm's *Primitive Rebels* came out in 1971, Carlos Castaneda's *The Teachings of Don Juan* was translated in 1972, Mircea Eliade's *The Quest* in 1973, Carl Jung's *Man and His Symbols* in 1975, Thomas Luckmann's *The Invisible Religion* in 1976, and Norman Cohn's *The Pursuit of the Millennium* and Peter Burger's *The Secret Canopy* in 1979. Isomae Jun'ichi (2019a: 2–3) argues that scholars in Japan reacted to these works by considering the possibilities that religion offered for a kind of anarchic world, free from the rules of the real world (*genjitsu sekai*). The lay religious groups that appeared throughout the nineteenth century, especially Konkōkyō, Tenrikyō and Ōmotokyō provided the model for such possibilities. These groups presented the commonalities described by Araki, but contrary to his Eliadean search for the 'essence of religion', scholars such as Yasumaru Yoshio studied these groups for answers to questions such as how humans acquire freedom and what is expected from humans during processes of social emancipation (Isomae 2019b: 26). The founders of such lay movements attracted attention because of the possibilities manifested in their successful attempts to lead popular religious movements into a modern era of upheaval. Hence, the focus by researchers at the time on compounds of the word *naoshi* (renewal, healing), such as *yo-naoshi* (world renewal), *kokoro-naoshi* (curing the heart) and *byōki-naoshi* (healing of illness) (Shimazono 2020: 149).

In retrospect, the idea that the alternative to increased social control could only be a promise for bottom-up renewal and healing seems to reflect a feeling of hope on the part of researchers, rather than how these movements actually interpreted this renewal. Takashi Miura demonstrates that the concept of *yonaoshi* bore various meanings depending on the events it became associated with, and not all of them expressed the subversive qualities that were later attributed to the term (Miura 2019). To cite just one of his examples, in the late 1830s two bureaucrats loyal to the Tokugawa regime were deified as *yonaoshi* gods by their local subjects who wanted to express 'gratitude and [to] honour their benevolent rule' (84). Miura also hints at the idea that the model of new religions employed by many scholars might have relied significantly on the millenarian beliefs of one group, Ōmoto, whose utopian and eschatological doctrines came to symbolize everything that 'world renewal' meant within the later framework of the study of new religions. This is developed further by Nagaoka Takashi (2020), who argues that the *minshū shūkyō* perspective, originally promoted by historians Yasumaru Yasuo (1934–2016) and Murakami Shigeyoshi (1928–91) in the first decades of the post-war period, stemmed specifically from studies of Ōmoto (212). Ōmoto's complex and sometimes contradictory ideology was simplified to fit a concept of popular religion meant as a critique of post-war Japanese society, which was seen to be leaning towards conservatism and pervasive capitalism under the influence of the Japan-US Security alliance and Japan's 'economic miracle' (297).

Nagaoka points out that, running parallel to this view of new religions' salvific potential, the post-war field of religious studies in Japan had also, ironically, inherited the viewpoint of the pre-war special political police (*tokkō*), which had employed theories of abnormal psychology to emphasize the biological and genetic origins of the discontent and dissatisfaction expressed by popular religious movements and of their 'anti-social ideologies' (252). Through its emphasis on the counter-cultural dynamics of new religious movements, the *minshū shūkyō* approach therefore unintentionally reproduced a pre-war model of popular religion that over-stressed its 'anti-social' qualities. This meant that, unlike 'established' religions, new religious movements continued to be seen in the post-war period as challengers to the (now secular) spheres of education and politics (Baffelli 2017) and their tendency to engage with more conservative political streams was, for many years, overlooked. Until at least the end of the 1990s, the pacificism of new religious movements was emphasized as a legacy of their pre-Second World War persecution (Kisala 1999); groups that had been quick to espouse nationalist views after the war were considered exceptional cases (Nakano 1990). Thus when 'new' religious shifts came to be associated with the emancipation of the 'common' people from the dire consequences of Japan's early-twentieth-century imperialism, the evolutionary idea of religion adopted by scholars of new religions and later spirituality ended up being bounded to the hopes of a new Japanese nation.

Bellah's legacy: Spirituality and Japan-making

The *minshū shūkyō* approach reflected the political and social concerns of the scholars who forged it in the post-war period and would remain central to Shimazono's ideas about new religions and what he saw as their successor, spirituality. To explain his use of the term Shimazono (2004) emphasizes that 'spirituality' ought to be employed because 'people in these movements consider that they belong to a new age ... that is to follow the age of religion' (297). This new age is characterized by 'a sense of a revival of something religious in a broad sense for the individual in present times ... to overcome the defects of both traditional religions and rationalist modern science' (299). Although this may sound like a description of the New Age movement, Shimazono is quick to point out that, unlike Judeo-Christian societies where spirituality movements differ significantly from the dominant religious culture (277), in Japan, 'as a form of popular religion, new spirituality movements share many common elements with Japan's folk religion and the Buddhist and Shinto traditions' (278). For Shimazono, contemporary social developments provoke new religious shifts, but these are essentially popular reactions to authoritative systems of thought and control.

In her discussion of the impact of the Second World War on the study of religion in Japan, Fujiwara Satoko notes: 'At the end of WWII, the utmost task of Japanese intellectuals became the criticism of the State Shinto system and the installation of democracy. Naturally, the task led to a value judgement with regards to religions ... [and to the attempt] to reform Japanese society, modelling it after the idea of modern Western society' (Fujiwara 2016: 199–200). This comparison with a mostly American West still haunts studies of religion today. For example, a recent, cheaply available and popular short book titled *Religion and the Japanese: From Funeral Buddhism to Spirituality Culture* (Okamoto 2021), written by a young prolific sociologist of religion, dedicates its first chapter to an explanation of the theory of secularization, based on the example of decreasing church attendance in the United States. The chapter ends with the argument that when it comes to the spread of religion outside religious institutions, Japan and Euro-America[14] have a lot in common, but, since Japanese traditional religions do not require their followers to espouse adherence to their belief systems, religion in Japan could be called a 'faithless religion' (14–15).

Foundations for this kind of comparative imperative in the study of religion in Japan had already famously been laid out by Robert N. Bellah in his *Tokugawa Religion* (1985 [1957]). Bellah stretched Eurocentric narratives of modernity to argue that the popular values of Edo period Japan – what Yasumaru (1974) called 'popular morality', exemplified by virtues such as diligence, thrift, humility and filial piety – had played a role analogous to the Protestant ethics of Weber's thesis on the rise of capitalism. Here, Bellah was mirroring the work of the political theorist Maruyama Masao, who during the same period 'envisioned a moral social order capable of radical self-transformation and constant renewal through the critical reappropriation of its own original form and consciousness – its religio-political archetypes' (Barshay 2019: 201–2). Amy Borovoy (2016: 483) argues that Bellah had sought 'to imagine a liberal secular politics that could be animated by a sense of oneness, social trust, national ideals, and overarching moral commitments'. Japan, she argues, was identified as a locus of comparison for what Bellah regarded as the excesses of American liberalism and individualism (488).

In the 1970s and 1980s, a shift towards a critique of modernity resulted in a rejection of the applicability of Weber's thesis among religious studies scholars in Japan. However, I argue that the appeal of a lay morality capable of transforming and 'saving' society remained at the heart of the study of new religions and the 'new' spirituality culture that was pitted as their successor. Shimazono's starting point was the counter of Weber's thesis, especially in its classic interpretation of the 'elimination of magic' as the characteristic feature of modern industrialized societies. Shimazono interpreted the vitalist outlook of new religious groups as an attempt to recover the bonds tying human to human, and human to the world and nature – bonds that Weber had argued modern societies had liberated themselves from (Shimazono 2004: 52). Here one cannot but sense Shimazono's commitment to Bellah's belief in the existence of a 'dormant' moral social order.

Shimazono (1991: 401) notes that it was Bellah who had approached him to work on the Japanese translation of *Habits of the Heart*, published in 1991. Given the complex nature of the original (Bellah et al. 1985), which was both a sociological analysis and a philosophical argument with novelistic undertones, it took Shimazono and his co-translator, Nakamura Keishi, five years to complete. He also mentions several influences that he shared with Bellah, including the argument developed by Herbert Fingarette (1972) that the Confucian concept of ritual (*li*) proved that the power of ritual manifests itself in everyday interactions such as handshaking, and not in the precepts that we usually associate with purely 'otherworldly' traditions, such as Christianity, Islam or Buddhism (Shimazono 2014: 220). Shimazono (1991: 397) understood that it was from this that Bellah had developed his concept of 'habits of the heart' to denote 'the ritualistic patterns of American life' and notes that Bellah had also found ritualistic patterns in the essence of Japanese culture in his *Tokugawa Religion*. Bellah attracted criticism for equating America with the White middle class (Thomas 2019: 31–2). Shimazono was clearly aware of this, noting that Bellah had remarked in a private conversation that the term 'civil religion' – which had been inspired by the phrase 'American Shinto' (Gaston 2019: 210)[15] – was no longer appropriate and that he was now more inclined to think in terms of a mutual echoing of diverse traditions (*tayōna dentō no hibikiai*) (Shimazono 1991: 398). Yet, even twenty years later, Shimazono (2014: 223–4) remained inspired by the critical and therapeutic functions that Bellah attributed to religion and that he himself had identified in his study of 'new' religions in Japan.

In contrast to Yasumaru's *yonaoshi*, Shimazono's focus was on *kyūsai* (salvation). For him, the so-called new religions were salvation religions, like Christianity, Buddhism and Islam, since they all expressed awareness of an actuality (*jitsuzai-sei*) in which it is difficult to escape from 'evil' (*aku*) (Shimazono 2019: 371). The study of new religions in Japan allowed him to provide a Japanese lens on the processes of development of salvation religions and, by extension, to problematize Yasumaru's argument that popular ethical reform in the early modern period had rejected magical elements (377).[16] Shimazono soon noticed, however, that the principles of salvation had shifted with modernization and that even the concepts of salvation and difficult-to-escape-evil were becoming obsolete. This is where 'spirituality' came in as 'the generic term for all thought and practice from which individuals can choose and pick when seeking communities, practice and thought that once "salvation" used to offer' (Shimazono 2019: 379). For Shimazono, spirituality was thus the successor to salvation; religion continued to offer salvific promise for Japanese people and, ultimately, humanity. In his short introductory book *Contemporary Religion and Spirituality* (Shimazono 2012), the reader can sense how much the March 2011 earthquake, tsunami and nuclear disaster in north-eastern Japan had affected Shimazono's hopes in the possibilities of spirituality. In a chapter on 'The New Spirituality and Peace', the author quotes from environmental awareness raising workshops and NGOs promoting 'holistic education' to note the ideological crossovers between new spirituality culture and peace activism (85). And it ends with examples of Buddhist organizations and spiritual care projects supporting those bereaved by the '3.11' triple disaster, which Shimazono interprets as 'religion=spirituality's turn to fill the loss of meaning that occurred in public spaces as the result of secularization' (131).

Bellah's legacy extends beyond Shimazono's work. Horie Norichika, for example, highly praises Bellah's chapter on 'Religious Evolution' (1964), arguing that it ought to be a classic of twentieth-century religious studies scholarship (Horie 2004: 277). Its wide and functional definition of religion as 'a set of symbolic forms and acts which relate man to the ultimate conditions of his existence' (Bellah 1964: 359), Horie (2004) argues, allows for the consideration of contemporary religious changes as symbolic expressions of humanity's ultimate conditions.[17] Horie considers that Bellah's theory of religious evolution, inspired by the fate of historic religions, can be read as a double structured argument about religious generation and proliferation (not degeneration). He is particularly keen to stress that Bellah not only described the rise of an alternative religiosity (*daitai-teki shūkyōsei*) tied to secularism, but also predicted a religious revival, even before the world witnessed the Iranian revolution or the rise of the Religious Right in 1980s America (279). In fact, Horie's (2009) *magnum opus* on the history of the discipline of the psychology of religion,[18] relies on Bellah's theory to argue that the self-actualization theories promoted by the rise of psychological thought in 'advanced societies' of the twentieth century correspond to a 'new spirituality' that reflects Bellah's 'modern religion', the last stage in his scheme of religious evolution: 'The historic religions discovered the self; the early modern religion found a doctrinal basis on which to accept the self in all its empirical ambiguity; modern religion is beginning to understand the laws of the self's own existence and so to help man take responsibility for his own fate' (Bellah 1964: 372). In an earlier publication Horie (2000) had already applied this schema to healing:

> Techniques of 'healing' (*iyashi*) originate in primitive religions (*genshi shūkyō*), but as historic religions developed, they came to form 'a small tradition' of practices that catered to sudden changes that normal rituals could not deal with. Then, for people today (*gendaijin*), who think of the mind and body as one, i.e. the 'self', healing was rediscovered as an effective form of modern religion. (Horie 2000: 70)

The salvific and therapeutic undertones of spirituality as contemporary religion stemming from a non-elite, small and popular core are evident in Horie's (2019b) recent collection on *supirichuariti*, titled *Pop Spirituality: Mediatized Religion* (*Poppu supirichuariti: media ka sareta shūkyōsei*), which includes his previously published writings spanning over a decade. Horie uses the term pop spirituality to refer to the spirituality of the people (*minshū*), not in the dismissive sense of popular as common, but in the sense of the 'spirituality held by people with a pragmatic consciousness of using what is useful for understanding and solving problems of the heart and soul' (Horie 2019b: viii). We immediately see here the implicit reproduction of a division between popular and official religion, as well as echoes of the therapeutic or salvific function attributed to popular religion in the *minshū shūkyō* discourse of post-war religious studies in Japan. As encapsulated in the book's subtitle, pop spirituality is 'mediatized religiosity'; Horie explicitly warns that the book only treats spirituality that is selected for being popular and easy to understand and use *and* that is circulated by people through media platforms such as SNS (viii). This highlights the great paradox that I described in the Introduction: the circulation of the spiritual through the media (=mediatized religiosity) is presented as evidence of the presence of a non-mediatized (hence a 'not-religion') spirituality. But there is also an additional slippage, since Horie reads this spirituality, freed from the constraints of 'religion', as representative of a kind of essential and timeless religiosity.

Religion, Horie argues, has always been a medium and continued to be so during the modern period, particularly 'through writings that would convey and share uniform teachings'. What 'religion' did, according to Horie, was to construct 'abstract concepts and doctrines' out of 'the world of hearsay and lore' from which 'both the Christian bible and the Buddhist scriptures stemmed'. Becoming 'a believer', he states, involved turning to a medium, a missionary (*fukyō*) who transmitted that religion. The 'mediatized religiosity' that is contemporary pop spirituality is different; it is *not* religion. Instead it represents something closer to religiosity before religion:

> There are people who try to express and convey a sense of values that are important to them but that, relative to 'religion', are not religion. The world of pop spirituality that is daily updated by such people is a contemporary phenomenon, but it might be closer to a state of the spiritual life (*seishin seikatsu*) of the humanity that preceded 'religion' and for that matter was antecedent to [the invention] of writing. (Horie 2019b: x–xi)

In short, Horie uses 'spirituality' to identify both the 'new' religiosity that he is trying to describe and a primordial (hence timeless) pre-religion state. Both Shimazono and Horie thus represent a more common and unflinching teleological view of religion in the *minshū supirichuariti* discourse, which carries on the legacy of *minshū shūkyō* in its implicit hopes for an alternative that can ameliorate the perceived loss of a moral-social order in Japan, and that hearkens back to an imagined popularly shared religious essence constantly capable of countering such losses. These concerns are made even clearer in a collection of chapters published by the University of Tokyo Press (Horie 2019a), in which several senior figures of religious studies in Japan reflect on the seventy-year post-war history of religion and society, concluding with a lengthy dialogue between Shimazono, Horie and a scholar of intellectual history Kurozumi Makoto (b.1950). This dialogue is predicated on the idea that post-war Japan has been characterized by both secularization and religious revival. Horie links this to his conceptualization of the post-war period as having a 'two-fold temporality' (*nijū no jikansei*): the formation of modern civic society based on democratization and freedom of religion has been contradicted by an 'opposite course' (*gyaku kōsu*), namely the drift to the right and regression to a pre-war authoritarianism (Horie 2019a: 5). All three scholars seem to be concerned with the role religion has played in such circumstances, revealing in their dialogue a fierce critique of what they consider to be old organizational forms, such as the state, capitalist institutions, and even those religious groups that have failed to reflect on the possibility that what happened in Aum could have occurred within their ranks too (309).

Their arguments reflect an evolutionary conceptualization of the relation between religion and society in Japan, albeit one that sees the pre-war top-down system (*jōikatatsu*) as having survived throughout the post-war period. This perspective can be summarized as follows. Folk rituals and beliefs of village society weakened as agriculture became less important and people moved to cities. New religions gained prominence in the post-war years because they provided faith communities for these new urban populations. As the third sector strengthened and people formed new bonds from the 1970s onwards, such organized social movements weakened to be replaced by spirituality, a movement more focused on individual therapy and care (Horie 2019a: 314). The problem, however, was that these post-war developments did not eliminate the idea of the primacy of the nation above all other social movements, including religious groups. This resulted in the re-enactment of a pre-war, conservative top-down approach to social organization summarized by the Meiji slogan 'enrich the country, strengthen the army' (*fukoku kyōhei*) (334). In support of this argument, Shimazono draws on the notions of group utilitarianism (*shūdan rikōshugi*) and the predominance of political over social values (*seijiteki kachi no yūetsu*) that Bellah associated with modernization. Then, as the nation's economic drive came to a halt in the 1990s, lateral bonds weakened and people, including politicians, prioritized financial benefits at the expense of solidarity, hence the conservative turn of society (315). But, if the 1990s had announced the end of *kyōhei*, Fukushima's nuclear disaster put an end to *fukoku* (335) and opened the possibility for a 'spirituality of publicness beyond national communities' (*kokka kyōdōtai o koeru kōkyōsei no supirichuariti*), a civic ideal independent of individual beliefs (344). This was a spirituality capable of bringing about not just the reconciliation between victims and perpetrators, but between humanity and the world environment (*sekai kankyō*) (318). In short, if spirituality had the potential to save Japan, it could save humanity.

The missed chance of *supirichuariti* studies

The rise of a field of spirituality studies centred around the salvific and therapeutic role of contemporary religion was, I argue, a misconstrued and mis-constructed attempt to provide evidence against the idea that 'legitimate' religion can only arise out of established religious traditions, whether in the form of religious organizations or local folk religion. It started with Shimazono's critique of the shortcomings of the popular religion perspective, in which he castigated historians of religion for their narrow-focused analyses of religious founders and their biographies at the expense of the lives of common believers (Shimazono 1995: 167). This is reminiscent of the beginnings of the Euro-American critique of 'popular religion' among proponents of the study of religion in 'ordinary' life, who pushed for a focus on the embodiment and enactment of religion regardless of the officiality of where that happens, expressed in various terms as 'vernacular religion' (Primiano 1995), 'implicit religion' (Bailey 1998), 'everyday religion' (Ammerman 2007) or 'lived religion' (McGuire 2008). Spirituality scholars were receptive to this shift in methodological approach, having seen how religious concerns could be found in self-development seminars (Haga and Yumiyama 1994), psychotherapeutic techniques and nutritional movements such as macrobiotics (Tanabe, Shimazono and Yumiyama 1999). But, instead of debating the causes or describing the formats of the co-existence of 'religious' and 'non-religious' concerns within contemporary human activities – not to mention questioning the religious and non-religious as scholarly categories – they simplified their task by assigning to the notion of spirituality a panacean function of religion-making. In other words, if a self-development seminar or a new nutritional product promoted some sort of apparently religious message, it automatically became proof of the spread of a new spirituality culture.

This becomes relatively clear in Yumiyama's defence of *supirichuariti* studies at the 2014 JASRS conference, when he argued that work in this field could be said to have inspired three avenues of research. Some researchers focused on practices such as meditation or ascetic training (*gyohō*), in which they themselves engaged. Others attended to spirituality in other fields, such as education or care. Finally, there were scholars who turned to examine religion as social capital, focusing on its practice in localities rather than organizations (*kyōdan dewanaku, chiiki no nakade*) (Yumiyama 2015: 146). The contributors to *A Sociology of Spirituality* have indeed gone in distinct directions. Kashio and Itō, Yumiyama's co-editors, have both gone on to become practitioners and proponents of yoga and meditation (Kashio 2016, 2019; see also Kasai 2010). Yumiyama and Kasai Kenta, who originally worked on spirituality in the Alcoholics Anonymous movement (Kasai 2007), have since published on education and spiritual care (Becker and Yumiyama 2009; Kasai 2016). They have also collaborated with a third group of scholars, such as Inaba Keishin, who have worked on religion and disaster, especially since 11 March 2011 Tōhoku earthquake and tsunami; here religion is considered as a factor enhancing resilience (Minowa et al. 2016; Hoshino and Yumiyama 2019). The only member of that group who has consistently and expressly focused on what he sees as the bad aspects of spirituality is Sakurai Yoshihide, otherwise more famous as an established scholar of the 'cult issue' in Japan. But even he seems to view spirituality as, in essence, positive, given that several of his treatises concern how certain groups identified as cults have, in his words, 'ended up violently eroding spirituality' as they developed as organizations (Sakurai 2004: 216; see also Sakurai 2009b).

These scholars were less successful in establishing *supirichuariti* studies as a pioneering sub-field in the study of religion. In trying to explicate their argument based on a historically evolutionary framework, within which their case studies were the next step *after* new religions, scholars of spirituality fell into a double trap. First, they repeated the mistake committed by new religions scholars before them of having to exclusively associate the so-called new spirituality culture with contemporaneous social changes; the 'new' in religion had to mirror the 'new' in society. Perhaps more importantly, they failed to employ the heuristic value that they eventually attributed to the concept of 'spirituality' (Kashio 2000: 166) to question religion as a *sui generis* phenomenon (McCutcheon 1997). Instead, figures or communities taken as representative cases of the 'new spirituality culture' in Japan were defined by the degree to which their biographies could be used to assume links with so-called established religious traditions, while their words were abstractedly compared to a corpus of messages that had already been labelled New Age. This approach hid from view structural commonalities with trends beyond a *sui generis* religion. This can be illustrated through the example of Yumiyama's work on Satō Hatsume (1923–2016) and her lodging facility for the distressed, Mori no Ischia, founded in 1992, and the missed opportunity it represents.

At a presentation delivered at the 1999 workshop on 'contemporary religiosity/ spirituality (*reisei*)', Yumiyama had argued against Shimazono's theory that the new spirituality culture is not 'salvation religion' (*kyūsai shūkyō*), employing the examples of Satō and Daitokuji Teruaki, both of whom he called New Age leaders (although neither identify as such). Each, Yumiyama observed, uses their personal background in, respectively, Catholicism and Tenrikyō to argue for a universal religiosity beyond specific religious traditions and to offer advice to individuals who have come to know about them through cultural products (a film dedicated to the first and a novel written by the second). Although they are not heads of religious groups and would be considered 'unconventional' (*shinki*) by their respective religions, they do play a salvific role (Yumiyama 2000: 160).

Senior scholars did not disagree, but in the post-workshop discussion they expressed doubts about the novelty of what Yumiyama was describing (Kashio 2000: 164–5). Scholar of new religions Nishiyama Shigeru asked whether those individuals could not simply be referred to as 'a new type of *reinōsha*' and urged Yumiyama to 'consider the characteristics of the contemporary world they live in'. Ikegami Yoshimasa, a scholar of shamanistic practitioners, remarked that Satō, Yumiyama's first case, 'looks like a contemporary type of folk shaman (*minkan fusha*)'; shamans, he pointed out, also draw from religious traditions. Was Yumiyama's distinction solely based on Satō's 'use of a contemporary vocabulary' and the medium of film? In order to appeal for the legitimacy and novelty of the religious phenomena he was witnessing, Yumiyama responded by emphasizing the link between what he identified as New Age beliefs, such as individual transformation, and so-called contemporary social shifts, such as 'the generalization of affluence', 'individualism' and the rise of an anonymous public (Yumiyama 2002). In so doing, he was trying to stress conceptual continuity with a framework that was already flawed. 'It all becomes a bit superficial, doesn't it?', Ikegami asked. 'I agree', Yumiyama responded, 'but people are drawn to those individuals. So, even if "superficial", this is today's religious situation.'

In retrospect and admittedly with the advantage of twenty years-worth of scholarly research on the subject, Ikegami was right to the extent that Yumiyama's case studies presented nothing substantially new in terms of how 'shamanistic' practitioners employ a variety of knowledge resources and local networks to acquire authority and forge legitimacy (see Chapter 1). However, Yumiyama could have used those cases to demonstrate the blurring of activities that he identified as 'spiritual' with other concerns. In the first ever book written about her (Satō 1997), we learn that Satō was a primary school teacher concerned with children quitting school. This may shed new light on the fact that Satō first started her counselling activities in 1982, in the middle of a national panic about the so-called school refusal syndrome (Okano and Tsuchiya 1999). Her emphasis on a proper healthy diet and her recipes for rice balls (*onigiri*) and other 'traditional' Japanese daily food, can be located within the national twentieth-century movement that emphasized a proper Japanese diet for a healthy mind (Hong 2017). Attention to the broader context and relational dynamics with contemporaneous phenomena and ideologies would have allowed Yumiyama to find religion beyond 'religion' and make the study of spirituality in Japan truly revolutionary.

To be clear, this is not a problem peculiar to 'Japanese' scholarship. As Itō (2003: 160) notes, Shimazono's description of the evolution of religion in post-industrial societies is similar to James Beckford's (1989) description of the new type of spirituality that he saw developing both within and without religious institutions in Western Europe and North America. They both owe a lot to the Habermasian turn, namely the conceptualization of religion as a cultural resource in late capitalist societies (Beckford 1989: 145–53).[19] As illustrated by Bellah's legacy, however, there was (and still exists) an additional dimension in Japanese scholarship in the genuine wish to provide *alternative* scenarios to 'Western', which often means Christian Protestant, theories. Even if more recent research clearly demonstrates that historical contacts make it impossible to argue for specifically 'Western' or 'Japanese' religious aspects in the twentieth-century societies that scholars attempt to describe (Kurita, Tsukada and Yoshinaga 2019; Dake, Ohmi and Yoshinaga 2020), many *supirichuariti* studies were developed and continue to be argued in response to a 'Western', mostly American, imaginary; their value is comparative (Horie 2019b: 2). At the same time, they claim to counter the Western hegemony of scholarly theory by presenting alternative models of socio-religious development.

Whether as a cause or effect of this comparative thrust, many *supirichuariti* studies, often unwittingly, associate religiosity as a sui generis phenomenon with a sui generis Japaneseness. Previous research has already shown the pitfalls of the essentialist tropes in these discourses (Prohl 2007), but there is something more in this than just an issue of culturalism. There is a problem in how scholars claim to speak for a population's moods and values, while being aware that these are co-constructed by (global) mediatized messages of which everyone is both a consumer and, increasingly today, a producer. Enmeshed in scholarly accounts of the fall of religion and the rise of spirituality, one can sense feelings of anxiety regarding not only where to find 'religion' in a secular world (Thomas 2019), but also how to account for the 'local value' of case studies in scholarly work that is increasingly required to answer to global theoretical shifts. It is this double anxiety that produces the paradoxical exegeses discussed in this chapter, which seek to present cultural phenomena such as the *seishin sekai* as relevant signs of global religious change but simultaneously wish for a differentiation between a cultural/Japanese and a 'non-cultural'/universal dimension of spirituality. What Rots (2019) refers to as 'Japan-making' arguments in academia are always connected to 'Japan-relevance' arguments. If religion-making narratives express a worry about the continuing relevance of normative religion in a changing world, Japan-making approaches illustrate continuing anxiety about the relevance of Japanese case studies in a predominantly Euro-American scholarly world.

Conclusion

The Aum affair undoubtedly changed how scholars could talk about 'religion'. Notably, it led to a lack of academic voices in the debates that developed over the 'cult' issue (Baffelli and Reader 2012: 17). But it did not ultimately change the way that religious studies researchers approached their field. Just as postwar scholars had sought to positively interpret what they saw as thoughts and behaviours peculiar to 'popular' religion (*minshū shūkyō*), *supirichuariti* studies scholars looked for the positive salvific and therapeutic potential in 'contemporary' (*gendai*) religion. For figures such as Shimazono Susumu, the new spirituality culture was a continuation (not a split) from the religiosity of new religious movements; a single evolutionary line that Shimazono describes in detail in his most recent book (Shimazono 2020). Shimazono finds the salvific opportunities of spirituality in self-help groups, which have inherited the religiosity of new religions but, contrary to salvation religions like Aum, do not become permanent communities (287). His book ends with an analysis of the thought of famous social activist, Sugimoto Eiko (1939–2008), who dedicated her life to rebuilding the communal ties of Minamata, the city of her birth. Early post-Second World War environmental pollution had turned her neighbours against each other after leaving many, including Sugimoto, with a neurological disorder known as Minamata disease. Shimazono notes that Sugimoto had been inspired to rebuild local bonds by the words of her fisherman-father, which she later interpreted through the Buddhist teachings of the new religion, Risshō Kōsei Kai. In Sugimoto, Shimazono found someone who had managed to connect traditional religion (=Buddhism) with new religions (=Risshō Kōsei Kai) and the post-1990s self-help movement, an amalgam which he calls the 'spirituality of *yonaoshi*' (2020: 296).

In this chapter, I have argued that the rise of the field of spirituality studies was a missed opportunity. Cases like those of Sugimoto Eiko, whose experiences were informed by environmental pollution, industrial disease, national economic imperatives and social discrimination, cannot and should not be reduced to expressions of a timeless religious essence, always ready to surface and rescue people from the various losses of modernity. As I have illustrated, the intellectual nexus from which this interpretation of contemporary religion arose has its roots in the post-Second World War socio-political climate in Japan and scholars' adoption of the concept of popular religion to identify the anti-establishment potential of a populace that had just come out of a terrible war. Picked up later by sociologists of new religious movements, who sought to explain their rise in conversation with Euro-American theories of secularization in post-industrial societies, the concept of popular religion was soon reduced to a salvific essence, which became the common denominator for the role of religion in contemporary societies. Although the study of spirituality was originally framed as a reaction to an institution- or tradition-based idea of religion, the next generation of scholars could not shed the idea that religion is essentially functional: it is there to bind us together and save us from natural and social disasters.

Such conceptualizations of 'salvation' and its successor, 'spirituality', are based on the premise of belief. Shimazono and other researchers of spirituality assume that individuals wholeheartedly believe in whoever or whatever is going to save them, whether a religious founder, a New Age leader, a text promising self-development or a practice leading to the transformation of the self. However, as noted by Ikegami (2020: 376) among others, this view reflects a Protestant-based monotheistic understanding of religion, which ignores the (often complex) feelings of doubt that accompany these experiences. As he points out, people might hesitate to respond 'yes' to a survey asking whether they believe in the after-life and they might be 'left with a sense of mere performance at the back of their head when they pray for the dead'. Even so, praying for the dead can still be meaningful and give them 'feelings of satisfaction and understanding by thinking that they might contribute to bringing a little peace to those they miss or have lost' (377). The reality is often messier than it looks. This was already evident in my discussion of spiritual therapists in the previous chapter, but will become even more so in the next, when I consider the personal ideals and lives of publishers and translators involved in the creation of what I call 'print spirituality' through the publishing industry.

3

Print spirituality

Ms Uehara was working as an editor at the small publishing house, Jiyūsha, when it published the Japanese version of Shirley MacLaine's popular New Age classic *Out on a Limb* (1983) in 1986.¹ Translated by the Yamakawas, a couple now renowned as 'legends' of the spiritual world in Japan, this book became a bestseller associated with the boom in *seishin sekai* literature in the 1980s to early 1990s. *Seishin sekai* is the book category that Shimazono Susumu appropriated to name the 'new spirituality culture' that he saw as the precursor of contemporary spirituality. In their articles in *Star People*, both Shimazono (2009) and Kashio (2009) mention the translation of *Out on a Limb* as being a milestone in popularizing New Age ideas in Japan. Yet, in an interview on 2 December 2020, Ms Uehara argued that the books that Jiyūsha was publishing in the 1980s were intended for a 'general audience'; they were not alternative or counter-cultural: '[Even though] *Out on a Limb* was sold as a *seishin sekai* book … it is really a book about life and human existence (*seikatsu-bon*). It's the story of the author that is important. Their motivations.'

While spiritual therapists engage with various forms of media, one of my first observations when I started investigating their business activities was that their interest in this kind of practice often seemed to be related to, if not instigated by the reading of the Japanese version of *Out on a Limb* or another New Age classic of Anglo-Saxon literature. Roger Chartier (1991: 68) argues that 'If the French of the late eighteenth century fashioned the Revolution, it is because they had in turn been fashioned by books'. The same could be claimed for the study of 'spirituality' at the turn of the twenty-first century. From Wouter Hanegraaff's ([1996] 1998) seminal study *New Age Religion and Western Culture* to Craig Martin's (2014) critical exegesis of contemporary spirituality culture in *Capitalizing Religion*, the analysis of popular literature has formed an essential component of the scholarly study of modern spiritualities. In Japan too, even the earliest attempts to identify a 'spirituality culture' or, for that matter, a 'New Age movement' relied on the writings of a few insiders who seemed to have played the role of gatekeepers of the popular and scholarly narratives that eventually became both associated with and representative of those phenomena.[2] Their analyses seem to confirm Olav Hammer's (2010: 60) claim that 'New Age religion is generated, reproduced and distributed by a small set of "religious virtuosi"'.

But what about the publishers like Jiyūsha who decided to take on the books written by those authors, and the translators like the Yamakawas who made them accessible to the Japanese market? What were their concerns and interests, and what did the spiritual mean and do for them? The *seishin sekai* and, more recently, popular *supirichuariti* literature has thrived relative to the overall situation in the publishing industry in Japan. Why and how did those books come to be popular, to the extent that the spirituality sector of the print market continued to grow when much of the rest of the market was in decline? The use – and sometimes establishment – of publishers by religious groups, as well as the reliance of alternative culture more generally on print material to propagate its ideas is a relatively well-known phenomenon. Yet, the middlemen, namely the translators, editors and publishing house founders or managers, have largely been ignored, almost as if books are independent products written, printed and distributed out of their authors' offices.

In this chapter, I reconnect spirituality to the context of the commercial publishing industry and delve into the role of these middlemen in the production and circulation of didactic narratives of self-cultivation that came to be marketed as 'spiritual' and that scholars later considered as alternative religious ideas and practices. I argue that the label of spirituality, which is easily assigned to various contemporary beliefs and practices, may be less about what those beliefs and practices are than it is about a larger totalizing media market that gains from having yet another set of beliefs and practices become part of a so-called global new spirituality culture. My aim is not to offer yet another moral critique of religion's subjugation to neo-liberal market powers; I do not believe that there is an 'authentic' spirituality that has been co-opted by capitalism and media consumerism. Rather, I show how the production of spirituality is intimately related to the structures of and changes in the publishing industry, the role of which has thus far been overlooked, as well as to the personal lives and concerns of individuals within that industry.

Books of the *seishin sekai*, which were originally an amalgam of a great variety of genres, slowly came to be associated with the growing self-help literature, or as Makino (2012: 71) argues, with personalities such as Ehara Hiroyuki, who became synonymous with the 'spiritual boom' and formed access points for people to become familiar with self-development ideas. One could thus argue that the popular *supirichuariti* literature was an extension of the *seishin sekai* literature, which tried to remain relevant in a climate of suspicion of religion and the occult by emphasizing the notion of self-help and self-development. But, as I explore in the first part of this chapter, there is a more subtle history to be told through the publishers who made their name in publishing such literature. I suggest that if it was not for certain small publishers' interest in the life paths and autobiographies of successful personalities and their belief that reading about certain life philosophies may make a better world, there might not have been a space in which 'alternative' religious messages could have reached a wider audience in Japan. The *seishin sekai* literature, as a predecessor of the popular spirituality literature, was therefore not a distinct field that later came to be associated with the self-development genre. It was an offshoot of a much longer tradition of Japanese self-cultivation (*shūyo*) books, and its 'alternative' religious discourse was in fact a reflection of *shūyo* concerns. In the second part of the chapter, I highlight the equally important influence of translators, through a close examination of the vital role that the couple Yamakawa Akiko (b.1943) and Yamakawa Kōya (b.1941) have played in translating and simultaneously 'configuring' alternative religious discourse in Japan from the late 1980s until today, including its therapeutic message of hope.

Religion, self-cultivation and commercial print culture

Reading, writing and commercial print culture are all intimately related to religious practices and institutions. Similar to connections between the Church and writing cultures in Europe, in Japan, up until the sixteenth century, the main producers of text were large shrine-temple complexes such as Todai-ji and Mount Kōya. Even after the arrival of print technology in the seventeenth century, it was the sale of Buddhist texts that supported the proliferation of publishing businesses (Wakao 2015: 9, 13). Among such religious texts, Japan saw the publication of spell books and occult (*hiden*) manuals very early on. These were not only used to attend to personal problems, but were also believed to transfer powers to the person who copied them (Koike 2015). This echoes beliefs about the merit-generating power of *shakyō* (sutra copying), but also reflects later variations of the practice, such as the copying of passages of *The New Human Revolution* by members of the lay Buddhist group Soka Gakkai

(McLaughlin 2019: 95). The example of Soka Gakkai, and its powerful publishing and audiovisual companies, is in fact typical of the intimate relationship between the (print) media and religion since the nineteenth century.

On the one hand, the multiplication of media into magazines, periodicals and newspapers in the second half of the nineteenth century was initially dependent on the critical stance that these media expressed towards the rapid social changes in Japan at that time. This included fierce attacks on new religious groups that often sounded like nostalgic reactions to the perceived degeneration of an otherwise invented Japanese religiosity (Gaitanidis 2019: 78). Similar arguments have been made in other locales, such as the United States, where, in the post-war period, 'the American religious fringe' was consistently constructed against a 'normative mainstream that was white, upper middle and middle class, male, and religiously liberal' (McCloud 2004: 28). On the other hand, religious groupings, from book-reading circles to newly founded religions, have tended to invest in self-published materials that respond to negative images found in other outlets, and that of course propagate their ideas and activities to both members and non-members (Baffelli 2016: 31–5). Beyond reaching a wider audience and earning income, however, reading and writing have also been essential to forming religious emotions and defining what being religious in this or that tradition 'really' means.

In his study of the business of evangelical books in America, Daniel Vaca (2019: 3) convincingly argues that 'contemporary evangelicalism took shape and steadily expanded through commercial efforts to generate new media markets and build successful media corporations'. Vaca avoids the classic, albeit problematic separation of economy and religion as distinct ontological categories. In the same vein as religious studies scholars who encourage a focus on the corporate form (McLaughlin et al. 2020), Vaca considers religion as a type of 'public'. In the case of the Evangelicals, this public is formed through group bible readings, but also, and more significantly, through the presentation by publishers and booksellers of 'book buying and reading as primary disciplines of authentic Christian faith' (Vaca 2019: 15). Reading not only helps individual introspection, but also 'idealizes both the merit of the book's content and the virtue of a book's reader' (14). In her study of the theosophical global print culture, Lori Lee Oates (2020) demonstrates that textual engagement simultaneously popularized and propagated theosophical ideas through, for example, Helena Blavatsky's and Annie Besant's publications, and partially supported the society financially through the establishment of publishing houses and the commissioning of translations of its books.

Vaca and Oates arrive independently at the same conclusion: the establishment of 'commercial religion' through the medium of book publishing in the nineteenth century provided the mould for how, even today, the world engages with religious ideas presented as new and alternative. There are, however, two further inter-related and important points that are seldom made. The first is that publishers established by religious groups have often been responsible for introducing into the market texts other than those written by the groups themselves. For example, Hirakawa Shuppan, the publishing arm of the new religion Agonshū, has been known since 1971 for the books authored by the group's founder Kiriyama Seiyū (Baffelli and Reader 2018: 64). But in the 1980s and 1990s, it was also responsible for translating famous thinkers usually associated with the contemporaneous New Age movement: Rudolf Steiner, Hermann Beckh, G. I. Gurdjieff, Jiddu Krishnamurti and René Guénon.[3] In their evaluation of Kiriyama's ability to catch the underlying concerns and trends of the time, Baffelli and Reader (2018: 55) note that in the 1980s, the group 'framed its teachings and practices in the context of the *seishin sekai* ... [and] frequently used the word *seishin sekai* in its publications'. Another case in point is Nipponkyōbunsha, which has mainly published works by Taniguchi Masaharu, the founder of the NRM Seichō no Ie, but was also responsible for introducing Theosophical, New Thought and occult texts to Japan in the immediate postwar period, mostly in translation. A third example, which is not related to a religious group *per se*, is that of Jimbunshoin, a publisher established in Kyoto in 1922, famous for its highly valued collections of translated works by famous French and German novelists, such as Pascal, Baudelaire, Racine, Goethe and Hesse. In 2013, one of publisher's staff discovered copies of the magazine *Nihon Shinrei* in storage and realized that the predecessor of Jinbunshoin was the Japanese Society of Spiritualism (Nihon Shinrei Gakkai), a group active in the early twentieth century and centred around individuals interested in alternative, psychic or spiritual therapies (see Kurita 2020).

In other words, publishers associated with particular religious institutions do not necessarily abide to normative notions of what a religious text is but are instead concerned with what it is supposed to do for the reader. For this, as well as for more prosaic commercial reasons, they tend to publish beyond the range of texts that they were originally established to promote. This brings me to my second point. Analysis of the connections between publishers and religious or spiritualist associations needs to be supplemented by an analysis of how their concerns and interests reflected and also impacted on wider socio-ideological shifts to which books contributed as sources of knowledge, bringers of authoritative literacies *and* products of a capitalist market. As this chapter will unfold, the market in books that came to be labelled as *seishin sekai* can be traced back to a concern with self-cultivation among key figures in publishing, rather than to a concern with 'alternative' religion.

Kōdansha, one of the three leading companies in Japan's publishing industry today, was one of the key contributors to ideas and methods regarding self-cultivation (*shūyō*), which became particularly popular in the Taishō period (1912–26) (Ōtani 2020: 12). It established the major trends that we see today in the self-development literature, of which, I argue the *seishin sekai* and spirituality books can be understood to be a part. The first appearance of the term *shūyō* in the modern period is found in the 1871 translation of Samuel Smiles's *Self-Help* (1876 [1859]), a Victorian era bestseller extolling its readers to build their character and seek success through perseverance (Kurita 2018: 68). The depiction of ordinary family life and work as the ideal context for personal and social improvement or *shūyō* had already existed in early modern Japanese discourse of the late eighteenth and early nineteenth centuries, leading to the establishment of the first 'new religious movements' (Sawada 2004: 7). But *shūyō* underwent various reinterpretations at the turn of the twentieth century, as it kept appearing in contemporaneous debates about the relation between religion, education and morality, and the state. It is this national concern that made *Self-Help* a bestseller in Japan. According to Kinmonth (1981: 20), the book's 'chief attraction' for its translator, Nakamura Keiu, was Smiles's assertion that: 'National progress is the sum of individual industry, energy and uprightness, as national decay is of individual idleness, selfishness and vice' (Smiles 1876: 3, cited in Kinmoth 1981: 20). Nakamura's translation cut and compressed certain chapters of the book, making it even more of an ethical treatise than the English original (Kinmonth 1981: 26).[4]

Up until 1890, *shūyō* carried Smiles's Christian flavour of encouraging an 'independent mind', but in the last decade of the nineteenth century, an internal sense of morality became the key message of *shūyō* literature (Kurita 2018: 68–70). Its nuance shifted again in the first years of the twentieth century to emphasize an ethical imperative that was to be achieved through practical means, such as sitting meditation (*zazen*) and internal contemplation (84).[5] Publishers at the time were particularly keen on such practical means to success and on the idea of learning through concrete examples from the lives of successful individuals. Translations of books by such authors as Orison Swett Marden (1848–1924) and Ralph Waldo Trine (1866–1958) brought many New Thought ideas to Japan, but according to Kawakami Tsuneo – a researcher at the publisher PHP Kenkyūsho, famous today for self-development literature – only those books that were not overtly spiritual found larger audiences (Kawakami 2012: 24).⁶

By 1909, when Noma Seiji (1878–1938) founded the publishing company that would be renamed Kōdansha in 1911, *shūyō* had become an established popular category, spurred in large part by bestsellers dedicated to it. In 1911, Nitobe Inazo, already famous for his *Bushido: The Soul of Japan* (1900; see Benesch 2014), published the monograph *Shūyō*, in which he exhorted 'ordinary people', such as farmers, to consider daily difficulties as potential sources for success (Nitobe 1911, cited in Takeuchi 2005: 220). If Nitobe was the bestselling author in the *shūyō* category at the turn of the century, notes sociologist Takeuchi Yō (2005: 219), then Noma Seiji deserves this accolade during the early Shōwa period, from 1925 to the end of the Second World War. The journalist and non-fiction writer, Uozumi Akira (b.1951), who has published the definitive history of Kōdansha's Noda family based on recently discovered documents (Uozumi 2021), paints a vivid picture of Noma Seiji as a man deeply invested in cultivating a youth section at his publishing company for adolescents as young as twelve years old, who he would encourage in the following way: 'It is not necessary to enter a secondary school to become important … What is the most necessary thing to become an important person? It is not learning. It is not wisdom. It is the character of the person' (Noma Seiji, cited in Uozumi 2021: 276).

Uozumi explains that popular publishers like Kōdansha, which focused on traditional storytelling, *rakugo* (a one-person comical performance) and *naniwa-bushi* (narrative singing with mostly sad themes), specifically targeted the growing numbers of youth unable to access the narrow and competitive route to success via the highly selective imperial universities.⁷ By 1918, nearly all children aged up to fourteen would complete their compulsory primary school education, but less than 20 per cent would proceed to junior high school (Uozumi 2021: 275). Economic and educational disparities had created a significant pool of readers ready to consume messages that promised them ways of 'making it' *despite* the system that had failed them. Precarity and exclusion have always been important motivations for self-cultivation.

By the mid-1920s, more than twenty adolescents entered Kōdansha's youth section each year, spending the next three to five years as apprentices, after which they worked as associate employees for a further two or three years before joining the regular workforce. By 1930, their daily schedule as apprentices (cited in Uozumi 2021: 279) was as follows: wake up at 5.45 am; clean until 7.00 am; practice kendo or attend classes to learn daily tasks such as letter writing or making phone calls until 8.00 am; breakfast until 8.40 am; work in the garden and on maintenance of the building until 6.00 pm, with a one-hour lunchbreak and ninety minutes of kendo practice during the day; dinner at 6.00 pm, followed by two hours of self-cultivation, which included reading anecdotes and stories about significant personalities, as well as training in speeches, debate, writing exercises and calligraphy, arithmetic, character evaluation and self-reflection, and a bath at 9.30 pm. Everyone was in bed by 10.00 pm, but some boys had to stay on duty to read a novel or magazine to Noma Seiji or his colleagues who would come to listen to them at their bedside. This task sometimes lasted until 2.00 or 3.00 am. Uozumi (2021: 280) cites from a 1932 pamphlet from Kōdansha's apprentice school, which guided members to bow their heads every time they entered a room with Noma Seiji's photo on the wall 'as if they were meeting him in person' and encouraged them to consider the morning call as a kind of prayer. 'Look at the photo of our master and pray for something', it extoled. '"You do not have to go to secondary school to become great" was a powerful message for young people excluded from an education-conscious society', Uozumi observes. 'But its simplicity left no room for a critical view of the State or of society; the objective was to get promoted and make money and the means was the accumulation of self-cultivation' (276).

When Ruth Benedict dedicated an entire chapter to *shūyō* in her post-war culturally essentialist exegesis of Japanese society commissioned by the US Office of War (Benedict 1947: 228–52), the concept had become so enmeshed with pre-war legitimizations of Japanese as imperial subjects that it had lost its appeal (Kurita 2018: 179). Its principles, however, survived. In 1946, the founder of Panasonic, Matsushita Kōnosuke (1894–1989), established the publishing company PHP Kenkyūsho, an acronym of 'Peace and Happiness through Prosperity Institute'. Originally focused on the publication of a monthly life ethics and prosperity magazine full of transcripts of Matsushita's speeches, the publisher started expanding its activities in the 1960s, when several of Matsushita's books became (and continue to be) bestsellers.[8] In his sociology of self-development (*jiko-keihatsu*) in Japan, Makino Tomokazu notes that Matsushita's message in all of his writings is very simple: 'He calls on people to master a frame of mind (*kokoro-gamae*) through which, with a modest heart and without letting difficulties dishearten them, they will devote themselves sincerely, positively, enthusiastically and with speed and energy to the work entrusted to them' (Makino 2012: 45). Matsushita's writings of the 1960s formed the stepping stone for the self-help publishing business that expanded in the 1970s and 1980s (Makino 2012, 2015), and survives today despite the serious decline in the book market in Japan over the last thirty years.

According to Kiyota Yoshiaki (2019: 149–52) – editor of publishing industry periodical *Publishing News* from 1961 until its closure in 2019[9] – in the early 1970s publishers switched their interest from books with strong ideological and political messages, to texts that aimed to foster the intellect and general education of larger audiences. A key event marking this shift was the entrance in 1971 of none other but Kōdansha into the pocket-size paperback market (*bunkō*), which had until then been limited to the re-edition of bestsellers.[10] This presented a business opportunity for book shops, which had mostly relied on periodical publications such as comics and magazines. Due to the price increase of paper after the 1973 oil crisis, books also became 20 per cent more expensive, making cheaper *bunko* editions more attractive to consumers. With more and more bookstores managing to negotiate with publishers over their profit margins, the book industry experienced a double-digit growth every year from 1973 through 1975. During the same period, and more rapidly from the end of the 1970s, a diversification into multiple niche topics, and hence markets, saw a sudden increase of periodicals with approximately 2,000 new titles hitting the stores during the 1980s. The impact on the industry was tremendous, with giant bookstores opening their doors one after another. By the early 1990s, books were even being sold at convenience stores. It is during these golden years of the publishing industry that, I argue, the market, in what came to be labelled *seishin sekai* books, arose out of a sustained and expansive interest in stories about people's lives (*jinsei-ron*).

Seishin sekai books within the growth of the self-development publishing market

Library classifications tend to separate what today is labelled *supirichuariti* from 'religion'. In the Nippon Decimal Classification (NDC) used by the majority of Japanese libraries to categorize books, one often finds spirituality books classified under one of two labels: 'parapsychology and spiritualist research' (category 147) or 'rules of life, practical ethics' (category 159), which covers the self-help and self-development literature. The NDC's ten general categories of books were originally inspired by the American classification system devised by Charles Ammi Cutter, who labeled the second category (i.e. books in the 100 range) 'philosophy'. The Japanese system dedicates the 140 range to 'psychology', 150 to 'ethics and morality', and everything beyond 160 to 'religion' (Shinto for the 170s, Buddhism for the 180s, and Christianity and Judaism for the 190s).[11] But as already indicated, quite where spirituality as 'not religion' belongs remains vague. This is exemplified by the classification of Ehara Hiroyuki's publications. While most are listed under cat. 147, one of his more popular books, *Spiritual Counseling for You* (2004), which relates the author's advice to twenty-four of his typical clients, is categorized under cat. 159.[12] This ambiguity is, I suggest, indicative of a more profound connection between the *seishin sekai* publications of the 1980s and 1990s and the wider burgeoning of interest in self-development during the same period, partly as a result of the expansion of the publishing industry and its focus on 'successful life stories'.

A search on the database of Japan's National Diet Library reveals that, as of 30 October 2021, 20,337 titles have been published in cat. 159 and 9,387 titles under cat. 147 since 1945. Most of these titles have appeared since the mid-1970s. An indicative comparison between these two NDC categories and category 148, which includes all content related to divination and fortune telling, shows that not all categories of books saw the same growth during the expansion of the publishing market and the peak years of the 'spiritual boom' (Graph 3.1). Although a slight jump is observed in cat. 148 during the 'golden years', it is far less obvious than the growth in the other two categories. We see evidence of the general slump experienced by the industry in the late 1990s across the board, but in the 2000s the number of books in cat. 148 returns to pre-1970s levels, while 147 and 159 experienced significant growth.[13] The apparent strength in the market for *seishin sekai* books is intimately linked to that of the self-development genre.

In the 1970s and 1980s, some publishing companies started to expand into genres they previously had not worked with, including and prominently

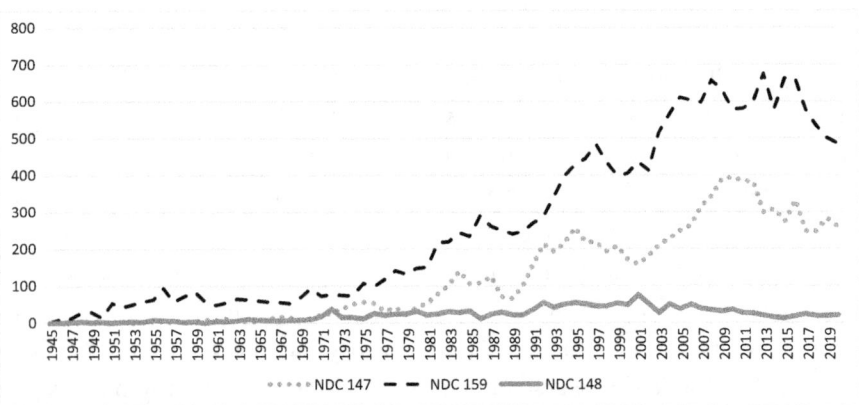

Graph 3.1 Number of NDL entries of book-length publications in NDC categories 147, 148 and 159 since 1945. Compiled by the author.

self-development. This was almost always due to charismatic and visionary managers who did not hesitate to break barriers and change existing company structures to fit their plans. A key example is the aforementioned PHP Kenkyūsho, established by Panasonic founder Matsushita Kōnosuke, which is the most popular publisher in the self-development category, with 1,632 titles in cat. 159 (and 124 titles in cat. 147). Another is Mikasa-shobō, which has 1,379 titles in this category (and 147 titles in cat. 147). Originating from a 1933 small house specializing in the translation of English novelists such as Ernest Hemingway and A. J. Cronin, the company went bankrupt (for the second time) in 1968. Thanks to the efforts of a young salesman, Oshikane Fujio, a former employee of the *Yomiuri* newspaper, it was given a new start. Oshikane managed to sell all of the publisher's stock and, after taking the reins of the company in 1979 at the age of thirty-eight, turned his attention to more profitable genres, such as the novelization of film scripts and television dramas, and eventually self-development books. It was the latter that made Mikasa-shobō successful and, according to historian of Japanese publishing Shiozawa Minobu (2003: 289), one of the winning survivors of the continuous crisis faced by the rest of the industry from the 1990s onward. Similar one-man success stories can be seen in the rise of other publishing houses, including Tokuma-shoten (327 titles in cat. 147; 175 in cat. 159), founded in 1954 by former *Yomiuri* journalist Tokuma Yasushi, which eventually reached unprecedented success especially in film production (Shiozawa 2003: 552–4). Diamond-sha (596 titles in cat. 147; 40 in cat. 159), a pre-war magazine publisher, which at the end of the 1960s hit a five-year long period of continuous deficit, was saved by a manager who shifted the company's focus to publishing 'business information that will contribute to the correct development of an industrial society' (162). The publisher Kadokawa-shoten (73 titles in cat. 147; 92 in cat. 159), which has published translations of New Age classics by Shirley MacLaine, Paulo Coelho and James Redfield among others,[14] similarly reinvented itself after Kadokawa Haruki (the son of the founder) became company president in 1975. He expanded the business into film production and, in the 1980s, into manga and business periodicals.

Many of these men later acknowledged that they had been inspired by classic self-development literature and the autobiographies of famous entrepreneurs. For example, Mikasa-shobō's Oshikane claims to have been influenced by the autobiography of famous Japanese landscapist Honda Seiroku (1866–1952), *The Secrets of My Life* (*Waga shosei no hiketsu*) (Shiozawa 2003: 289),[15] while Kadokawa Haruki confesses to having been inspired by the best-known work of

Napoleon Hill (1883–1970), *Think and Grow Rich* (1937), which was translated into Japanese as *The Thirteen Requirements to Build a Fortune* (*Kyofu o kizuku jyūsan no jyōken*). In an interview, Kadokawa recalls writing the sentence 'I will make Kadokawa the biggest publisher in history' on the side of his bed and narrates how he had come to believe in the power of thought by reading that sentence aloud every day and 'drilling' it into his subconscious (cited in Shiozawa 1985: 252).

At the same time, we see the establishment of dedicated publishers. Daiwa-shobō (14 titles in cat. 147; 503 titles in cat. 159), for example, started in 1961 as an offshoot of the publisher Seishun Shuppan (75 titles in cat. 147; 384 titles in cat. 159), but by the end of the 1960s had made its name as a specialist publisher with a best-seller titled *Ai to shi o mitsumete* (*Staring at Love and Death*), which narrates a three-year correspondence between two university students, one of whom had been diagnosed with bone sarcoma and died at the age of twenty-one (Ōshima and Kōno 1963). It followed this with several non-fiction books, categorized at the time as life-perspective (*jinseiron*), and later, in the 1990s and 2000s, with life-advice essay collections with a psychotherapeutic, 'healing' (*iyashi*) flavour that mainly targeted a female readership. Sunmark Shuppan (110 titles in cat. 147; 450 titles in cat. 159) is another company that came to specialize in fringe science and spirituality books, such as Haruyama Shigeo's (b.1940) *Nōnai Kakumei* (Haruyama 1995), which argued that positive thinking releases good hormones from the brain and can make people more successful. As of December 2020, this book was in the seventh position in the list of bestsellers in Japan.[16] Sunmark Shuppan was originally founded in 1971, but after trying its hand at various genres decided to focus on books with 'energy', namely books that are not easily perishable and do not treat ephemeral topics, but are long-sellers because they have a special power to attract readers even if they are written by anonymous authors (Shiozawa 1998: 239). A former editor at Tokuma-shoten, Ishii Takeshi, founded his own small company in 2010, Hikarurando (498 titles in cat. 147; 33 in cat. 159), focusing exclusively on new spirituality topics.

When we dig even deeper, it is evident that the structure of the book trade had at least some impact on the types of books and number of copies printed. In Japan, powerful book and printed materials distributors called *toritsugi* are responsible for choosing how many copies of each publication should be delivered to which stores, calculated on the basis of each store's point-of-sale data.[17] While this system limits the stocking choices of store owners (Steinberg 2019: 248), it also protects them from making a loss. Distributors buy copies from the publisher in advance based on sales predictions and hand them out to the stores at fixed prices (new publications cannot be discounted). If the stores do not sell all of their copies, they can return them to their distributor at no cost and the distributor will then ask the publisher to pay back the difference. This system originally prevented the more established publishers from taking too many risks.[18] As a result, the golden days of the print industry saw the appearance of companies that encouraged self-publishing and eased the connection between bookshops and relatively small publishers who could not convince the *toritsugi* to sell their books to the bookshops. These companies effectively opened the book market to 'alternative' topics by unknown authors that more established publishers would not take the risk investing in. The representative example is Seiunsha (317 titles in cat. 147; 244 titles in cat. 159), founded in 1979. The company is not a publisher *per se*, but a seller (*hakkō-moto*) or 'publisher responsible for circulation' (*ryūtsū sekinin shuppansha*). Seiunsha effectively works as a proxy publisher, taking on the responsibility of persuading the *toritsugi* to distribute other publishers' books. A later significant player was Bungeisha (406 titles in cat. 147; 556 titles in cat. 159), founded in 1996 by Uritani Tsunanobu, the son of Uritani Yūko who established Tama Shuppan (395 titles in cat. 147; 40 in cat. 159), the first postwar publishing house to specialize in occult and spiritualist books. Bungeisha specialized in self-published writers and offered several options that benefited first-time authors.

The power of the *toritsugi* becomes especially apparent in the establishment of the label *seishin sekai*. As a book category, it first appeared at an eponymous fair of 'Books about India and Nepal's Spiritual World (*seishin sekai*)' held in the Shinjuku branch of the bookseller Kinokuniya in June 1978. In a series of articles about the *seishin sekai*, published in the national newspaper *Yomiuri* in 1985, the journalist Kobayashi Takakazu offers some fascinating details about the origins of that appellation. When coming up with a name for the fair, its organizers had been looking for a new label for books that they could not fit into existing categories, a classic example being the translation of Bhagwan Shree Rajneesh's *The Search*, which had appeared that same year. Since the fair was a surprising success, Kobayashi tells us, it encouraged one of the two largest *toritsugi*, Tōhan, to copy the name and open similar fairs around the country, thus establishing the *seishin sekai* as a new category of books. 'The [*seishin sekai*] boom was instigated by the publishing industry' concludes Kobayashi (1985: 11).

However, the golden years did not last forever. The burst of the bubble economy at the end of the 1980s and the arrival of personal computers and mobile phones into peoples' homes from the mid-1990s are usually offered as significant reasons for the slow down and eventual decline of the publishing industry.[19] In 2019, the advertising giant Dentsu reported that the markets for books and magazines had, in 2017, shrunk to half the size of its peak year of 1996 (Yuzawa and Amano 2019: 13). Under these circumstances, and to avoid having to refund distributors for unsold books, publishers rushed to put new titles out to make up for the margin that they constantly owed to distributors (Urushibara 2012: 125). As a result, there were growing numbers of titles on the market, but fewer and fewer copies of each, leading to the ironic situation of a shrinking market in which the number of new titles doubled from 40,000 per year in the early 1990s to over 80,000 in 2012 (Nose 2019: 180). This situation was also fuelled by the increasing share held by the self-publishing market, which has continuously grown since the 1980s in stark contrast to that of the established houses; 132 publishers closed their doors between 1990 and 2020, only fourteen of them voluntarily (Nose 2019: 156).

Such changes naturally impacted on the content of books, reflecting what had already happened in the American and British book markets where, as sales shifted from small booksellers to chain stores in the 1990s and 2000s, the focus fell on 'fast-selling titles by brand-name authors at the expense of those titles that would add depth and range to the store but that would have much slower stock turns' (Thompson 2012: 35). In Japan, publishers' need for more titles increased the number of translations, which were almost monopolized by the field of self-development from the mid-1990s to the early 2000s, accentuating the attention given to 'methods to control or change the inner self' (Makino 2012: 59, 2015: 262). In the late 1980s, self-help books for businesspeople were only entrusted to editors that could not work on more 'serious books' such as exegeses of market trends or specific industry-related textbooks. One editor (cited in Urushibara 2012: 57) explains that while there was no need to have any specialized knowledge to edit a self-help publication, there was a particular psychology according to which this self-development literature worked: keeping up with the latest trends in self-management became part of what it meant to be an active worker who, consequently, should not worry too much about the price of books that promise to make them more efficient and successful. These books are not novels or non-fiction books that will be read for entertainment, the editor points out; they are books that are 'work-related' (cited in Urushibara 2012: 19). This, coupled with the ongoing economic downturn from the late 1990s onwards, made self-help books increasingly attractive to publishers.

At the same time, the inter-organizational rivalry that tends to produce a degree of homogeneity among book firms who publish in the same area (Thompson 2012: 10) leads to the constant re-creation and reinterpretation of a certain type of discourse through a process of reflective monitoring. Editors continually check how their interpretations of the key concepts used in the latest publishing trends compare to those of other publishers. They then try to add new twists to those interpretations in order to sustain a sense of originality in the new publications that will be launched under those same trends.[20] I argue that this is what happened with the publishers who focused on messages of self-help and self-development but who later came to be associated with the *seishin sekai* and more prominently with *supirichuariti*. Just as the spiritual came to be a label attached *post-hoc* by therapists to alternative therapies already in usage in Japan (Chapter 1), so too did it become attached to publishers and the literature that they were interested in as didactic stories.

There are of course other examples of small publishing companies that have specialized in the production of *seishin sekai* and new spirituality books and magazines, but also in workshops, audio products and the like. VOICE, founded in 1988, and Natural Spirit, founded in 1997 (245 titles in cat. 147) are both companies that came to prominence in the 1990s and 2000s thanks to a mixed-media model that saw them inviting non-Japanese figures of the New Age to Japan, organizing seminars and talks with them, and also translating their books into Japanese. After more than thirty years, VOICE still represents the famous channeler Darryl Anka in Japan, having published at least twenty-six texts authored by either him or the multidimensional entity that he channels, named Bashar.[21] Misawa Yutaka, former editor at Hirakawa Shuppan and owner of the website *seishin-sekai.com*, which provides information on the latest media trends related to *seishin sekai* and spirituality, lists what he considers to be thirty-seven specialized publishers.[22] These include those already mentioned here, but also others that mostly specialize in the publication of Buddhist texts, some of which (e.g. Hōzōkan Shuppan and Yanagihara Shuppan) have a history of several centuries. Regardless of whether these other publishers would associate themselves with categories such as the *seishin sekai*, Misawa's listing illustrates how neither editors nor readers necessarily make the distinctions that scholars have tried to establish. This is even more evident when we turn to consider two publishers specializing in books categorized under this genre: Jiyūsha, which had published the Japanese translation of *Out on a Limb*, and Tama Shuppan, a specialist publisher of occultist and spiritualist books.

'Alternative' publishers?

In my interview with Ms Uehara, the former editor at Jiyūsha, she argued that their interest in publishing, and more specifically in publishing materials advertised as *seishin sekai*, had not stemmed from a search for alternativity. 'We were not counter-cultural', she recalled. 'We just published about how we thought things ought to have been (*honrai kō de aru beki*).' She explained: 'If these [books like *Out on a Limb*] are indirectly inspiring readers to change their lives, that is something else. We never aimed for "this is how you ought to live"-type of books here, but we did want to avoid being categorized as "occult".' I interpret Ms Uehara's comments to mean that these small publishers built themselves in conjunction with contemporaneous trends and did not aim for a general critique of society. More importantly they did not think of themselves as alternative or fringe, as their unwillingness to be categorized with the occult or, more recently, the spiritual reflects. 'I feel like that with the more recent *supirichuaru* trend, authors have gone back to targeting a specific type of reader addicted to (*hamachatta*) certain kinds of topics. In contrast, the books that we published in the 1980s were for a general audience', argued Ms Uehara, with a hint of nostalgia for a time when messages like those promoted by Jiyūsha did not have to be categorized under labels that she felt limited the scope of their books.

Jiyūsha was founded by Masuda Masao in 1982 to support authors that 'live by the wisdom of life (*inochi*) ... a latent natural force that can be found in everyone' and used to solve all kinds of problems and build a perfect society.[23] The detailed charter of the company, dated October 1982, is even more revealing of Masuda's belief in the innate capacity of humans to become independent of any former guidance by religions, culture and the like, and walk along 'the age of self-awareness' (*jikaku no jidai*).[24] Masuda had been an editor at another publisher, Hakujusha, which had originally focused on treatises by pioneers of welfare and education, but had also published works by intellectuals who would become famous abroad for popularizing 'alternative' ideas in their respective fields, one example being the Sōtō Zen priest, Uchiyama Kōshō (1912–98). In the 1980s, Masuda and at least three other editors at the company left to establish their own publishing houses. According to Ms Uehara, Masuda had quit Hakujusha because he had wanted to continue publishing books by Wada Shigemasa (1907–93), an intellectual active in contemporaneous debates about home schooling (*katei kyōiku*).

Wada's emphasis on the natural potential of humans appealed to Masuda's environmental concerns for nature and his interest in the role of women in society.[25] The concept of *inochi* used by Masuda figures prominently in Wada's critique of the loss of such power to live, to strive forward, to imagine and to collaborate among the youth of the post-war period (Wada 1982: 54). In an interview uploaded to YouTube on 3 April 2015 (Chiwaki no Mori 2015a), Masuda says that he believed such power to be essential for humans to rid themselves of the restrictions of various social ideologies and to become independent beings living harmoniously with nature. He therefore considered that the next step in humanity's progress would be to harness the wisdom of people who had already managed to achieve that. Like Wada's emphasis on how mothers can educate their children (especially children with disabilities) to use their *inochi*, Masuda wished for his publication of such success stories to change societies. This was reflected in the company's decision to publish the Japanese translation of *Out on a Limb*. Masuda says that he was initially reluctant to take on a book that sounded like a banal success story, but he nevertheless agreed to read the manuscript and he and his staff eventually decided that it would fit the company's profile. 'Our first book was titled *The Era of Mothers* (*Haha no Jidai* by Wada Shigemasa) ... and we thought that this one was similar ... a woman who thought by herself and could be someone autonomous in today's society ... and also a human story of independence' (Chiwaki no Mori 2015a).

As an editor and publisher, Masuda's fundamental endeavour was therefore to connect Hakujusha's concerns with education and welfare to a larger message of human independence and environmental protection. As one of the translators of *Out on a Limb*, Yamakawa Kōya, later recalled, this association of ideas could be retrospectively interpreted as a typically New Age framework (Chiwaki no Mori 2015b). However, at the time publishers were not really concerned with specific religious/secular dichotomies nor with identifying themselves with specific movements. Rather, they had personal ideologies that often presented themselves as narratives of therapy and healing, linking a great variety of experiences under one editorial roof. Editors and publishers like Masuda are therefore more than nodes of connection in a wider network of practitioners, activists and intellectuals; they are essential actors whose own concerns informed the way that ideas that later came to be considered 'alternative' have been associated, explained and conveyed to wider audiences. This is what Ms Uehara's negation of 'counter-culturalism' means.

A similar dynamic can be found among publishers who had associated themselves with religious movements much more explicitly than Masuda. Tama Shuppan, founded in 1969 by Uritani Yūko, was the first post-war house specializing in the production of occultist and spiritualist books. It originally started with translations of the seer Edgar Cayce's texts and later expanded into unidentified flying objects (UFOs), supernatural powers and other topics categorized under the occult. Its current editor-in-chief, Nirasawa Jun'ichiro (b.1945), a UFOlogist, has been a relatively well-known face on Japanese television variety shows where he often makes extraordinary claims regarding the occult, engaging in often comedic heated debates (perhaps prearranged) with his arch-enemy, the physicist and equally well-known debunker of the paranormal, Ōtsuki Yoshihiko (b.1934). Uritani, however, seems to have had different concerns. In his autobiography (Uritani 1990), he paints a very vivid picture of his life and that of his wife, using pseudonyms such as S-san and O-san and expressions such as 'one religion' and 'another religion' to anonymize the characters and organizations involved.

Uritani's family's businesses had benefited from Japan's occupation of China but went bankrupt with the end of the war. In the process of having to make a living, Uritani and his wife sought comfort with various religious individuals and groups in the 1950s and early 1960s. A close reading and comparison of dates of key events reveals that he was a fervent follower of the Church of Perfect Liberty (PL Kyōdan) from 1953 to 1957; during this period he donated a large portion of the proceeds from the sale of his house to the construction of their headquarters in Osaka.[26] Pushed by his wife's interests, he says that he visited various fortune tellers, psychics and religious groups before becoming a member of a group that would become the religious organization Sekai Mahikari Bunmei Kyōdan.[27] He remained in the group from about 1962 to 1968, becoming its PR representative, but left when he and his wife felt that it had become 'too restrictive'. This did not prevent him from receiving a substantial sum of money from top-ranking member Sekiguchi Sakae (1909–94), which allowed Uritani to save the publishing section of his bankrupt paper-making company and turn it into Tama Shuppan in 1969. Sekiguchi would become leader of the religious group in 1975.

Uritani explains his involvement with the publishing of *seishin sekai* books as a path away from religion or as 'ditching religion' (*datsu-shūkyō*). By this he means that religions, as institutions with obligations to grow, to distinguish themselves from others and to present a cohesive image, eventually become limiting, especially for those like him who want to keep searching for existential and spiritual answers in life. Uritani's view of the *seishin sekai* as the antithesis of 'religion' was, he says, inspired by the humanistic psychology of Erich Fromm, particularly his books *Man for Himself* and *Psychoanalysis and Religion* (Uritani 1983: 13). This reinforces my argument that 'alternative' religious discourse can be considered part of *shūyō* concerns rather than a new type of religiosity. Uritani's ideas do not reflect a process of secularization through the psychologization of religion.[28] He explicitly credits the Church of Perfect Liberty for teaching him that bad things happen because of ourselves rather than others. In Sekai Mahikari Bunmei Kyōdan, he says, he found the more complex vocabulary and imagery that he needed to grasp the afterlife and the world of the spirits. Ultimately, however, Uritani argues that each individual needs to find his own *seishin sekai* and follow his own path.

Echoing the association between corporations and religion commonly made at this time (most famously by Matsushita), Uritani saw the spiritual world as indistinguishable from running a successful business. He dedicates an entire section of his autobiography to the relation between the *seishin sekai* and entrepreneurship (Uritani 1990: 111–38) and mentions at least two rules common to both business-making and *seishin sekai*'s ideology: 1) never allow yourself to depend on others and 2) use your own resources to the maximum (127). For Uritani, publishing eventually became equal to a search for truth in order to advance towards the independence of his soul (*tamashii no jiritsu*) (96). In his autobiography he writes that:

> Of course, the primary significance of books is their content, but as objects, their vibration (*hadō*) is also important. In many cases, the strength of vibration is directly proportional to the content, but it is said that the force of the author's and publisher's thoughts contributes to that strength too. That is why it is worth always keeping good books by one's side. (Uritani 1990: 100)

In contrast with Jiyūsha, Uritani explains that when he opened Tama Shuppan he was aiming precisely for the genres that at that time were very minor and sometimes frowned upon: spiritualism (*shinrei*), parapsychology and the occult.[29] According to him, the ensuing popular interest in these topics seems to have shifted how they were popularly interpreted. Rather than being perceived as external phenomena, they were now seen as internal; they and associated practices such as yoga and meditation were understood to connect to 'one's inner world' (*jibun no sekai*), which is the ultimate definition Uritani gives to the *seishin sekai* (Uritani 1983: 35–7). This shift made his house a pioneer of *seishin sekai* books (33). As one reads through Uritani's collection of thoughts on the *seishin sekai*, it becomes obvious that individuals who had interiorized their existing religious beliefs, such as Edgar Cayce who had made Jesus his own, had particular appeal for Uritani because of his previous experiences with religious groups. Unwilling to reject such a past and fascinated by the extraordinary powers that he believes to have witnessed in others committed to religious paths, Uritani's publishing dreams resemble those of Masuda and others in that he considered his role to be that of a gatekeeper of stories of extraordinary individuals who ought to inspire his readers to solve their issues and better themselves, by any means possible.

In some respects then, the so-called global spirituality culture that the *seishin sekai* is seen to represent can be seen as just another label for what the media market has historically relied heavily upon for its success: didactic and moralistic stories. This can be traced back even further than the modern concern with *shūyo*, to when books starting conveying an economic view of value. Laura Moretti, for example, describes how seventeenth-century popular literature in Japan contains many examples of 'how to become rich' manuals. These started placing more emphasis on individual responsibility than medieval deterministic notions of fate in a manner that recalls much more recent self-development literature. Readers are not taught exactly how to become rich: 'Rather, the text seems more concerned with reinforcing the ideal of human nature' (Moretti 2020: 229). In the same way that the burgeoning *seishin sekai* literature has been interpreted as 'proof' of a new spirituality culture, those Edo period texts could be seen as Confucian manuals linking frugality and morality, but, as Moretti points out, none of the texts guaranteed such a link. Similar to the so-called New Age literature, what is characteristic of this didactic ideology is the space that it leaves for more answer-seeking.

Translating spirituality

The practice of the therapists I interviewed was often inspired by or related to the reading of books published by the houses discussed so far in this chapter. The books most commonly mentioned were Japanese translations of classic New Age Anglo-Saxon literature: Marianne Williamson's *A Course in Miracles* (Kiseki no gakushu kōsu, [1976] 1998), Shirley MacLaine's *Out on a Limb* (*Auto on a rimu*, [1983] 1986), Brian Weiss's *Many Lives, Many Masters* (*Zense ryōhō*, [1988] 1996), James Redfield's *The Celestine Prophecy* (Sei naru yogen, [1993] 1996) and Neale Donald Walsch's *Conversations with God* (*Kami to no taiwa*, [1995] 2002). Three of those five books were translated by Yamakawa Kōya (b.1941) and Yamakawa

Akiko (b.1943), who have become the 'sages' (*chōrō*) or 'legends' (*rejendo*) of the spiritual world in Japan. Since 1986, they have produced nearly a hundred translations and twenty-five self-authored books (sometimes in the format of recorded conversations with others), openly using what in trade publishing parlance is called a 'platform' (Thompson 2012: 86) as gatekeepers of the *seishin sekai*. The Yamakawas estimate that their translations have sold in total 10 million copies (Yamakawa and Yamakawa 2018: 4). This may not be an exaggeration since a detailed look at their personal website reveals that at least twenty-two of their books have been republished in pocket paperback editions (*bunkobon*).[30]

The editors of the volume *Translating Religion* argue that 'religion and the academic study of religion are fundamentally translation enterprises' (DeJonge and Tietz 2015: 5). Beyond the literal translation of religious texts upon which the majority of scholarly endeavours depend, the field of religious studies itself has been interpreted as translation, or better termed, interpretation, based on 'sightings from particular geographical and social sites whereby scholars construct meaning, using categories and criteria of their own making' (Tweed 2002: 257). Jeffrey J. Kripal (2010: 25) has gone even further, suggesting that 'paranormal phenomena are, in the end, like the act of interpretive writing itself, primarily semiotic or textual processes'. Hence, we find the practices of 'automatic *writing*' or what spiritualists call 'psychical *readings*'. Although the ultimate argument that Kripal wants to make about human unconsciousness lies beyond the scope of this monograph, history shows that writing, reading, editing and translating are fundamental religion-making and unmaking endeavours.

Drawing on my interview with the Yamakawas on 2 May 2016, as well as several books in which they recall their career (notably Yamakawa, Yamakawa and Kokusai 2015; Yamakawa and Yamakawa 2018), I argue that the Yamakawas were instrumental in fashioning and forging *supirichuariti* through their translations and subsequent personal lectures, workshops and writings on therapy and healing, which were often informed by the books they were contemporaneously translating. As photos illustrating their personal website show, they have been responsible for introducing to Japanese audiences an impressive list of key New Age authors. Their translations include eight of Shirley MacLaine's books (at least 800,000 copies sold in hardback edition),[31] nine of Brian Weiss's books (approx. 1.2 million copies in all editions),[32] six of Paulo Coelho's books,[33] all nine of James Redfield's books,[34] and four of Rhonda Byrne's books (with Sano Miyoko),[35] as well as the autobiography of co-founder of the Findhorn community, Eileen Caddy[36] and four of Osho's books, which the Yamakawas personally negotiated with the Osho Foundation to translate.[37]

They have even worked on a children's book by the famous German poet, Hans Magnus Enzensberger.[38]

Like the majority of individuals translating New Age spirituality literature,[39] the Yamakawas are not professional translators. Their sustained effort to introduce this particular body of literature to the Japanese market – at roughly three books per year for thirty years (1986–2016) – has not been a response to social crisis akin to, for example, the early-nineteenth-century shogunate-sponsored 'crisis translation' of military texts, which was spurred by a growing sense of external threat (Clements 2015: 177). Rather, as insider-translators who have preached and practiced the ideas that they have translated, the Yamakawas have been a significant player in the translocal movement of religious ideas and practices. Although they only started writing their own books from 1999 onwards, they have been organizing regular workshops and lectures since the late 1980s, as soon as their first Japanese-language editions of Shirley McLaine's books became a hit.

The Yamakawas's role has been somewhat comparable with that of D. T. Suzuki (1870–1966), another famous translator and significant player in the global image of 'Japanese' spirituality, albeit working in the opposite direction, from Japanese to English. Studies of and about D. T. Suzuki have significantly increased in the last ten years. They reveal a sustained effort on Suzuki's part to popularize a certain understanding of Zen Buddhism in the Western world, fashioned by Suzuki's own life and varied interests within and without contemporaneous Buddhist thought. The tools that he used for such popularization were translation and later his own writings. His strength, as Rossa Ó Muireartaigh (2012: 292) argues, stemmed from 'his immersion in a network that he did not create, but which he could dominate and influence through the adoption and adaptation of its cultural capital by skillfully using its charged symbols in his translation work'.

The Yamakawas's played a similar role in the establishment of a spiritual (therapy) narrative in Japan, which they adopted, adapted and – perhaps even more so than Suzuki – propagated through networks that they sometimes inadvertently created themselves. To give just one example, the spiritual convention SUPICON, which journalists and scholars frequently cited as the quintessential manifestation of the 'spiritual boom' in the first decade of the twenty-first century, was started by a group of men who met at a monthly book club called The Lazies' Reading Circle (Namakemono Dokusho-kai). This exclusively men-only club was started by Yamakawa Kōya in 1997, a year after the couple were admonished by an American shaman to attract more Japanese males into the *seishin sekai*. In a remarkable feat of narrative-making, the Yamakawas have framed all of their activities through an endless story of illness and healing that has continued well into their eighties, and which seamlessly blends personal issues, transformative experiences and ideas made popular through the books that they have been translating. If, to understand D. T. Suzuki's success, we might talk of a 'Suzuki effect' (Faure 1993: 54) to refer to how Suzuki's ideas both produced and were produced by positive Orientalist discourse in the early to mid-twentieth Anglo-American West, we should perhaps also talk of a 'Yamakawa effect'[40] through which the Yamakawas both produced and were produced by the positive spin assigned to *supirichuariti* as self-help and self-development in late twentieth and early twenty-first-century Japan.

The Yamakawa effect

Like many narratives of self-transformation, including those encountered among spiritual therapists (see Gaitanidis and Murakami 2014), the Yamakawas identify a threshold moment that split their lives into a before and after structure. In 1981, Kōya participated in a workshop in Kobe with the intention of brushing up on his English language. The workshop turned out to be a 'self-awareness' seminar run by Duncan Callister, a former lawyer and co-founder (with Robert White) of Life Dynamics, a Japan-based offshoot of Werner Erhard's Mind Dynamics seminar company (York 2009: 121). Such seminars inspired by the human potential movement had started spreading to Japan in the mid-1970s, but only really became popular in the late 1980s. By 1989, 'Life Dynamics had established seven centres throughout the country and graduated a total of more than seventy thousand people' (Haga 1995: 285).[41] Among these was Kōya, who, according to his wife Akiko, returned home from the 1981 seminar as a new man. Eight months later, on the insistence of her husband, Akiko also took part in the seminar. This was a couple who had graduated from the top Japanese university (University of Tokyo) and worked in elite positions as, respectively, a high-level bureaucrat in the Ministry of Finance (Kōya) and a manager at a foreign-owned enterprise (Akiko). During my interview with them in May 2016, they swore that they had never been interested in religion, philosophy or the 1970s occult 'boom'. What had made them change their mind?

For Kōya the seminar put into question his choice of career, making him rethink what he really wanted to do and who he was. For Akiko, the experience was even more dramatic. On the third day of the five-day seminar, having consistently been unable to find a partner for the games included in the daily workshops, she fled back to Tokyo where she was living while her husband was temporarily posted in Kobe.[42] Crying and blaming herself for being unworthy, she locked herself in the apartment, refusing to pick up calls from her mother, sister and husband. When, after several hours, she eventually talked to her family, she launched into an hours-long series of accusations against her husband for ignoring her wishes and wants during their past fifteen years of marriage. Then, she writes, the people, the buildings and everything around her started shining radiantly. She felt relieved and happy and noticed that her attitude towards others had changed for the better and she became a more flexible person (Yamakawa and Yamakawa 2018: 15–18).

Sociologists and other scholars interested in the motivations of participants of 'alternative religion' have often employed the 'individualist card' and focused on an empowerment narrative. Haga (1995: 290), for example, argues that such seminars may have been appealing to a Japanese audience as they promoted a 'thoroughly achievement-oriented individualistic worldview in which everyone has the potential to realize happiness regardless of circumstances, and in which everyone is totally responsible for the reality they have created for themselves through their own choices'. This worldview gives trainees 'a more positive sense of their capabilities in effecting change' and, when internalized, enables them to 'discover an approach to reconstructing their own lives that is different from any they have known before'.

The framing of Haga's argument is problematic. First, it seems to share a common culturalist assumption that 'Japanese society' was an importer of American individualism, which allegedly shook the core of the rather 'conservative' Japanese youth. This ignores the relatively long history of translocal exchanges between Asia and North America, and their influence on American self-development seminars such as *est* (Laycock 2014). Second, it overlooks at least two significant elements. The first is hinted at but not developed by Haga, who observes that the same elements that make self-development seminars attractive can be found 'in other aspects of youth culture, including pop music concerts, discos, computer communications, and certain telephone dial services' (Haga 1995: 299 n. 9). Once again we find that the alternative in religion is not really the alternative of religion, but 'the alternative' *tout court*, a rider that is common across several human activities. It bears value precisely because it is not unique to the particular epistemic field it is attached to. The second element that is overlooked is that the therapeutic narrative and healing experiences with which alternativity has been mainly associated are less about empowerment than they are about the precariousness of physical, psychological and social health and the need to performatively communicate this precariousness. This is illustrated through Akiko's account of her life – a life in which she painstakingly and continuously tries to come to terms with her relationships with her mother and, more importantly, her husband, who for several years refused to acknowledge her as his equal in their translation work and remains, to this day, the frontman and main representative of what has in practice been a shared professional career. If the 1981 experience opened the door to alternative existences for the Yamakawas, these existences have required constant healing.

A life in need of healing ... and translation

When the Japanese Ministry of Finance gave Kōya a three-year posting at the World Bank in 1982, Akiko quit her job and moved with him to Washington, D.C., She took with her the new self she had acquired through the 'self-awareness' seminar in Kobe. Her mind was preoccupied by memories of her mother telling her that, as her third daughter, everybody wished she was a boy. Reflecting on her feelings of self-worthlessness, she decided on arrival in America that she had already wasted forty years of her life hating herself; it was time to change. While in the United States, partly thanks to connections they had made at the Kobe seminar, the Yamakawas took part in Alexander Everett's (1921–2005) Mind Dynamics courses and other lectures and events later ascribed to the New Age movement. Then, sometime in 1984, Kōya, who confesses to having been an avid reader of autobiographies, found on his secretary's desk a copy of Shirley MacLaine's *Out on a Limb* and brought it home.

Kōya and Akiko found *Out on a Limb* mind-opening, feeling that it revealed to them everything they had always wanted to know. Several months later, Kōya floated the idea of translating it into Japanese, having taken into consideration Shirley MacLaine's relative fame in Japan at the time; MacLaine was married to Steve Parker (1922–2001), a Japan-based theatre and film producer who had produced *My Geisha* (1962), with Shirley MacLaine in the lead role. After a quick phone call to the American publisher, Kōya acquired their permission on condition that he find a Japanese publisher willing to buy the rights. After a polite rejection from Kōdansha, an American history professor at Sophia University, Matsuo Kazuyuki (b.1941) suggested that they contact Jiyūsha.[43] Matsuo happened to be the Japanese translator of the New Age movement's 'bible', Marilyn Ferguson's *The Aquarian Conspiracy* (1980). Kōya's description of their encounter in one of his self-authored books (Yamakawa 2009: 63–7) is very telling of the associations that the Yamakawas would start to make between their lives and the contents of the books that they were translating. He narrates that he came into contact with Matsuo after finding in his office a register of around thirty Japanese residents of New York who had, like him, been born in 1941, and who held informal gatherings at the embassy. Matsuo, born the day before or after Kōya, proceeded to give Kōya his translation of *The Aquarian Conspiracy*. Kōya felt that it spoke to him and that he should look for a greater purpose in life. The message of a new aquarian era in which it becomes important to know oneself and connect to a spirit (*seirei*) is repeated twice in the short translators' note included at the end of the Yamakawas's Japanese translation of *Out on a Limb*.

Jiyūsha, which had opened two years earlier in 1982,[44] ended up buying the rights to *Out on a Limb* for US$2,000. Kōya translated the first half of the book, which dealt with the importance of knowing oneself, but according to Akiko, he did not much like the content of the second half, in which the author has several supernatural experiences, including an encounter with a UFO. Akiko was rather more interested in that part of the book and was the one to translate it. Kōya makes two important observations regarding the translation process. First, he claims that he cut out the foreword and reduced the first section (in which MacLaine describes a love affair with a British politician named Gerry) at the request of the Japanese publisher. This is denied by Ms Uehara, who states that these cuts were Kōya's decision. Since the book remained substantial in length it is indeed hard to believe that the publisher had asked for them. Secondly, and even more significantly, as a beginner at translation, Kōya remembers struggling with the Japanese rendition of some words. Having learned with his wife to listen to their instincts, it was eventually 'as if the words just wrote themselves. We translated "spirit" as *seirei* and tried to limit the usage of ominous-sounding (*odoroodoroshii*) terms, such as *reikai* or *reiteki*' (Yamakawa 2009: 70). When MacLaine talks of either her own spirit or the human spirit, the Yamakawas use the term *tamashii*, whereas they render the adjective 'spiritual' as *seishinteki*. What perhaps made their translation even more approachable to their Japanese audience was their decision to simply leave out references to 'spiritual' or 'spirituality' if they were not the focus of the sentence.

In a key passage of the book, David Manning, the character composite of various spiritual teachers MacLaine had met during her life, connects Christianity to a universal idea of spirituality. MacLaine (1983: 93) quotes him as saying: 'Christ and the Bible and spiritual teachings don't concern themselves with social or political questions. Instead spirituality goes right to the root of the question – the individual.' A literal back-translation of the

Japanese text shows that the translators omitted this idea of 'spirituality': 'Jesus, the Bible and various spiritual (*seishinteki*) teachings do not directly deal with social or political problems, but are directly related to the human individual (*ningen kojin*) who is at the basis of these problems' (MacLaine 1986: 83). It is clear from the structure of the sentence that the Yamakawas considered the association between Christian teachings and the individual to be more important than the 'spiritual' nature of these teachings. Like the other biographies of extraordinary individuals that both they and their publisher were interested in, the Yamakawas took MacLaine's message as one of empowerment in the vein of their human potential workshops. This subtle but important (re)interpretation is directly related to the act of translation. Translation involves reading a text with awareness of its various meanings and layers; this is not how everyone else usually reads. But, this is precisely how 'translation becomes the phenomenon that it is, the means by which the surplus and unseen meanings in source texts become once more foregrounded as a text marches on through history' (Ó Muireartaigh 2015: 162). This history is definitely the Yamakawas's history. They slowly started embodying MacLaine's narrative of self-transformation, to the extent that translation became the means by which they could experience MacLaine's life.

The Yamakawas translation of *Out on a Limb* took three months, but it was not published until 5 March 1986, nearly one year later, after the Yamakawas had returned to Japan. What happened in between is indicative of how the couple's career and lives were intertwined both discursively and experientially in a typical print spirituality narrative. On 1 July 1985, the Yamakawas were about to leave the US and return home when Kōya, on the recommendation of an American friend, decided to meet a channeler after work. The channeler was Lia (aka Aruna) Byers, who two weeks earlier had participated in a channelling school in New Mexico and suddenly found herself able to connect with the spirit of Count Saint-Germain. Saint-Germain was a historical figure from eighteenth-century Europe who later became a mythical Master appearing in nineteenth-century occult novels and theosophical writings (Fuller 2006: 1022–4). Akiko describes Kōya coming home that night with a pale face, whispering in her ear that he was told very curious things (*fushigi-na koto*). Speaking through Byers's mouth, Saint-Germain had claimed that it was he who had made MacLaine write *Out on a Limb* and who had made the Yamakawas come to Washington and translate that book; 'the world is about to change', he had said, 'and you two will be the ones who will bear that transformation on your shoulders' (Yamakawa and Yakamawa 2018: 33).

At the invitation of the spirit of Saint-Germain, Akiko went to see Byers the following day to work with him to change the world.

These events seem to have had a tremendous impact on the Yamakawas who switched gears and started considering their translation work as fulfilling not just a personal interest, but a sort of destiny. The book did not become a bestseller overnight. First, on Byers's admonition to find a bigger publisher, the Yamakawas tried to get Jiyūsha to sell on the rights, but Masuda's angered refusal forced them to consider alternatives. Finally, a phone call from Kōya to Shirley MacLaine convinced them that it would be better to stay with Jiyūsha. Second, Kōya originally planned to list only his name as a translator and to thank Akiko in an afterword, because 'I am the one who, by the word of the spirit (of Saint-Germain), changed the world's consciousness' (57). Akiko reluctantly accepted this, since she believed, she said, in the will of the Spirit. However, the publisher insisted that her name should be listed, since the original author was a woman and Akiko had translated half of the text. In the published version, the translators' afterword is sole-authored by Kōya. Among those to whom he expresses gratitude are familiar names such as Duncan Callister, Alexander Everett, Lia Byers and even Saint-Germain. There is no mention of Akiko, who only figures on the cover as one of the two translators.

The first print run of 4,000 copies sold quite quickly. The only attempt to advertise the book came from the Yamakawas who, in what they explain as a response to the admonition of the spirit of Saint-Germain, sent approximately a hundred copies to celebrities and famous people. The fact that a high-ranked government official had translated a Hollywood actress' book soon attracted the attention of the media, with the *Asahi* newspaper dedicating an entire page to the book (see Figure 3.1). The Yamakawas were soon in demand and Akiko started co-organizing short seminars around the country, often in collaboration with local personalities of the *seishin sekai* such as Asano Makoto.[45] She also replied to the three or four letters that she received daily from readers of MacLaine's book, and frequently received people at her home, transmitting to them what she believed to be messages from spirits of saintly figures.[46] However, the asthma attacks that Kōya had started having during their stay in Washington became debilitating. The couple refused to seek professional help, partly through fear of the side effects of steroid-containing drugs, and partly because they believed they were receiving spirit messages encouraging them to seek non-medical help. The result was three years (1986–9) of significant pain for Kōya, who had no choice but to quit his job in 1987 at the age of forty-five. Akiko also faced significant challenges. While caring for her husband, she also became the

Figure 3.1 *Asahi* newspaper article on the translation of Shirley MacLaine's book by the Yamakawas (*Asahi*, Morning Edition, 18 May 1988).

breadwinner, translating by herself Shirley MacLaine's next two books (although her husband's name also appears on the covers) and continuing to offer lectures. Fortunately for them, an employee of Sony put particular effort into advertising and selling an eponymous ABC television series based on *Out on a Limb* starring MacLaine, directed by Robert Butler and first broadcast in 1987. Suddenly the translations of all three of MacLaine's books became genre bestsellers in Japan, with combined total print runs of 560,000 copies as reported by Jiyūsha. In niche markets such as that of the *seishin sekai*, it is not uncommon to consider books that have sold more than 50,000 copies bestsellers.

The Yamakawas's career as translators and importers of the spiritual in Japan only really picked up in 1990. Until then, they had basically worked as the Japanese translators of Shirley McLaine. In 1989, when several failed attempts to cure Kōya's condition brought them back to the doctor, a novel prescription of treatment against asthma improved Kōya's situation significantly and allowed him to go back to work. It was then Akiko's turn to fall sick from exhaustion. She experienced motor issues that took another two and a half years to cure. In a typical auto-hagiographical statement characteristic of translators of New Age material, Akiko recalls that 'those years of living with illness were for us, who have been fated to introduce spiritual books to Japan, a chance to start shifting our consciousness' (Yamakawa and Yakamawa 2018: 105).

In many ways the Yamakawas's activities resemble those of Terry Hu and C. C. Wang, two of the forerunning translators of the same New Age literature in Taiwan. According to Paul Farrelly (2019: 57), Taiwanese authors and translators like Hu 'gave readers more than just ideas and philosophies for self-exploration and understanding'. They wrote themselves into the New Age movement 'through spiritual auto-hagiographies where they augmented their own experiences with the authority of those they translated … [becoming] figures relevant to Taiwanese society that interested readers could model themselves on'. Similarly, the Yamakawas embodied and represented the texts they worked on and, like Terry Hu (70–1), clearly considered their translation work to be a spiritual activity that had 'healing potential'. Their experiences of illness and other discomforts and disappointments have been continuously enmeshed in a constantly evolving and open-ended dialogue with both the ideas that they have translated and the requests made to them by editors and publishers to write about such thoughts under specific themes. This was especially the case from 2005 onwards, when the Yamakawas's career was at a point where reflection on and acknowledgement of their significant contribution to the *seishin sekai* could be discursively and practically linked to the so-called spiritual boom that was occurring at that time.

Although they have translated more than hundred books, the Yamakawas built their popularity on their flair for bestseller authors such as Brian L. Weiss, whose first book, *Many Lives, Many Masters*, Kōya brought back from a brief visit to the United States. The Yamakawas interpreted Weiss's books as a psychiatrist's version of *Out on a Limb*, and proceeded to seek their own past lives through trips to Europe and the rest of the world (Yamakawa 2018). Next, on the request of Jiyūsha, they translated Paulo Coehlo's *The Alchemist* and proceeded to co-organize his visit to Japan, where over 800 people gathered to listen to his talk. On the request of Kadokawa-shoten, they translated James Redfield's *The Celestine Prophecy*, which sold out immediately with hardly any advertisement.

In a kind of snowball effect, the more the Yamakawas translated popular New Age Anglophone literature, the more invitations they received for translation jobs, as well as lectures targeting readers and fans of their work. Nearly all of their self-authored books include in their afterword messages of gratitude to the editors or other individuals who had asked them to write about themselves. They both continued to seek new experiences. Kōya, for example, visited the Esalen Institute several times in the early 2000s and brought back to Japan what he calls spirit dance. Akiko made yearly trips to Hawaii to take part in swimming with dolphin tours. But their extensive network kept bringing them new translation jobs. Yamazaki Yoshinobu, a long-term student of Osho (the Indian NRM leader formerly known as Rajneesh), brought them to India and connected them with the Osho foundation. One of the workshops that Kōya organized in 2007 for aspiring translators of *seishin sekai* texts led them to meet Sano Miyoko, with whom they translated Rhonda Byrne's books.

The Yamakawas's activities remained interconnected with health issues. In 2007, which happened to be the peak of the so-called spiritual boom in Japan, both Kōya and Akiko experienced several incidents of what at first seemed to be fatigue, but in Akiko's case developed into myodesopsia and other temporary impairments of her eyes and ears. With early signs of depression also showing, but no drugs having any effect on her conditions, Akiko narrates how disappointed she felt at her feelings of guilt for asking her husband to help. She writes that a year later, after being diagnosed with cancer (later revealed to be a benign tumour), she found some kind of peace with herself, but acknowledges that she had always been jealous of her husband. He had been able to constantly better himself, while she never managed to get rid of a sense of competition towards him. 'I did not need a doctor. I needed counselling and healing' (Yamakawa and Yakamawa 2018: 183). Thereafter followed further new discoveries of self-development methods, workshops and books (e.g. American motivational coach Brandon Bays's *The Journey* and German psychotherapist Bert Hellinger's *Family Constellations*), all of which looked for personal or family traumas, even in previous generations. Akiko writes that at the age of nearly seventy, still seeking answers on a visit to a counsellor in Hong Kong, she was told (and again realized) the same thing she had been told in all of the treatments she had tried: she had still not accepted herself 100 per cent. 'I needed to keep trying to forgive myself', she says (221–2).

Print spirituality: Feeding on the counter-cultural legacy

The idea that *supirichuariti* became popular in Japan as a reaction to a deteriorating image of religion in the post-Aum era does not take into account the early pioneers of *seishin sekai* literature, such as Tama Shuppan's founder Uritani, who were looking for a path away from 'religion' (but not rejecting it) well before Aum had made a name for itself. Even more importantly, the idea that the spiritual was a way of avoiding ominous associations with the character *rei* is less an analysis than a repetition of how early gatekeepers like the Yamakawas have explained themselves to an audience looking for something else, but not necessarily an alternative to religion. The Yamakawas have been writing for people who are interested in healing and empowerment or self-betterment no matter the means. Their association with the New Age or with spirituality is secondary. The Yamakawas and their ideas are part of a mainstream culture of self-development that has relied heavily on the publishing industry to thrive since the 1980s, and has fed on a therapeutic narrative that gains from being associated with 'alternative' scenarios, such as that of the spiritual but not religious. Moreover, the constant enmeshment of their life struggles and successes with the books they translated has further reinforced the association of alternative religion with a therapeutic message of hope.

In his discussion of the contemporary use of spirituality, Boaz Huss (2014: 53) argues that the concept is a new discursive construct 'establishing current ways of classification and different modes of understanding the world and acting within it'. Huss rightly refuses to consider spirituality as an etic concept, but rather describes it as an emic postmodern cultural category that has raised awareness about the contingency of the 'old' categories of religion and the secular (56). This has also led it to being criticized 'for being part of late capitalistic consumer culture and for enhancing neo-liberal ideology' (58). However, I believe that Huss could have gone further. He seems to be trying to separate the contemporary spirituality that 'emerged in the context of Western, globalized consumer culture and express[es] the cultural logic of late capitalism' from 'the people who engage in New Age practices [and] do not necessarily accept neo-liberal values' (57). But I believe that it is impossible to separate the two since they are in constant interaction. We have seen this interaction in the lives and practices of the translators, editors and publishing house founders who have featured in this chapter, and in the activities of those making a living from providing spiritual therapies in Chapter 1. Moreover, as I will unfold further in the second part of the book, both globalized late capitalist culture and countercultural narratives feed on each other's alternativity, meeting at the nexus of an audience constantly needing healing and growth.

4

Alternative therapies in the age of attention

In 2006, at the age of thirty-one, Ms Kawasaki was diagnosed with depression. She told me that she had probably been depressed for a while, having been born into a family drowning in debt and growing up with a mother with a chronic disease who was constantly fighting with her father. She described herself as having been a pessimist child, full of complexes from growing up with so many unfulfilled wishes and lacking in self-esteem. She had spent her twenties filling temporary positions in the service industry before deciding to launch herself into the manga business as an artist. 'I would shower once per week and take a day off once per month, during which I would just sleep through', she explained. 'One day I just could not handle it anymore. I had just got married but still had family issues to deal with and, well, just collapsed.' Although prescribed antidepressants and hormone balance therapy, Ms Kawasaki remained dissatisfied. 'When I was younger, people did not know the word "depression". They would say "you are lazy". So I was happy that it was finally recognized, but the side effects of the anti-depressants were severe. I developed a kind of diabetes and experienced losses of memory.'

This lasted for about six months until, one day, Ms Kawasaki saw the television programme *Unbelievable* (FujiTV) hosted by the famous comedian, actor and director Takeshi Kitano, which narrated miraculous experiences, often veering on the paranormal, in an infotainment style. That day, the programme had focused on the past-life regression therapy of Brian L. Weiss, whose books were translated by the Yamakawas (Chapter 3). 'I thought "that's it!" Ms Kawasaki recalled. 'I found a hypnotherapist nearby and got a session. [Pause] I felt like I had found myself. I was really surprised there existed such a good technique and went again, for a second time. Then I thought, with my service industry skills, I can do better. I want to learn.' Quitting her low-paid job as a manga artist, Ms Kawasaki returned to a temporary service industry position so that she could pay for more hypnotherapy sessions and, eventually, for the various certificates that would allow her to open her own salon two years later.

In the first half of this book, I analysed why and how the *supirichuaru* and *supirichuariti* came into usage at the start of the twenty-first century through a critical examination of the concerns that these concepts reflected in three inter-related fields: the complementary and alternative therapy business, academia and the publishing industry. In this second half, I turn to focus on the lives and activities of spiritual therapists, many of whom – like Ms Kawasaki – entered the spirituality business during the so-called spiritual boom after experiencing what they considered to be new ways of thinking about themselves that involved paying attention to their lives, feelings and emotions. What did the 'spiritual' mean in practical terms for these individuals and how did it relate to the social conditions that they faced from the end of the 1990s through the early twenty-first century?

As a first step in answering these questions, this chapter discusses the therapeutic milieu of Ms Kawasaki and other spiritual therapists in early-twenty-first-century Tokyo, providing an overview of the range of therapies that they provided and, more importantly, analysing the therapeutic culture underpinning their practice – that is, the interaction between therapist and client, patterns of disease causation and justification, and expectations of healing. As we have seen, spiritual therapists use the label 'spiritual' as a discursive strategy that positions their therapeutic milieu in relation to biomedical settings; the therapies that they provide are not medicine (Chapter 1). As this chapter discusses, this framing resonates with how the rise of today's alternative therapy culture, both globally and more specifically in Japan, has often been interpreted in academic studies as a reaction to scientific medicine and a post-1970s rise of healthism. Yet, the actual practice of spiritual therapy, I argue, shares the same format as all contemporary therapeutic interventions (biomedical, alternative and complementary). At its core lies the imperative to pay attention to ourselves.

Spiritual therapies

When I met Ms Kawasaki on a late August afternoon in 2009, she was offering more than twenty types of sessions, even though her salon had only been open for about a year. These sessions were divided into the three categories commonly found in the spiritual therapy business: reading, healing and hypnotherapy. The purpose of reading (*riidingu*) sessions, usually the cheapest on a therapist's menu, is to diagnose the client's worries or issues and sometimes to heal them through a form of reiki. In some cases, the therapist examines a specific part of the client, such as their aura, chakras or energy levels, or a 'power stone/crystal' that they have carried with them or bought in advance from the salon. Alternatively the therapist might convey to the client information extracted from another source, such as the client's Higher Self, their guardian spirit, a god or an extraterrestrial being. Ms Kawasaki confessed that her 'reading the Light' (*hikari no riidingu*) session, priced at 6,000 yen for a one-to-two-hour meeting, had been the most successful. She was thereby alluding to her ability to converse with sources of knowledge that she called 'the Light' and that transmitted through her messages of advice and encouragement.

The second category are generally called healing (*hiiringu*) sessions. These vary from massage-based manipulation to more abstract or non-physical interventions that use counselling techniques and/or objects such as crystals to release (*kaihō*) the client from an energy or mental blockage and bring them into what is considered a healthier, ideal condition of balance (*baransu*). In this category, Ms Kawasaki's most popular technique, which she later developed into workshops that she offered around the country, was the melody crystal healing session, which she had learned from the American 'crystologist' A. Melody (d.2019), who Ms Kawasaki had met in Japan in 2007. Melody was one of the most famous proponents of the idea that some crystals have the ability to affect a person's physical and mental state if appropriately selected and positively 'charged'.[1] It is not unusual for therapists to generate a secondary income through the sale of objects associated with healing sessions, such as crystals, stones and oils, which can be employed by the therapist or recommended to the client for their private use (Figure 4.1). As companies such as Gwyneth Paltrow's Goop have demonstrated, the value of such objects stems from the conditions of their production and authorship; *how* they are supposed to work remains largely secret, if not unknown (Crockford 2021b: 209).

The third, and usually most expensive type of session that most spiritual therapists offer, is hypnotherapy. As a category of therapies, hypnotherapy includes past-life regression therapy, age regression therapy and several goal-focused therapies that claim to treat trauma, anxiety and other specific psychological issues. What they all share is an Ericksonian approach to hypnotherapy, which involves the use of indirect (most frequently, conversational) techniques to encourage the client to participate in the induction of a trance state by responding to the therapist's questions and casual suggestions. Typical of these hypnotherapy sessions are a relaxed atmosphere, the use of simple phrases or

Figure 4.1 A booth at the Iyashi Fair in 2012, selling healing crystals, power stones and other objects used in spiritual therapy sessions. Photo by the author.

body manipulations (such as the hand levitation technique) and the idea that whatever comes out of the client's mouth *spontaneously* is an expression of their subconscious. Websites of hypnotherapy salons in Japan emphasize the conversational character of these therapies to pre-empt any impression among prospective patients that they will lose their decision-making abilities during a session. The majority of the spiritual therapists whom I interviewed had been licensed by an institution called the American Board of Hypnotherapy, which was founded in 1982, in California, by A. M. Krasner, who shared the typical Ericksonian belief in the empowering potential of hypnosis. In his most popular book, *The Wizard Within: The Krasner Method of Clinical Hypnotherapy* (first published in 1990 and translated into Japanese in 1995), Krasner argues that all hypnosis is, in fact, self-hypnosis (Krasner 2002: 17). The key inspirator for these ideas (referred to several times in Krasner's book) was the hypnotist Emile Coué (1857–1926). Deeply embedded in the positive-thinking ideology popular at the time, Coué had argued that by repeating the sentence 'every day, in every way, I'm getting better and better' several times per day (the so-called Coué method), one could, through optimistic auto-suggestion, actually get better and better.[2]

Reading and hypnotherapy sessions largely rely on the therapist's ability to build a coherent narrative that appeals to their client. Hence, like fortune telling, their perceived quality increases as the therapist acquires more experience. In contrast, healing sessions require the therapist to have a substantial amount of prior knowledge; Melody's books, for example, identify more than 700 types of crystals. But, regardless of type, practitioners will have had to make an investment in texts, tools, workshops and classes for most of the therapies offered. One needs to acknowledge the tenacity of Ms Kawasaki and others who seemed to become avid collectors of all kinds of certificates during the peak years of the 'spiritual boom' from 2005 to 2009. Roughly half of the sixty-five therapists whom I interviewed in 2008 and 2009 had opened their salons from 2005 onwards, the year Ehara Hiroyuki launched his television show (Gaitanidis 2010: 148). Certification cost them both time and money – often several tens of thousands of yen – since it could be acquired only after attending courses, usually between two and six hours long, which they might have to travel some distance to attend. During this period, Ms Kawasaki completed an Aroma Environment Association of Japan aroma advisor course, a hypno-navigator course at the Japan Hypno-management Association, a hypno-reading counsellor course at the Japan Spiritual Association and an aura-reiki healing course at the Aura Reiki Academy.[3] These were in addition to her finishing both levels of Melody's crystal healing course, for which she acquired certificates in 2009; in 2011, she would even travel to Arkansas, where Melody had opened her own mine (Melody Green Mine) from which visitors were invited to extract their own crystals.

On their personal websites and in the stories they told me during interviews, as well as in scholarly exegeses on spirituality, practitioners' sudden and fast-paced switch to a life centred on spiritual therapy is often explained (out) with reference to a trigger event. In Ms Kawasaki's narration of her pathway into the spiritual therapy business, it was during her first hypnotherapy session – a form of regression therapy – that she was struck with the realization that she needed to transform her life:

> I saw myself living a poor life, sometime in the Middle Ages, writing tracts at home and distributing them in the street. I then saw myself being married to a rich man so that I could save my family from poverty and I thought: That is what I am doing right now. I am sacrificing myself for my family. This has to change!

In this respect, we might think of spiritual therapists as shamanistic practitioners and place them within the long history of 'wounded healers'

(Gaitanidis and Murakami 2014). But, beyond this, we also need to consider how that trigger event is reflected in their subsequent practice of spiritual therapy and in the socio-therapeutic context in which they perform. In this chapter, I want to understand Ms Kawasaki's discovery of the effect of hypnotherapy not just as a reflection of what she thought of herself, but as an expression of the therapeutic milieu that she found herself in. It is obvious that her visions of a past life were associated with her predicament at the time of her first session, but this does not explain why the practice of hypnotherapy had the 'liberating' effect that it did on her, prompting her to quit her job and open her own spiritual therapy salon. Leaving the debate around the scientific basis and effectiveness (or not) of hypno- and other therapies to specialists, I explore what it was that made people who tried out a spiritual therapy during these peak years of the 'spiritual boom' turn their lives around and decide to launch themselves into a new business endeavour.

Is therapy culture an expression of healthism?

The global therapeutic milieu in which Ms Kawasaki was practicing when I met her has often been framed as a reaction to scientific medicine (Kelner and Wellman 2000; Tovey, Easthope and Adams 2004). The standard narrative starts with the 'golden age of scientific medicine', which spanned sixty years, from 1910 to 1970 (Turner 2004: xiv). This so-called golden age ended when health, for the first time, came to be defined as more than the mere absence of disease or infirmity and when striving for a better condition of health became a right and responsibility of the modern individual. More importantly, this signified a 'turn inwards' to explore and attempt to discover through attention to the self what there is to 'fix' through healthcare. This transformation of the concept of health prepared the ground for two consecutive elements in the development and consolidation of today's global therapy culture.

First, there was the appearance of medical consumerism. Arthur W. Frank claims that this made of health the contemporary basis of what Max Weber had referred to as 'the theodicy of good fortune' (Frank 2002: 27). Weber argued that by treating suffering 'as a symptom of odiousness in the eyes of the gods', religion had traditionally met a general psychological need, reassuring the fortunate that 'he has a *right* to his good fortune. He wants to be convinced that he "deserves" it, and above all, that he deserves it in comparison with others' (Weber 1958: 271, cited in Frank 2002: 27). Frank proposes that medical consumerism 'instantiates this good fortune in the body', making the individual believe that each person is responsible for their own health and thus deserves it. This interpretation of the effects of healthcare consumerism, namely the shift of authority from without to within, has been reproduced in religious studies to support the idea that the self has become sacralized in late modernity, as exemplified by the New Age movement (Heelas 1996: 82). As Shimazono (2002: 17) puts it, the rise of spirituality and rise of contemporary therapeutic culture are like two sides of the same coin. Second, the more the individual focused on improving their health, the more it became obvious that the manipulation of individual predispositions can affect health, that is, that 'health care is a matter of cultural modelling rather than scientific truth' (Cassidy 1996: 31). As people's health expectations surpassed what scientific medicine and the pace of its innovation could offer, they started turning towards old and new types of therapies and healing, provoking a surge in CAM and other alternative therapies. As I will go on to discuss, the idea that Japanese society became more healthist in the 1980s and 1990s, driving an upsurge of interest in alternative therapies, became something of a truth among sociologists, who referred to it as the health (*kenkō*) or healing (*iyashi*) boom.

It has been suggested that the 'subjective turn' in health-seeking behaviour and consequent infatuation with alternative therapies stems from the rationalization of the doctor-patient relationship during the golden age of scientific medicine and the resulting absence of the patient in the process of their diagnosis. Here, I am reiterating a well-versed argument eloquently summarized by Michael Taussig (1992: 87–8) as the denial of the social facticity of facts: the moral and social components of disease are concealed by the use of the natural science model, which regards the results of a diagnosis as 'solid, substantial things-in-themselves'. Hence, medical practice inevitably produces grotesque mystifications in which we all flounder, grasping ever more pitifully for security in a man-made world that we do not see as social, human or historical, but rather as consisting of *a priori* objects that are beholden only to their own force and laws – laws that are dutifully illuminated for us by professional experts such as doctors (89). In contrast, CAM practitioners believe in the interrelation of mind, body and spirit through a universal vitalism and tend to focus on the underlying causes of illnesses, often relying on the body's assumed self-healing and self-regulating capacities. This integrative conceptual framework is meant to prevent the patient from floundering in a purely biomedically framed, man-made world.

Or so the argument goes. But what if non-biomedical interventions were already being pushed *during* the golden age of medicine, well before they were allegedly rediscovered after the 1970s? We now know that the so-called golden age was accompanied by the increased popularity of the paramedical and popular therapy sector, which in Japan saw a significant growth from the 1920s that continued in the post-war period (see Kurita, Tsukada and Yoshinaga 2019). Far from disappearing, history shows that non-biomedical therapy (popular, alternative, complementary, spiritual) was strengthened with the advance of biomedicine. The current use of hypnotherapy in many spiritual therapy salons in Tokyo, for example, draws its origins from a French technique of autosuggestion that became world famous in the 1920s and was later propagated through professional and lay hypnosis credentialing organizations in the United States from the 1950s to the 1970s (Eichel 2010) before reaching the Japanese shores in the 1980s. To understand the basis for the therapy culture experienced by people like Ms Kawasaki in the early 2000s, therefore, the question is not whether non-biomedical therapies were 'rediscovered' in and became more popular from the 1970s onwards, but whether people like Ms Kawasaki were turning to them because they had become more health conscious.

From the 1980s, if not before, it was considered a truth among Japanese sociologists that Japanese society had, from the 1970s onwards, become healthist; the proof of this was the exponential increase in publications related to health topics and health-gaining techniques. In a series of single- and co-authored articles published between 2003 and 2008, Kuroda Kōichirō, professor of sociology at Ryukoku University, put this truth into question. Fujioka Masayuki, who later summarized this debate in some detail (Fujioka 2015: 107–43), notes that Kuroda's argument relied on a precise analysis of nationwide health awareness statistics, which showed the Japanese population to have been more concerned about its health at the end of the 1950s than from the 1970s onwards. According to Kuroda, the misinterpretation of the post-1970s data stemmed from increased public criticism in magazines at the time *against* healthist attitudes. Contemporaneous scholars and commentators seeking to understand why such voices had appeared sought to explain them as a reaction to what they mistook to be a 'health (*kenkō*) boom' (Kuroda, cited in Fujioka 2015: 134–5).

While Fujioka agrees with Kuroda on this point, he nevertheless argues that there had in fact been a proliferation of magazine and periodical publications about healthy lifestyles. Based on a statistical analysis of the ratio of this type of publication to the total number of publications in the post-war period, Fujioka finds that between the end of the 1960s and the mid-1970s, and then again in the mid-1990s, there occurred what could only be described as a healthist publishing boom (Fujioka 2015: 189). Sociologist Matsui Takeshi's (2013) study of the 'healing (*iyashi*) boom' suggests that the explanation for the second of these upsurges might be at least partly found in the marketing strategies of companies operating in a post-bubble economy, rather than in a post-1970s healthist turn in society.[4]

Based on a discourse analysis of nearly 40,000 newspaper and magazine articles and books framed around the concept of *iyashi* (Matsui 2013: 73–4), Matsui notes that, between 1988 and 2007, the word came to be attached to every experience and product available on the Japanese market, from shopping to traveling and from the pet-robot AIBO to music CDs. In contrast to many commentators, including religious studies scholars, Matsui identifies this trend as a marketing strategy rather than as a reflection of a need for healing. Economic stagnation in the 1990s increased the imperative to find new ways of attracting consumers, especially among companies that dealt with non-vital services, such as hotels, the music industry or gift shops. They looked to the *seishin sekai* for ideas and, as a result, became pioneers of *iyashi* by recognizing its potential marketing value. Matsui identifies several starting points, including the opening of two shops that advertised themselves as providing 'total healing' (*tōtaru hiiringu*) in the late 1980s in Tokyo's rich district, Daikan'yama; one sold accessories and the other organic food (88–9). The marketing professionals of larger companies, such as Sony, would subsequently employ the word *iyashi* – a more neutral concept than the transliteration *hiiringu* – to raise the value of their products, a classic example being Sony's AIBO pet robot (93). This was a purely strategic move to ride on the *iyashi* wave by adopting a term that was trending, Matsui explains. These companies were not seeking to meet the therapeutic needs of their customers nor even necessarily promoting their products as having healing effects. It was the media that developed the narrative that the Japanese population was in need of healing in order to explain the popularity of *iyashi* products. This narrative was then internalized by consumers, journalists and eventually academics.

Matsui (2013: 240) observes that the meaning of *iyashi* shifted around the turn of the millennium. It had originally been understood as an active seeking of healing for one's worries and issues, but eventually came to be conceptualized in more passive terms as an experience that one is given by others. As such, an *iyashi*-based therapy culture did not in practice function as an alternative to the culture of biomedicine and its model of the specialist acting on the patient. Fujioka's findings similarly complicate the idea that health was becoming de-medicalized. Based on a content analysis of magazine and periodical publications about healthy lifestyles, Fujioka (2015: 225) stresses what he calls a paradoxical phenomenon: the great variety of healthist publications seemed to support a certain autonomy of choice on the part of consumers and hence a de-medicalization of everyday life, but, *at the same time*, they fostered a normative medicalist sense of what health is and ought to be.

In short, both Fujioka and Matsui deny the existence of an especially heightened health awareness in Japan from the 1970s onwards. They also note that the increased consumption of narratives, products and services meant to heal their buyers seemed to reproduce the normative and passive therapeutic experience of the man-made world that Taussig so vehemently decried. People are offered *iyashi* experiences. What these entail is attention to the self. *This* is precisely the therapeutic culture that Ms Kawasaki experienced when, diagnosed with depression, she discovered hypnotherapy and became a practitioner herself. Ms Kawasaki and others like her were not turning to non-biomedical therapies in the first decade of the twenty-first century because they had become more health conscious. They were turning to them as an opportunity to pay attention to and master their suffering – and to then offer the same opportunity to others – in an early-twenty-first-century culture of what medical anthropologist Kitanaka Junko (2012) calls 'socializing medicalization'.

Depression and socializing medicalization

Spiritual therapists shared the 'mainstream' biomedical narratives of depression and other social malaises that had originally brought many of them and their patients to a spiritual therapy salon. At least twelve of the therapists I interviewed sought help for depression in the early 2000s, while many others identified depression as the reason why clients came to them for therapy. 'In the early 1990s, no one knew about depression', Ms Miwa explained. 'So even I did not know I had it.' The same theme emerged when I asked Ms Shibata if she had seen a difference in her clients' cases since she had started learning spiritual therapies a decade earlier. 'Depression', she immediately responded. 'Most of the people that come now are just depressed.' Mr Matsuyama and Ms Natsuda, who had both been providing therapeutic services for over thirty years, independently made the same observation, claiming that the majority of recent cases were linked to depression. Ms Takashima, who had attempted to take her own life on three occasions in the 1990s when she was in her early twenties, felt that she had become a specialist in the treatment of depression. She reasoned that her personal experience had contributed to her deeper understanding of such cases; that is why, she explained, she was popular. When I interviewed Ms Takashima in early July 2009, she was already fully booked until mid-September, a rare case in the spiritual business. Ms Fukuyama, who had spent several years learning psychological counselling, criticized practitioners like Ms Takashima for believing that they knew something because they had been through it, even though they might themselves still be in a state of recovery. But she too commented on the increase in depression cases at the start of the millennium. As Kitanaka (2012: 2) observes, it was clear that depression had, at the turn of the century, become a 'national disease'.

Margaret Lock and Nguyen Vinh-Kim (2010) locate the medicalization of 'feeling down' and 'being gloomy' in Japan to the 1990s (74). This was a time when other somatized behaviours, including school refusal and social withdrawal, also became the target of professional counselling and biomedical intervention (78). Antidepressants had only reached Japanese shores in 1999.[5] According to contemporaneous commentators, they were presented as a drug that changes personality in accordance with the American-type competitive lifestyle (Kirmayer 2004: 169), showing how the American therapy culture imported into Japan spanned the entire spectrum of therapies, from New Age channelling to pharmaceutical substances. *Utsubyō* (depression) had been known in Japan since at least the Edo period (1603–1857) as a condition of accumulated sorrow, excessive contemplation or silent endurance. However, the advent of German psychiatry in the late nineteenth century provoked a stigmatization of 'abnormal' psychological states and rejected certain conditions, like depression, as mere complaints; hence, Kitanaka (2012: 38–9) argues, the 'rediscovery' in Japan after the turn of the millennium of depression as 'disease', a status it had until then been denied by biomedicine.

Several factors contributed to this rediscovery, but one of the most significant was the death of Ōshima Ichirō, an employee of Dentsū, perhaps the largest advertising and public relations company in Japan. Approximately one year after starting work at the company, Ichirō hanged himself in his bathroom in what was later concluded to be a state of depression caused by stress and overwork. Ichirō's family subsequently sued Dentsū. Their initial victory at the Tokyo District Court in 1996 was probably the first time that the Japanese public heard that suicide could be the result of a mental illness called depression (Kitanaka 2012: 157). Based on an extensive study of psychiatric journals, interviews with psychiatrists and participant observation at psychiatric hospitals and various conferences and study groups, Kitanaka concludes that as the new antidepressants were introduced, they were absorbed into a social narrative produced by government and health experts. This narrative linked recession ('Japan's lost decade' and the effects of the Asian economic crisis of 1997), suicide (the number of yearly deaths exceeded 30,000 for the first time in 1998) and depression, creating 'a culturally infused image of collectively depressed bodies under siege, while crystallizing people's prevailing sense of loss and anxiety in the name of depression' (177).

Kitanaka calls this phenomenon 'socializing medicalization'. She notes a significant gender gap between psychiatrists' sympathetic portrayal of overworked salarymen and their assessments of 'undiagnosable' women whose storylines were considered less straightforward than those of men, often navigating around what Kitanaka identifies as three types of 'lack': a lack of social and medical cognition, a lack of trust in medical professionals and a lack of certainty in the meaning of their depression (140–1). She nevertheless describes in detail how psychiatrists managed to get patients to reproduce narratives 'with surprising uniformity and consistency, not necessarily because they have thoroughly persuaded patients and transformed their consciousness, but because they deliberately leave much unexplored' (127). This is illustrated in Kitanaka's description of how psychiatrists dealt with suicidal patients:

> First, they 'extract' the underlying psychopathology and urge patients to objectify their own body, cultivating an awareness of how fatigued and even alien their body has become; second, they de-existentialize suicidal urges by showing suicidal patients how not only their bodies but also their minds change through biological interventions. They encourage patients to regard their suicidal intention as a departure from their 'normal' selves … and third, … psychiatrists also call attention to the social pressures driving the breakdown, thereby suggesting patients' victimhood. In this final step, psychiatrists effectively merge the biological and the social in their particular construction of psychopathology, which culminates in a generic framework that at times effectively translates individual misery into a sign of social suffering. (Kitanaka 2012: 127)

The rise of depression as a national illness and the effects that it had on the practice of psychiatry spread quickly and widely beyond the walls of psychiatric hospitals and private clinics. They soon influenced the way people described and experienced healing in general and impacted on how the media sought to explain the 'needs' of consumers of healthy lifestyle magazines, CAM and anything with an *iyashi* effect. A 'looping effect' was then responsible for the exponential increase of the market for CAM and other alternative therapies, which was driven by both marketing strategies and media exegeses of *iyashi* products *and* psychiatric and national warnings of a depression 'epidemic'. A brief analysis of the annual editions of the *Therapy All Guide* (TAG) will illustrate how these phenomena transformed the way 'spiritual therapy' came to be introduced to and experienced by consumers.

Healing through attention

The *Therapy All Guide* (TAG) is a catalogue of alternative therapies that was published between 1997 and 2013 by BAB Japan, a publishing house renowned for its bimonthly magazine *Serapisuto* (*Therapist*), first published in 2001. TAG was typically divided into three sections. The first carried interviews, testimonials and practical advice from therapists, the second consisted of a catalogue of therapies introduced over a two-page spread and the third was a short section of advertisements from salons, shops and producers of *iyashi* consumables. In its fourteen-year run, the magazine decreased in size from approximately 250 to 130 pages but its first section grew from a few pages to occupy one-third of the publication, reflecting a change in TAG's purpose. It had started as an annual special supplement of BAB Japan's *Ki no mori* (lit. *Forest of Energy*) magazine (thirty-eight volumes between 1993 and 2005) and had functioned as a source of information about spiritual therapy salons, workshops and schools. But with the increasing number of websites providing such listings for free, the editors of TAG shifted the focus to introducing therapies and therapists that were successful enough to attract a readership (Figure 4.2). Before going on to analyse testimonials published in this section as illustrations of healing as socializing medicalization, it is first worth reviewing TAG's catalogue section and the variety of therapies it introduced. These data provide a clear overview of the overall shift in therapeutic culture as we enter the years of the 'spiritual boom'.

Graph 4.1 shows the fluctuation in the number of therapies listed in the magazine based on TAG's own four categories: body, mind, nature and art. To this I have added a line indicating the fluctuation in the number of publications listed in the catalogue of the National Diet Library of Japan that included the word *supirichuaru* in their title. This line represents the occurrence of the so-called spiritual boom. While the overall number of therapies decreases over time, during the 'spiritual boom' the category of mind therapies remained fairly constant and more popular than the other three categories, suggesting that mental and psychological concerns have been at the core of the spiritual

Figure 4.2 *Therapy All Guide* catalogues. Reproduced with permission. Photo taken by the author.

business. There are also more subtle patterns, especially in the kind of therapies that disappeared from TAG's catalogue section and in those that remained or were introduced after the end of the boom.

As the number of therapies listed in the first issue indicates,[6] techniques originally spanned a wide spectrum and sought to appeal to a very large audience, which was perhaps looking for new experiences as well as for healing. The first issue, which lists horse-riding as a body therapy, even includes an interview with Kayama Rika, a psychiatrist who would go on to become a staunch critic of the *supirichuaru*, but who, at the time, sought to draw attention to the then increasingly popular practice of counselling (see Chapter 1). 'Channelling' was listed until the 2004 edition, being recommended for people 'who have a problem that they cannot solve on their own and who, therefore, might want to listen to the voice and opinion of a being (*sonzai*) with a more objective and expansive perspective' (TAG 2002: 142).[7] Another mind therapy that disappeared after 2004 was 'energetic medicine', suggested for 'people who want to live their lives proactively and who want to heal their illness and problems at the energy level' (TAG 2003: 120).

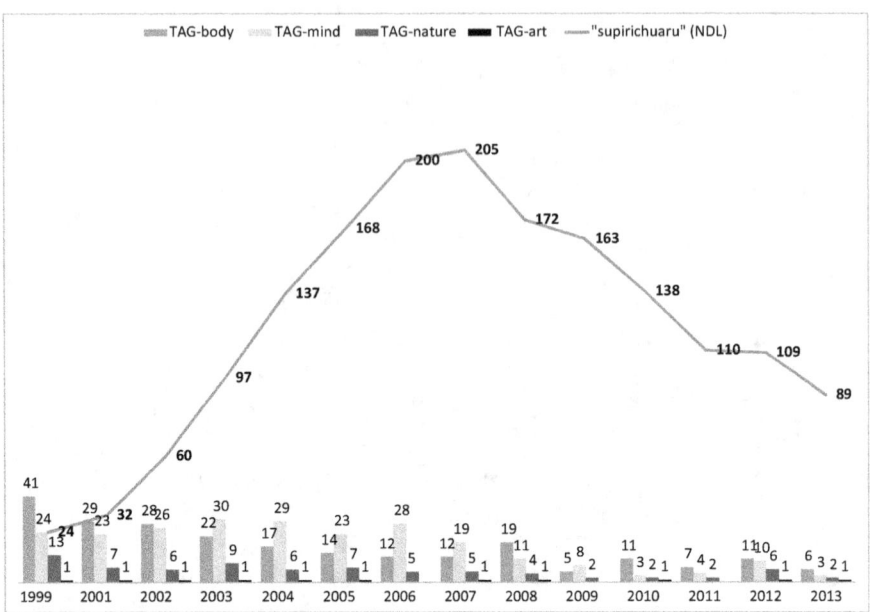

Graph 4.1 Categories and number of therapies listed in the *Therapy All Guide* catalogue between 1999 and 2013. Compiled by the author.

While mind therapies such as channelling and energetic medicine that had relatively vague descriptions soon disappeared, some of the body therapies that emphasized their effects on psychological issues remained popular throughout the run of the magazine. 'Three In One Concepts', for example, a type of chiropractic technique using biofeedback machinery, appears in nearly all of TAG's volumes, where it is claimed to 'heal the emotional stress that causes various issues of the body, mind and soul, and help people find new possibilities in themselves' (TAG 2013: 82). Meanwhile, popular mind therapies that had originally been promoted for their experiential originality more than their therapeutic value came to be entirely framed around a variety of psychological and psychosomatic issues. Hypnotherapy is a classic example. Whereas in 1999 it is recommended for 'relaxation, increased concentration and correction of bad habits (such as biting one's nails)' (TAG 1999: 142), in 2005 it is suggested for 'worries regarding relationships, lack of self-confidence and motivation, dysautonomia, anxiety, tension, stage fright, panic, social phobia, eating disorders, allergies and people who wish to know life's goals etc' (TAG 2005: 129).

As the descriptions of both body and mind therapies shift to interpreting all issues through psychological ailments, the clients' testimonies, regardless of the category of therapy used, reflect a pattern similar to that analysed by Kitanaka

(2012), in which narratives of healing follow the three steps of socializing medicalization: objectification of the body, de-existentialization of issues, and merging of the biological and the social. In the 2007 edition, a woman from Kanagawa talks about her visit to a salon offering vital reiki therapy (TAG 2007: 151), listed in TAG as a body therapy from 2002 to 2007. Like other testimonials in TAG, this woman's story reveals that she had been a regular user of such services, but this is not the reason she offers for trying vital reiki. She explains that her inability to cope with stress at work had pushed her to look for a spiritual-type (*supirichuaru-kei*) therapy. She then recounts how she spent the preliminary counselling session talking about issues at her workplace and was surprised when the therapist asked her if she was planning to have children. In response, she related the advice she had been given by another spiritual therapist, who had told her that her energy was too 'male' and that she would have trouble conceiving a child. Her new therapist said that this probably had to do with a problem in her past life, prompting her to book a past-life therapy session and to try out vital reiki. 'I was surprised at the effects. Slumps here and there in my body subsided and, as a result, I felt more stable and stopped being upset.'

Having objectified her body and externalized the cause of her distress as something that her past-self had committed – and for which she was therefore not directly responsible – she then de-existentializes her issues by linking her newly relaxed body to her mental stability. But the story does not end here. She goes on to describe how, during her third visit to the salon, she had a vision of an angel carrying a baby holding a four-leaf clover. This convinced her that having a baby would bring her and her husband luck and happiness. Not long after that, she discovered that she was pregnant and that the boss who had been harassing her had been moved to another office. She also found that her skills were being rewarded by her company, which was entrusting her with a new project. Her story ends with the suggestion that vital reiki therapy is a therapy that 'brings happiness', thus perfectly merging the biological and the social in both the causes of suffering *and* in the attainment of healing. We never find out what the problem with her former boss had been about, but we do acquire a sense that therapists constantly pushed her to pay attention to herself and, particularly, to the changes that *must* occur after she had turned her attention inwards.

Ms K. Y. provides a testimonial of another success story, this time of a mind therapy called 'crystal angel healing' (TAG 2004: 151). Her narrative starts with the death of her twelve-year-old dog, which leads her to seek the help of a salon. She describes how, lying down with crystals in her hands, she soon felt warmth spreading throughout her body accompanied by the scent of mint. She sensed her chakras being cleaned out by something like clear blue water and the swollen parts of her body becoming relaxed. An energy described as pink then descended from above into her body, returning it to a stable position 'united with the universe'. At the end of the session, Ms K. Y. writes, she realized that the death of her dog had revealed a deeper traumatic experience that she was finally able to take control over and infuse with her real self (*jibun ga shikari to haitteiku*). By de-existentializing the loss of a pet, which becomes nothing more than an opportunity for her to discover the trauma of another self, she collapses the social into the biological while leaving grief out of the healing narrative.

Kitanaka suggests that socializing medicalization may be a 'Japanese' phenomenon. I disagree. As I have already argued, it is hard to conceive of a point in time when this or that trend was specifically 'American', 'Japanese' or any other national-cultural category. The same narrative patterns of therapeutic experience have been flowing around the globe since at least the start of the twentieth century and can be found today in internationally renowned spiritual practices such as mindfulness. What is interesting is how they move around the globe and what they actually do to people who experience and employ them. Consider, for example, how compellingly similar the testimonials published in TAG are to the writings of the inventor of Mindfulness-Based Stress Reduction (MSBR), Jon Kabat-Zinn, who, Eric Braun (2017: 176–9) argues, conceptualizes individual pain as a sign of an everyday, generalized anomie stemming from a world that mindfulness practitioners have in advance conceived of as lacking inherent moral or spiritual significance. Medicalization, in this view, leads to life settings devoid of (and thus needing) meaning, but the meaning that students of mindfulness are promised they will find suffused in the world if they pay attention to their suffering demands no metaphysical commitments (Braun 2017: 179).

Like psychiatrists whose pathologization of suicidal intention leaves out cases that cannot be pathologized, spiritual therapists leave unexplored existential issues stemming from bad personal relationships, the deaths of loved ones, or what clients may consider life failures. In the case of psychiatrists this unwittingly supports the cultural discourse of 'suicide as resolve', that is, that a minority of suicides cannot be anything other than moral acts of self-determination (Kitanaka 2008). In the same way, by (re)producing the belief that one ought to be aware, attentive and in control of oneself, this socializing medicalization in the context of spiritual therapies results, for a minority of clients, in a 'realization' that they need to quit everything and start again from scratch if being aware, attentive and in control is not possible in their current lives. This,

I suggest, is where Ms Kawasaki's sudden self-determination came from. This process subdues and often effaces any explanation of malaise or disease that lies beyond the individual, whether in the specific actions of others (e.g. the boss who harasses an employee) or structural issues (e.g. inequalities). Instead, the precarity caused by their suffering is to be mastered by being attentive to the positive meaning to be found in their suffering. Clients are then encouraged to carry this positive meaning back to society to help others in similar precarious situations with their newfound messages of hope. This narrative subsists even in the case of hypnotherapy, a type of spiritual therapy that is predicated on the assumption that the solutions to the client's issues are in their subconscious and can only be revealed if one pays due attention to it.

Self-attention as ability

Sitting back on a comfortable chair with a towel covering the lower half of my fully-clothed body, I waited for Mr Yogino to close the curtains, dim the lights and seat himself on a stool next to me. At his request, I relaxed, started breathing slowly and closed my eyes.[8]

Mr Yogino:	Imagine yourself on your bed. How do you see yourself? Sitting? Lying down?
Me:	Lying down.
Mr Yogino:	Ok. Get up, look around the room and describe it. Are the windows or the door open? What do you see?
Me:	Everything is closed.
Mr Yogino:	Walk to the kitchen and open the fridge. What's inside?
Me:	A bottle of coke and cheese.
Mr Yogino:	You see! You saw this yourself. I did not tell you there is coke and cheese in the fridge. Some people say they find an elephant in the fridge. Ok. Now imagine yourself in a situation you really like and where you feel good. Where are you?
Me:	On the beach.

Mr Yogino, who, in our first meeting in 2009, had been practicing as a spiritual therapist for only one year, had invited me to participate in a hypnotherapy session so that I could experience his skills. He had learned his craft by attending a one-year course in Japan, at the cost of 700,000 yen, run by Hans Tendam, a self-proclaimed 'pioneer' of regression therapy,[9] who was frequently mentioned by my interviewees.[10] Regression here refers to the idea that clients, in a state of 'waking hypnosis', can be made to recall and relive past events in their past as well as present lives, based on the idea of reincarnation. Some hypnotherapists, including Mr Yogino, also believe that they can have clients travel into the future of their present or future lives in order to reveal their subconscious wishes.

Mr Yogino's conversation-based technique was typical of the Ericksonian approach to hypnosis common among hypnotherapists around the world today, which considers 'trance' to be similar to the state we may find ourselves in during the course of everyday life when we are deeply absorbed by something. It is an awakened dream-state induced by paying attention to what happens in our brains (Erickson 1980). To reproduce this state, Mr Yogino started with my visualization of a situation where I felt good. This conversation continued for ten or fifteen minutes with Mr Yogino constantly asking me to describe my surroundings and insisting that my responses should come instinctively (*chokkan de*). I therefore described what sounded like one of the typical Cretan seaside locations where I used to spend my holidays as a child. Then the conversation shifted:

Mr Yogino: Ok. Stop swimming. Come back out and if you feel ready, go home. Who's there?
Me: My mother and my sister.
Mr Yogino: Can you see their faces?
Me: No.
Mr Yogino: What are you doing?
Me: Watching TV and getting ready to eat.
Mr Yogino: Where's your father?
Me: Outside.
Mr Yogino: Call him. Can you see his face?
Me: Yes.
Mr Yogino: Does he resemble anyone you know?
Me: Yes, my father.
Mr Yogino: Is the TV black and white?
Me: [Pause] Yes.
Mr Yogino: So, maybe you're in the 1920s! OK, now think of a situation where something happened (*dekigoto no atta toki*). Where are you?

We repeated this cycle four times, with Mr Yogino asking me to imagine a situation and then providing a series of questions or prompts that allowed him to locate that situation in a specific time-place, in what he considered to be either a past life or the future of my current life. He kept encouraging me to say whatever came first to my mind, but I felt that I could not simply repeat what I had said before. I needed to be constantly creating new scenarios. All of the images that I conjured ended up being of a 'future self'. I first 'saw myself' as a thirty-year-old driving a bus on the island of Crete, then as a forty-year-old businessman returning by car to Scotland from Switzerland where I had just closed a deal. Next, at fifty, I was traveling through the United States where I was again driving cross-country, and finally I saw myself at the age of seventy sitting under a tree, feeling sad. Our conversation had by now lasted perhaps forty or fifty minutes and I sensed that the session was coming to an end. This was, after all, a trial. Usual sessions, Mr Yogino told me, often lasted double the time and cost 20,000 yen. But there was one final scenario that Mr Yogino prompted me to imagine – my death.

Mr Yogino: Now imagine that you die. Where does your soul go? To the sky or to some other place?
Me: Nowhere. It just stays under the tree.
Mr Yogino: Ok. Return to your room and imagine that you are facing that self who has just died. Does he have any advice for you regarding, let's say, relationships?
Me: He's angry.
Mr Yogino: Can you see his eyes? Are they human?
Me: Yes. He's just probably always been lonely.
(*Mr Yogino checks whether I have a girlfriend*)
Mr Yogino: Tell him that you are not [lonely] and that you have a girlfriend now.
Me: He says that I will never marry.
Mr Yogino: Hug him and tell him that you are going to be alright.
(*Session ends*)

A book titled *Welcome to Past Life Therapy* or *Zense ryōhō e yōkoso* (Okuyama 2005) presents descriptions of sessions very similar to mine. The author, neurosurgeon Okuyama Terumi, owns a clinic in Osaka and promotes integrative medicine. In his book, Okuyama provides ten transcripts of particularly successful sessions that follow exactly the same structure as Mr Yogino's: after an initial period of relaxation, the patient is asked to imagine themselves in a situation and describe the surroundings and the people they meet. Then the patient is asked to jump forward or backward in time twice or thrice until either the time of their death, when they climb to the sky and meet a dead relative or acquaintance, or until they face what is assumed to be the dead-self of their previous life. Closure comes when the patient finds the reason for their present distress in something that they did or endured in a previous life or something they fear that they might undergo in the future. For example, Okuyama presents the case of a woman with constant headaches who finds solace when she realizes that, in a previous life, she was a man named Marko, a Christian priest who was stoned to death (hence the headaches) by the adepts of a new faith group that had invaded his village (14–26). From the transcript, we gather that not only was the woman's health problem healed, but she also went home with the conviction that her weakness in standing up for herself had been inherited from Marko's inability to promote his faith to his fellow villagers (22).

My session did not conclude in such a salvific manner as we had not set up in advance a specific issue that I wished Mr Yogino to treat. However, my experience, along with the hundreds of testimonies published on the internet by people who have gone through hypnotherapeutic sessions, clearly demonstrate the significant effort that is required by the 'hypnotized' to sustain the imageries that they are constantly asked to produce. In the process, the client is automatically forced to employ informational resources calibrated around their self. The ability to do this – and therefore to be hypnotized – is a skill. This is particularly pronounced in the Ericksonian hypnosis that I underwent with Mr Yogino, which forces the client to pay significant attention to themselves. Nicholas J. Long's (2018) extensive analysis of Indonesia's hypnosis boom at the start of the twenty-first century illustrates the extent to which being hypnotized is valorized as a skill rather than considered a passive state.

Indonesia's hypnosis boom was spurred by the establishment of the Indonesian Board of Hypnotherapy (IBH), modelled after its American counterpart founded by Krasner, which has played a central role in training Japanese hypnotherapists. In his observation of IBH seminars targeting hypnotherapists-to-be, Long (2018) found that responsiveness to suggestion was framed as an ability, 'something at which one can be good, or bad – rather than a trait which may be "high" or "low"' (79). This infused the seminars with a motivational dynamic and competitive atmosphere, which was not about who could hypnotize better, but rather who could *be hypnotized* better. Long observes that, after their training, many hypnotherapists started practicing what they called 'waking hypnosis', like the one I underwent at Mr Yogino's salon. Taking the Ericksonian approach to its extreme, they had come to understand all conversation as inherently hypnotic (85). This waking hypnosis promotes a conversational mode 'in which even mundane social interactions could be understood as reflections of one's hypnotic prowess or vulnerability' (86). As I have illustrated, Mr Yogino was very keen to convince me that I was in a mental state appropriate for a hypnotherapy session. His framing of my imaginary narratives sustained a climate in which every instance of paying attention to my thoughts could be nothing other than a sign that I was hypnotized since I saw things that only a hypnotized person would be able to see.

The contemporary popularization of this self-attention-based hypnosis can be traced back to the 1980s and 1990s, when past-life regression therapy attracted audiences in the United States and subsequently in Japan through books such as Brian L. Weiss's *Many Lives, Many Masters*.[11] Again, however, these trends may not be that novel nor in fact unique to an alternative therapeutic milieu. The psychologist Nicholas P. Spanos (1996: 3), for example, argues that hypno- and psychodynamic therapies that seek illness aetiology in the patient's past merely condition them to create 'a social impression that is congruent with their perception of situational demands, with the self-understandings they have learned to adopt, and with the interpersonal goals they are attempting to achieve'. And Ian Hacking (1995) reminds us that associations between memory, trauma and hypnosis have a long history, originating in the clinical settings of nineteenth-century French psychiatric hospitals. By 1888, for example, Pierre Janet had already published cases of hysteria produced by past but forgotten psychological trauma, which he argued could be healed by recollections induced in hypnosis (Hacking 1995: 193), while during the same period hypnosis also played a key role in the emergence of psychoanalysis (Mayer 2013). Given the global networks of knowledge transfer, it should not be surprising that hypnosis also attracted significant interest in late-nineteenth-century Japan, albeit accompanied by criticism from both the scientific community and the Buddhist clergy.

Hypnotism came to be known among Japanese intellectuals around the year 1885 through the translation of the writings of the American mesmerist John Bovee Dods (1795–1872). It was not long before authoritative scholars such as Inoue Enryō (1858–1919) started to explain hypnotic states rationally, using the psychological concepts of suggestion and belief. Their efforts, however, did not stop the popularization of theories of hypnosis that resorted to esoteric knowledge claims (e.g. the existence of subtle energies) to explain the therapeutic powers of hypnotism, some of which survive today. Another short, but influential boom of publications on the subject occurred in the first years of the twentieth century, but in 1908 a law was introduced that prohibited the 'abuse' of hypnotism, pushing the practice further into the field of unorthodox healers (Yoshinaga 2021: 231–3).

Particularly relevant for my argument here are the debates that occurred at that time about what a truly hypnotic state corresponds to and how it is supposed to act on attention to the self. Yu-Chuan Wu (2018) describes how disagreements between psychologists, Buddhist scholars and occultists regarding hypnosis gave birth to new theories and practices that sought to compare hypnotic states with Zen meditative states and to bridge theoretical differences by harnessing psychological vocabulary. For example, Murakami Tatsugorō, a scholar in agricultural ethics, argued in the 1910s that hypnosis essentially consisted of an extraordinary state of intentional attention and even claimed that self-hypnosis was a more efficient and reliable method of Zen cultivation than sitting Zen (Wu 2018: 486–7). He also advised his students to undergo regular hypnosis or self-hypnosis 'to experiment with all kinds of hypnotic phenomena, including catalepsy, hallucination, personality change, planchette, and mind-reading, contending that they were all attention-training methods in themselves and were effective for the improvement of intelligence, morality, and willpower' (487). Fast-forwarding 100 years, we find scholar-practitioner of mindfulness Inoue Vimala and hypnosis expert Ōtani Akira arguing, in a published conversation, that the two techniques share a common characteristic: they both 'help the person to maximize their vital power by shifting a warm *attention* (*atatakai chūi*; my emphasis) towards the core of their living self' (Inoue and Ōtani 2018: 116).

Popular hypnotism has always essentially been about knowing oneself to heal oneself and to better oneself. That attention and the ability that it requires to pay attention in certain ways and at certain times has found new grounds for legitimacy in the current era of attention overload. Attention, illustrated by our 'like' activity on SNS, has become valuable capital. Anthropologist Joanna Cook (2018) has observed that in contemporary discourse, the 'human capacity for deep, sustained attention has become a cultural concern'. Among politicians, healthcare experts and regular consumers, she argues, 'we see calls for a skilful response to ambient advertising, smartphone addiction and rabid consumerism'. The perceived remedy for such 'attentional "hijacking"' is the development of 'sustained attentional control ... enabling people to choose when and to what they pay attention'. This attention crisis has, therefore, shifted our conception of freedom to that of having precisely the kind of reflective ability to control and use our attention with the purpose of self-betterment that hypnotherapists offer to elicit from their clients, hence the continuing popularity of opportunities to do nothing other than pay attention to oneself – for a price, of course.

Was I ever hypnotized during my session with Mr Yogino? Was I skilful in paying attention to myself? It is difficult to say. The majority of readers would probably assume that I was not in any kind of hypnotic state since I could sense and hear everything around me, from the cars passing outside Mr Yogino's salon to the flowery scent of the towel that he had laid on the lower half of my body. When I met Mr Yogino again in the spring of 2018, I asked what made him think that a client has really been hypnotized. His response was framed around emotions: 'When they are satisfied at the end of the session', he said. Like the testimonials in *Therapy All Guide*, a positive emotion at the end of hypnotherapy was not only supposed to confirm the therapy's effects, but also to legitimize how the therapy functioned. The healing power of crystals, vital reiki, spiritual counselling or hypnosis is intimately associated with the experience of relief and further life changes as the client continues to interpret post-therapy events *through* that particular session of therapy.

Ms Etō was one of the few clients I had the opportunity to interview on their own, without a therapist present. Aged fifty-five, she was married to a wealthy man and had two children in their twenties. In the early 2000s, she had decided to find a job and had become a cosmetics consultant, selling her products door to door and inviting customers to her house for demonstrations. 'It was a very stressful job. People always came late to appointments, they always complained, and my house became my office', she observed. Although she wanted to quit, Ms Etō was unable to find the courage to do so and had started consulting various spiritual therapists to solve her stress issues. Through this process she started accumulating reasons to change her lifestyle. Some therapists contradicted her commitments – for example, she hated the fortune tellers who had suggested that her husband's low income was responsible for her situation at the time. But a few reinforced her conviction that she was unfit for her current job. One day, Ms Etō met Mr Suzuki, the spiritual advisor practising near Shinjuku station. His 'kind manner' and 'understanding tone' encouraged her to take the final decision to quit her job. She did not remember the arguments that Mr Suzuki had made that had led her towards that decision. All she remembered was that Mr Suzuki had finally made her feel confident by 'telling me things I had never thought about'.

The authority of empirical experience and a heightened attention to individual emotions are frequently emphasized in research on holistic spiritualities for the central role they play in framing the effectiveness of New Age therapies. But these are not phenomena confined to so-called alternative therapies. Kitanaka (2015) argues that in Japan there is a national desire for controlling psychological health as expressed in the implementation by corporations of stress evaluation questionnaires and resilience training. Through this, she argues, 'Japanese workers adopt psychiatric language for scrutinizing their own moods, biorhythms, and cognitive patterns, [and] they come to see themselves with a novel sense of health – and of self' (253). The crisis of attention is therefore intimately related to a crisis of self-disclosure, which is itself a major object of attention. The sharing on SNS, internet blogs or in corporate workshops of the results of the introspection involved in our self-attention constitutes a large part of the information that we consume every day. Such increasing demands for self-disclosure both within and beyond the workplace result in 'a fundamental shift in ownership of self-knowledge … [and] a new understanding of what counts as a valuable secret' (Kitanaka 2015: 253). When the secrets revealed during hypnotherapy sessions – the bad deeds of a former life, the traumatic experiences of a younger self or the worries about a future career – become valuable information with therapeutic effects, they reframe ourselves. The ability to pay attention becomes the ability to change oneself. For some therapists like Ms Kawasaki, this is experienced as an ability to change their career and teach others how being attentive in a certain way can bring to them the same results. As I will show in the next chapter, however, a new life also means new secrets, like a precarious income and new gender disparities.

Conclusion

Hypnotherapy is, perhaps paradoxically, the perfect illustration of how 'attention to our self' lies at the core of today's therapy culture, from health periodicals to psychiatric interventions and spiritual therapy salons. The therapy culture that I witnessed spiritual therapists and their clients navigating in early twenty-first century Tokyo was far from *alternative* to that of contemporaneous biomedical interventions and social welfare policies. Despite the various ideological and theoretical underpinnings of spiritual therapies, which are often distinct from the content of the curriculum taught at most medical schools, the interaction between therapist and client, patterns of disease causation and justification, and expectations of healing remained common across the practice of therapy (in the widest sense of the word). Therapists were functioning in a climate of socializing medicalization, perfectly equipped to answer to the needs of a populace for whom self-attention was an expression of freedom, a therapeutic means and a harbour of valuable secrets.

The understanding of self-attention as an ability with positive therapeutic effects enhances the belief that it can be turned into a source of income. For the clients of spiritual therapies who eventually turn into therapists, like Ms Kawasaki, the reframing of their private selves around newly revealed secrets was experienced as the revelation of a new professional skill. In other words, Ms Kawasaki had discovered that she might be able to teach clients how to express their ailments so as to maximize the effects of their therapeutic self. In this way, she could be compared to a self-help guide, a motivational speaker or even a programmer of new emoticons. Ms Kawasaki, however, also functioned as a small business owner in a competitive consumer market. To fully understand what it was that made her and others like her quit their jobs to become therapists, we therefore need to look beyond their therapeutic milieu to examine more closely how the spirituality business works (and fails) as a strategy against social precarities in a highly gendered, neoliberal economy.

5

Precarities in the spiritual business

'I could really be free during the healing touch session', read one of the approximately thirty client impressions of similar style found on the website of the salon of Ms Michiko, a thirty-seven-year-old therapist who I met in August 2009. 'It was the freedom of just feeling the body and letting my consciousness play', the testimonial continued. 'Every time I was touched, that freedom expanded more and even though it was my body that was being treated, I came to feel as if my body was not there anymore.' Five months after I met Ms Michiko, her salon had closed down and she had started working at a friend's shop selling natural products. By the end of October 2010, after following her internet blog through three different platforms, I had completely lost track of her. I recalled then how she had complained that two years had passed since she had opened her business, but neither advertisements of her salon in relevant media outlets nor the client testimonials that she kept posting on her website had contributed to any increase in her clientele. 'Nothing has changed', she had said. 'Seventy percent of them still come on the recommendation of a friend who teaches courses on macrobiotics.' Ms Michiko's skills, it seemed, had not been enough to guarantee her a place in the spiritual business.

Precarity is a running theme in explanations for the rise of spirituality in Japan. Recall for a moment the crucial role that economic downturn and stagnation following the burst of the bubble economy played in scholarly narratives that linked the plight of the nation to the rise of spirituality through the needs of a precarious public, whether in positive or negative terms (Chapter 2). Recall also how the Yamakawas's rise to New Age translator-stardom depended on them embodying, through their decision to quit prestigious jobs, the precarity that their books sought to save their readers from (Chapter 3), and how explanations for the rise of the counselling profession (Chapter 1) and the *iyashi* phenomenon (Chapter 4) both heavily relied on the idea that people had been suffering economically, physically and mentally, and were in need of attention and healing. But what of the precarity that runs *through* spirituality as a phenomenon manifested in the spiritual business and represented by spiritual therapists like Ms Michiko?

This chapter considers how precarity in the spiritual business is associated with the nature of the business itself. I show that running a spiritual therapy salon requires entrepreneurial skills that not every enthusiastic therapist may possess. It also asks for a continuous investment of time and money in keeping the business afloat and monitoring the competition. As a service industry bound by the rules of consumer protection and dependent on the financial stability of both its providers and its clients, I argue that the business of spiritual therapy presents challenges stemming from a sort of 'cruel optimism' (Berlant 2011) associated with the coalescence of precarity, spirituality and therapy. Hope of freeing oneself from an (often heavily gendered) precarity is what brings many therapists into this sector. It is also what brings them many of their clients, to whom the alternative paths chosen by spiritual therapists are supposed to form a model for what a spiritual life is about. This spiritual life, however, remains dependent on the market conditions and social assumptions from which it seeks to escape. Like Berlant's cruel optimism, the hope offered by spiritual therapy is therefore a 'relation of attachment to compromised conditions of possibility whose realization is discovered either to be impossible, sheer fantasy, or too possible, and toxic' (Berlant 2011: 24). To practice therapy and promote spirituality, the professionals I interviewed need to endure precarity.

Spirituality and neoliberal critique

As Susannah Crockford (2021a) illustrates in her study of Sedona, the American Mecca of the New Age and holistic spirituality culture, neoliberalism and spirituality are similar in form. Having both emerged during the same historical period, the late 1970s to early 1980s, Crockford argues that they share the same four characteristics: financialization, privatization, deregulation and individual responsibility (27). The monetization of everything, including the self (financialization), with no institutional support nor corporate body of regulations (privatization), means that there are no standards determining valid practice (deregulation) and that everything that happens to the individual is the result of their own making (individual responsibility) (26–7). For many years, this shared form between neoliberalism and spirituality was misinterpreted, with spirituality seen either as a form of religiosity corrupted by capitalism

(=economization of religion) or as a salvific reaction to the corruption caused by capitalism (=spiritualization of the economy). Either way, religion and economy have been treated as ontologically distinct categories, with one being reduced to the other.[1]

In her analysis of the articulation of religion and economy in the New Age, Hildegard Van Hove (1999: 167) argues that the globalization of the market economy has produced a pluralism of choice. This ensures the functioning of this type of economy but has also led to a peculiar characteristic among modern individuals: people today construct their identity, their social life and their spirituality based on the choices they make. In the religious domain, the 'spiritual market' enables individuals to make choices without identifying themselves with any particular tradition or doctrine, such identification being counter to the ideology of the market economy (170). Van Hove coined the appellation 'spiritual market' to distinguish between two facets of the New Age: the 'religious' belief in the coming of a New Age or the Age of Aquarius, which spread among hippies in the late 1960s (Heelas 1996: 68); and the ensuing network of New Age ideas and practices from which 'consumers' could freely pick and choose, within which belief in the Age of Aquarius was only one among many observed trends and 'certainly not the common denominator' (Van Hove 1999: 164–5). Prominent scholar of the New Age, Michael York (2001) expands on this in his description of the New Age as a form of religion that 'is modelled upon, and is an outgrowth of, liberal Western capitalism' and is, therefore, essentially economistic:

> It is part of the same 'cultural logic of late capitalism' that asserts the right to free and unrestricted global trade. As an aggregation or congeries of client services and competing audience cults, New Age is part of what is described as the 'religious consumer supermarket' – one which thrives on competition and the offering of various spiritual commodities. Rather than a rejection of free market principles, New Age endorses a spiritualized counterpart of capitalism – one which seeks ever extended markets, new sources of marketable goods, and expanding products. In that the profit motive of New Age is fully financial, if not also oriented toward greater spiritual well-being, it represents a modern continuation of Calvinistic principles which exalt material success as a sign, reflection, or consequence of one's spiritual state of grace. (York 2001: 367)

These early arguments opened up important avenues for theoretical critique of the bifurcation between 'religion' and 'economy', firmly situating both domains in historical and social developments of the nineteenth and twentieth centuries. However, they were also haunted by the ghost of a *sui generis* religion.

They implied that New Age and holistic spiritualities were a different kind of religion, hence their mirroring of contemporary capitalist market trends. Rather than being treated as examples of a more general blurring of the boundaries between religion and economy, these early arguments and much of the work that has built upon them has taken spirituality as the exception: an entirely new religious development in the grips of neoliberal ideology. In many cases this reading of spirituality has been explicitly normative, a classic example being Jeremy Carette and Richard King's (2004) $elling Spirituality: The Silent Takeover of Religion. As I discuss in more detail in the next chapter, the idea that spirituality, or more specifically spiritual business, is corrupt or 'bad' religion is also found in scholarship produced in Japan (Gaitanidis 2020, 2021). The scholar to have most consistently taken this perspective is Sakurai Yoshihide, sociologist of religion and prominent member of the anti-cult movement that arose after the Aum affair. Sakurai (2009a: 241–2) argues that the vulnerabilities that lead contemporary Japanese to being duped by the spiritual business relate to four domains: social economy, identity, relationships and intelligence. In summary, Sakurai blames the popularity of holistic spiritualities on the lack of socio-economic stability and vision for a future. These conditions, coupled with the loosening of human relationships, drive young individuals to seek solutions to their problems and to their crisis of identity in new forms of community, such as healing networks and 'cults' whose value they judge based on their feelings, rather than on rational knowledge. Sakurai's critique mirrors Carrette and King's (2004: 125) claim that 'religious artefacts and language have "cachet value" for a society of isolated individuals hungry for packaged meaning'.

Paul Heelas (2008: 83) refers to this line of argument as the 'consumption strategy' of critics of holistic spiritualities, who have used it in the 'war against the increasing significance of the "sins" of capitalism' or 'to show that the sacred has taken corrupt forms under the influence of modernity'.[2] But its underlying assumption regarding the exceptionalism of the articulation of religion and economy under late capitalism also underpins the arguments of the opposite camp – the 'defenders' of the spiritual marketplace who see spirituality as an attempt to overcome the rationalization and disenchantment of the modern, economistic world. Stef Aupers and Dick Houtman (2010: 15), for example, suggest that New Age spirituality is 'a veritable religion of modernity', on the grounds that 'its participants collectively sacralize the long-standing modern value of individual liberty, and especially the ideal of an authentic self that distances itself from allegedly alienating institutions and traditions'. More recently, Itō Masayuki, one of the co-editors of A Sociology of Spirituality (see

Chapter 2), published a collection of his writings of the last twenty years, in which he takes the rise of interest in yoga, mindfulness and positive psychology as evidence that spirituality has become a 'culture'. Today's well-being is focused on spiritual richness rather than on material affluence, he argues, even if contemporary spirituality culture is not part of the economics of well-being in advanced capitalist societies *per se* (Itō 2021: 113).

That scholars have sought to critique market capitalism or neoliberalism through a critique of the spiritual business is not necessarily the problem here. The problem, as Andrea Jain (2020: 63) points out, is when such critiques reduce contemporary instantiations of spirituality to economy or religion by, for example, comparing commercialized forms of yoga, mindfulness and the like to idealized practices of the past, or by assuming that 'all spiritual consumers hold such simplistic aims as pleasure or escape from the reality of life under neoliberal capitalism'. What Jain suggests, and what Crockford does brilliantly by connecting Sedona's community to American white class struggles and neoliberal imaginations, is 'to take spiritual consumers seriously as religious agents and simultaneously evaluate them, and even critique them, as complicit in the expansion of neoliberalism and market capitalism in and through their institutions and practices' (Jain 2020: 66). With this in mind, I explore in this chapter how spiritual therapists in Tokyo talked about the precarities of their work and how they linked them to national and global socio-economic trends.

Precarity is/in the spiritual business

The first time I met Ms Jinnai, on a rainy day in June 2009, she had just the previous month rented and decorated a small apartment near Sendagaya station, a relatively wealthy area located southwest of Shibuya, and was launching herself into the spiritual business. I could sense her excitement. It became clear in our ensuing discussion that this was her second new start in life in the past five years. The mood was entirely different when I met her again in late April 2014, this time at a café in Kinshicho, the once 'sleazy' centre of East Tokyo, known for its many adult shops and bars, although it has been somewhat gentrified over the past decade. During this second meeting, Ms Jinnai seemed exhausted and unsatisfied with her life. She was living with her mother on her meagre income from working as a fortune teller two days per week in a tiny booth, crammed onto an intermediate landing between two floors of one of the luxurious shopping malls of Ginza. She blamed no one but herself for this turn of events but was very aware of the difficulties associated with the spirituality business. Her story exemplifies the precarities that she and other entrepreneurs stepped into when they entered the spiritual business as a strategy against the precarities they experienced in their everyday lives and work.

Ms Jinnai was born in 1968. At the age of twenty, she had married a British man who invited her to follow him abroad.³ For the next decade, she had a relatively good life, she said, touring the United States and Europe. When she returned to Japan in 2001, she immediately found a job using her language skills at a foreign-owned company, but her private life deteriorated and she filed for divorce in 2004. The rest of her auto biographical narrative is similar to that of Ms Kawasaki, who we met in the previous chapter. Depressed, Ms Jinnai tried various therapies including hypnotherapy, which she found liberating. She then decided to learn hypnotherapy herself and supplemented it with other credentials, though most of the sessions that she offered when she opened her salon in 2009 were variants of the past-life therapy that she said had saved her from her depression. It seems that Ms Jinnai had thought out her business plan. She knew that she could not ask for too much money for her sessions, since she had just started and 'the number of people in spiritual professions are increasing, so prices are going down'. But she also knew that, 'despite the economic crisis, people will pay for a good therapy session'. She hired a professional web designer who built her page based on a comparison with the advertising styles of other hypnotherapists, as well as aestheticians and professionals providing cosmetic services. She was particularly keen on making the website text easy to read and engaging (*kanshinka suru*). She also partnered with her hypnotherapy teacher and fellow graduates from that small spiritual therapy school to set up booths at monthly fairs to attract potential clients.⁴ But her salon did not last the year. It was not easy to find clients and, after a few months, she could not afford to pay for her rented space. The humiliation for her was in having to return to her mother's home at the age of forty-two. She could no longer support herself.

Spiritual therapists like Ms Jinnai were not naïve entrepreneurs. Having gone through the system themselves, spending hundreds of thousands of yen on books, manuals, workshops and certificates, they knew how the business worked better than anyone. Her attempts to attract clients through a professionally designed website and spirituality fairs demonstrated her awareness of the potential consumer markets for her services (a point to which I will return). Five years passed between Ms Jinnai's entrance into the world of the spiritual and her opening of a salon. She had seen dozens of therapists, participated in twice as many fairs and heard several times about the difficulties of the business. Like Ms

Kawasaki, she thought that she could do as well if not better than others. Unlike Ms Kawasaki, however, she failed. It is impossible to pinpoint the exact cause of her failure. Saturation of the hypnotherapy market or more general spiritual therapy market around Sendagaya might have been one factor. Another may have been Ms Jinnai's lack of experience on the job, beyond the twenty- to thirty-minute sessions she had offered at local fairs in a room full of other therapists. During her first month of work, her bookings consisted of only one session. She said that she needed at least eight to be able to pay the rent. Her hypnotherapy teacher, Ms Shibata, sent Ms Jinnai some new clients, but Ms Shibata ended up closing her school a few years later and working out of a rental booth in Ginza. The precarity of the spiritual business mirrored the precarity of its consumers. 'I thought that people would choose me because of my skills, but when people have a problem, they just want to solve it, regardless of who helps them', were Ms Jinnai's last words the second time we met.

The reasons that Ms Jinnai herself gave for what she clearly interpreted as a failure centred on two key factors. The first was an issue that very few therapists talked about, but which seemed to be an important element of keeping a successful business. Ms Jinnai called it 'maintenance': 'Maintenance costs money: yoga classes, fitness classes, massages, trips to hot springs, concerts, theatre and the like almost every week; I just need a lot of money to keep up being a therapist.' Appearance was of utmost importance for Ms Jinnai and many other spiritual therapists, who were spending two or three hours per session in a relatively small room with a person who might be paying several thousand yen for the service. They needed to be at what they considered to be the top of their game, but also to be aware of and able to recommend the latest in entertainment and healthy activities. Being a successful therapist was clearly about more than investment in training in therapeutic techniques and collecting professional certificates. To make a blunt comparison: no one wants to get their hair styled at a salon run by a dishevelled stylist who knows nothing about the latest fashion trends, regardless of where that stylist received their training. The second reason was more personal. Ms Jinnai thought that she was still too preoccupied with her own issues and had been unable to get past them during sessions with her clients: 'I just kept getting back to the same narratives, which sounded like what I would have liked to hear'. Ms Jinnai admitted that she had been wrong to think that simply because she was healed by hypnotherapy, she could do the same for others. But she had not given up. 'There is no future in fortune-telling', she explained during our discussion in 2014. 'I have started studying to get a [psychological] counsellor license.

This would allow me to expand my skills and perhaps find work outside the spiritual.'

Ms Jinnai's new strategy of training as a counsellor reinforces my argument that spiritual therapists primarily saw themselves as therapists. Yet, the various strategies that Ms Jinnai had employed in her attempt to create a successful business, as well as the reasons she expressed for her failure, illustrate how the practice of spiritual therapy existed at a threshold between the welfare, cosmetic and niche 'spirituality' consumer markets. Some clients sought answers for genuine psychological and physical worries, like Ms Jinnai had herself done when, suffering from depression, she had started trying out spiritual therapies. Others abided to a regime of bettering themselves. This second type of client approached a reiki or aura reading session in the same way as they would treat a running session on a treadmill or a relaxing walk in a park. Yet others were what therapists referred to as spiritual 'fans', that is collectors of spiritual narratives who would seek every new therapy on the market, sometimes sticking with the same practitioner for several years who they would look to for the latest trend, like a car aficionado buying a new vehicle every few years from the same dealer. Calibration of their practices and services along these different lines contributed to the precarity experienced by therapists such as Ms Jinnai, who clearly felt that she was there to 'heal' but not necessarily to indulge in spiritual storytelling. In an interesting overlap with more general critiques of holistic spirituality, many spiritual therapists clearly regarded spiritual fans with contempt. 'I despise those who come to a fair like the Spiritual Market (SUPIMA)', Ms Jinnai had told me back in 2009. 'They are not really serious; to them, it is just like going shopping.' But she and other spiritual therapists nevertheless relied on having at least some 'fans' as their regular clients to guarantee a (temporarily) stable income.

They thus found themselves in a situation in which they had to constantly offer new services and keep up with new trends, while also honing their skills on the therapies that they felt had the best results and on which they could build their reputations. Reviewing the dozens of self-development and spirituality-related books and magazine articles published every month, and trying to select what to incorporate and what to reject as untrustworthy, is a serious time-consuming endeavour. Very few practitioners seemed to be good at it. Many complained of their exhaustion after listening to people's life struggles on a daily basis, while also managing their internet presence (webpage, blogs, various SNS platforms), showing up at small events organized by fellow therapists to support them, running the finances of their business and, of course, meeting the demands of their personal lives, such as supporting their families.

At the same time, bound by the same professional ethics regulating other welfare professions, spiritual therapists could not divulge their clients' personal details, so it was often difficult for them to effectively employ client testimonials to legitimize the 'authenticity' of the experience they were offering. The multitude of (often anonymized) client testimonials that could be found on the webpages of spiritual therapy salons like Ms Michiko's were supposed to illustrate the abilities of the salon owners. However, like those testimonials published in the *Therapy All Guide*, they rarely emphasized the skills of the therapist *per se*. Instead, they mostly provided generalized descriptions of feelings and emotions experienced by the client during the session and the physical and social changes that they underwent post therapy. In our conversations, therapists also generalized the reasons why their clients had consulted them, such as 'bad relationships at work or in the family' or 'unfulfilled dreams'. Unless pressed and willing to share, they would rarely use specific examples to illustrate what they meant. This decontextualization signalled that they maintained client confidentiality and could therefore be trusted, but it also tended to trivialize the impact of personal issues on the perceived effectiveness of therapies, reducing them to standardized descriptions of healing processes and possible effects. This imperative to generalize meant that there was often a close resemblance in how spiritual therapists advertised their sessions, to the point that therapists sometimes complained to me that someone else in the business had copied their website content verbatim, by which they were almost always referring to the 'menu' descriptions of the therapies on offer. To attract new clients to their tailor-made spiritual services and products, therapists were therefore relying on an abstract vocabulary that prospective clients would hopefully interpret on a personal level and come to experience at its source of production, the salon.

They were also, like any other type of entrepreneur, more generally at the mercy of the economy. During the first quarter of 2009 (when Ms Jinnai opened her business), Japan's economy was still in retreat as a result of the global financial crisis – Lehman Brothers had collapsed on 15 September 2008. According to a survey by the Organization for Small and Medium Enterprises and Regional Innovation,[5] this was when the business sentiment of small and medium companies reached its lowest point, with the majority of respondents declaring negative earnings. Ms Jinnai had entered the business with the foreknowledge that as a result of the economic downturn she would not be able to charge 'too much'. Others, aware of their competition, tried to move to the east of Tokyo where salons were still fewer in number. This was a strategy employed by Ms Noda, a friend of Ms Jinnai and graduate from the same school of hypnotherapy, who had opened her salon a few months earlier, in February 2009. Ms Noda had done some market research and decided to rent a space in Asakusa for its proximity to the famous Sensō Temple. By locating her salon near to such a popular tourist attraction, she reasoned that she would be able to offer her clients more reasons to visit her. But she also had to reduce the prices. Her fee for a hypnotherapy session was only 75 per cent of that charged by Ms Jinnai in Sendagaya. Moreover, these higher-priced sessions were not her most popular. Ms Noda focused on (cheaper) reiki therapy and on teaching clients how to shift to a macrobiotic diet, 'because people here are common (*shominteki*)'.

Ms Noda's story follows the same pattern as that of Ms Jinnai. Before she opened her salon, she had worked as a tourist guide for nearly ten years and had travelled around the world – to more than a hundred countries, she said. She had then found a position in the sales management section of a toy company and, according to her, was very good at that job. Yet, she quit after a decade, feeling tired of doing the same tasks every day. Before leaving her job, she had attended a seminar on the macrobiotic diet and become infatuated with it. She continued to learn and expand the registry of therapies she could offer and only quit her main job in April 2009, after she had set up her business in Asakusa. She used her skills as an English-language speaker to take on occasional work as an interpreter to supplement her income, but spiritual therapy had become Ms Noda's main profession. She seemed to be astute in how she perceived the value of her services and how that value might be increased. By the time we met, in the summer of 2009, she was working on a plan to provide original sessions that would combine advice on macrobiotic ingredients (which she called macrobiotic healing) with aura reading. It was clear that Ms Noda understood how important the marketing aspect of her job was. But she too struggled to make a success of her business and, two years later, moved to her mother's house in Fukuoka in southern Japan. Yet, like Ms Jinnai she did not give up. In 2021, according to her blog, she was still offering the same sessions she had offered ten years before, and was moving between Okinawa, Fukuoka and Tokyo.

Practitioners complained about the precarious nature of the spirituality business, which, coupled with the unstable situation faced by many small businesses, made the running of spiritual therapy salons a truly challenging task, even for those like Ms Kawasaki with experience in other domains of the service industry. Yet, many of the same therapists framed 'regular' work as tedious, oppressive (especially in terms of hierarchy) and unfulfilling for people who would like to live life to its fullest. After all, many spiritual therapists had elected to quit 'regular' jobs to embark on a career in the spirituality business and, even in the face of failure, were not willing to give up. As the remainder of this chapter will unfold, this apparent contradiction can be explained in large part by the gendered economy of spirituality as a precarious business dominated by women.

Spirituality, precarity, therapy

According to the yearly surveys on life satisfaction conducted by the Japanese government's Cabinet Office,[6] throughout most of the 1990s and 2000s, approximately 55 per cent of the population were, when asked specifically, unsatisfied with their income. Approximately 60 per cent were unsatisfied with their savings and between 60 and 70 per cent experienced worries and uncertainties in their daily lives, more than 50 per cent of which had to do with either their health or how they would manage to make a living after retirement. Nevertheless, the percentage of people generally satisfied with their life seems to have progressively increased from 50 per cent in the mid-1970s to nearly 74 per cent at the end of the 2010s. Furthermore, in the new millennium, nearly 60 per cent of the population was content with their level of self-growth and skills, and about the same percentage felt that they had enough time for leisure. As with statistics about religious affiliation, these figures need to be read with caution. 'Satisfaction' is a relative concept dependent on context and timing. While I am generally satisfied with my work, if you ask me about job satisfaction after a long faculty meeting, I may reply otherwise. Surveys can perhaps grasp a mood, but they are not to be trusted as the basis of assumptions about how people live their lives. This is especially the case when dissatisfaction with social and economic conditions becomes almost a prerequisite to precarious work. Or, in other terms, when the value of one's labour rests on the successful enactment of the very assumptions that make that labour marginal, precarious and, in the case of spiritual therapists, gendered.

As already noted, fifty-five of the sixty-eight spiritual therapists that I interviewed in 2009 were women aged between thirty-five and fifty years old. Of those, nineteen were married and thirty-six were single, eight having divorced at least once. Eleven were only practicing spiritual therapies on a part-time basis, in the evenings and at weekends; two of those did not have any other paid work. The majority (thirty therapists) mentioned either office work or sales as their previous or present occupations. None had ever occupied a managerial or highly ranked position. According to the therapists, the overwhelming majority of their clients were women aged between twenty and fifty; thirty-eight therapists testified that their clientele was over 90 per cent female. These findings are in line with the results of an internet survey on the spiritual business conducted by a business consulting company, which found that spiritual therapies are more popular among women than men, and most popular among women aged between their early twenties and late forties (Arimoto 2011: 144–8).

The example of one particular therapist, Ms Godai, serves as a useful entry point to exploring spiritual therapy as a business fed largely by the precarities of such women and the normative assumptions upon which those precarities are built. As something of an outlier in terms of her own relative economic stability, Ms Godai's autobiographical narrative indicates that the implicit reinforcement of these assumptions is embedded within the logics of spiritual business, rather than being a mere strategy of economic need. Born in 1965, Ms Godai had been in the business of spiritual therapy for six years when I met her for the first time in the summer of 2009. She had worked as a study abroad counsellor after graduating from a private university in Japan, but then quit her job after she got married. Since being a housewife did not suit her, she said, she decided to use her English-language skills to find a job at a non-Japanese-owned multinational company. The work was initially very interesting, but, similar to other cases already discussed, when a change in her supervisor influenced her mental health, high levels of stress led her to try different therapies, including hypnotherapy. From there, she followed the familiar path of attending seminars and workshops, quitting her company job (in 2003), and offering therapies. Ms Godai had first offered hypnotherapy, then reconnective healing, which was her main session when I first met her in 2009, and then channelling followed by 'coaching counselling', which she considered to be one of her two main sources of income when we met again in April 2014. By 2008, she was doing so well that she even convinced her husband to quit his job and take a position that would allow him more free time, but the ensuing financial crisis forced him to return to his original workplace.

Despite the many similarities in her story and those of other therapists, there was an important difference: Ms Godai had a stable income from renting out several apartments that she owned, one of which she had turned into her salon. Unlike others, Ms Godai could therefore afford the precarity of her business and the fast-paced updating of sessions that she felt was required to keep her afloat in the market: 'I have always thought [that attending] spiritual therapy fairs and healing fairs was never about increasing my clientele. It was more about me finding out what is new, what is trending.' Ms Godai did not hesitate, for example, to jump on the opportunity to work as an interpreter for Eric Pearl, the creator of reconnective healing, when he first came to Japan; by 2009, she had trained to become one of the few Japanese then qualified to teach reconnective healing. That experience changed her thinking about the future direction of her business. 'The era of one-to-one sessions is over', she recounted on the second occasion we met. 'Today it is all about one-to-many. Teaching one's skills to others is a business in its own right. So, I decided to launch myself in a (second) business: that of cosmetics counselling.' Hence, in addition to the sessions she conducted in her salon, Ms Godai opened an online counselling service, advising clients on the best cosmetics products for them and, in addition, taking a cut of sales of those products. She explained this new business venture as complementary to the aims of spiritual therapy: 'In the end, before finding oneself, one needs to become an ordinary person (*futsū no hito*) and start fixing one's appearance (*gaiken o naosu*).'

There was also another side to Ms Godai's new endeavour, afforded by her relatively stable position, which exemplifies how spirituality and precarity coalesce to make the spiritual business. She did not perform the cosmetics counselling herself, but employed young women, most of them former clients whom she had diagnosed as 'not being able to fit society' and 'wanting to work at their own pace and lead the life they liked'. Ms Godai thereby linked the therapy and cosmetics sides of her business: 'I offer them an opportunity to make a basic living while they try to find what they want to do with life.' While spirituality informed her practice of spiritual therapies and how she framed her cosmetics business, it also permeated her idea of empowering her former clients by offering them a part-time job. Spirituality was not, however, the sole connector. Precarity played a role too. Precarity brought her a clientele on the one side and fuelled the pool of her employees on the other, while she herself could rely on an existing (third) source of stable and non-precarious income. This supported the lifestyle that was 'proof' of the empowerment afforded by spirituality. Indeed, if it were not for her regular real-estate earnings, Ms Godai would probably not be able to keep her salon, nor to support the 'alternative lifestyle' that feeds a cruel optimism among precarious clients in need of therapy and employees in need of earning a living.

In her monograph on sex work in contemporary Japan, Gabriele Koch (2020) demonstrates how gender and precarity seamlessly blend to obscure the roles of women in service-based industries and elsewhere as professionals. She employs the concept of healing (*iyashi*) labour to describe how 'sex workers view the reparative aspects of their care as necessary for the successful functioning of the male-gendered economy' (100). Mirroring my discussion on the popularization of *iyashi* in the 1990s, Koch links the emergence of the term with 'a growing adoption of psychiatric categories of mental illness and increased concern with forms of "existential alienation, loneliness, and loss of meaning" in the face of both national affluence and economic restructuring' (102–3). Sex workers interviewed by Koch expressed a concern for 'healing' the hard-working man, who supports the economy but is never cared for by his company or at home, especially after his wife becomes a mother and the frequency of sexual intercourse, it is assumed, decreases. So, although often looked down upon by the rest of society and working sometimes in precarious conditions, sex workers imagine their labour as playing a key role in sustaining the socio-economic conditions responsible for their marginalization:

> A sex worker's success rests in appealing to the customer on the basis of her girlish or young womanly charm ... the ability to create an atmosphere in which the sex worker's performance of normative femininity allows the customer to relax completely. As sex workers imagine it, they see the customer as ultimately craving recognition as someone hard-working, desirable, and fun to be around ... Although questions of productivity and value might seem ideologically separate from intimate performances in the sex industry, the point is precisely that they are not – the performance of an eroticized and maternal care that is understood to enable men's productivity, in other words, is the gendering of the economy. (Koch 2020: 120)

At first glance, women spiritual therapists appear to represent the antithesis of these sex workers. The way that many conceive of their work as healing labour bears clear similarities to Koch's observations, but their labour is primarily oriented towards themselves and other women, not towards enabling the productivity of men. They imagine themselves to be offering to their clients the kind of 'liberation' from the predicaments of women in a heavily gendered society and economy that they themselves experienced in a therapist's salon. Ms Godai was able to take this a step further than most in offering job opportunities to some of her clients. However, as intimated in the narratives of Ms Godai and the other spiritual therapists we have met in this chapter, the liberation afforded by spirituality therapies did not transcend or challenge the gendered economy within which they and their clients were marginalized and precarious; the spiritual business was very much a part of it.

Women in 'alternative' religion

The 'lost decades' of the Heisei era have been linked to every single social development, including the rise of *supirichuariti*, which is interpreted as religious change that is often seen as a process of economization. But observers seldom consider how this change is connected to the gendering of new and alternative religious practices through the gendering of the economy. Since the 1970s, the reality that women are more present and active, especially within novel religious frameworks (Roemer 2009: 304),[7] has progressively led scholars to emphasize how alternative religious movements empower women to form alternative networks to support themselves and others and to subvert the male-dominated status quo, by providing avenues for women to negotiate socially expected roles and 'modern' ideologies of empowerment.[8] Alex Owen (2004: 87), for example, argues that the rise of occultism in nineteenth-century Britain was entangled with 'a spiritualized vision of social change'. By drawing on ideals of regeneration and self-fulfilment, occultism 'offered a "new" religiosity capable of outstripping the conventional Victorian association of femininity with a domesticated spirituality'. At the same time, since it was a spiritual rather than political movement, occultism was not seen as challenging more conservative norms relating to 'women's place in the moral and temporal order of things'. Therein lay its potential for subversion. Helen Hardacre (1984: 212–17) presents similar findings in her study of the new religious organization Reiyūkai Kyōdan, founded in the 1920s. While the organization viewed women as inferior to men, this did not completely disempower them, Hardacre argues. Rather, it allowed them to pursue what she calls 'strategies of weakness' to achieve their objectives. She cites the case of a husband whose wife's 'unusual' conduct upon learning that he is having an extramarital affair forces him to terminate it. The wife, a member of Reiyūkai Kyōdan, did not scream and demand a divorce, nor utter any word of complaint. Rather, she seemed to blame herself for not properly fulfilling her duties. Her unexpected submissiveness seems to have motivated the husband to not only accede to her wishes that he terminate the affair, but also to eventually join her religion, which he had originally strongly opposed.

Hashisako Mizuho (2019) describes a very similar dynamic in her discussion of the propagation of fortune telling and magic charms through periodicals during the 1980s and 1990s, which she identifies as 'the first "religion" created specifically for women in Japan'. In her analysis of the *uranai* (divination, fortune-telling) magazine *My Birthday*, popular among a young female readership, particularly since the 1980s, Hashisako notes how the magazine's articles and the goods such as divination cards and charms that it promoted, provided a sort of 'map' of how to avoid being ostracized by friends at school during a period when bullying became a social issue reported in national news outlets (188, 190). The magazine could not solve these issues but, according to Hashisako, it provided a space for its readers to vent their worries about the loss of safe havens for adolescent girls. Yet it did not offer a critical stance towards nor attempt to change society, but was instead 'supported by adolescent girls and women as a guideline for how to adapt to a reality in constant flux'. Moreover, by associating itself with 'ideals of "femininity" (*josei-rashisa*, lit. woman-likeness) and "girlhood" (*shōjo-rashisa*, lit. girl-likeness)', the magazine served to reinforce gender biases (197).

Societal shifts and the continuous failure of policy implementations to respond to them have created paradoxical associations between the empowering functions that these and other new religious organizations or forms are assumed to offer to women, and self-fulfilling ideals about women still living in precarious working and economic conditions. In Hardacre's study, based on fieldwork in the 1970s, the empowerment of the women of a new religious organization came from their ability to both protect and subvert their traditional roles based on the 'good wife, wise mother' ideal, which had been adopted by the Japanese state in the nineteenth century. As Levi McLaughlin (2019) demonstrates in his extensive study of Soka Gakkai, the largest group among the so-called new religious movements in Japan, such institutions continue to perpetuate this ideal even if their justifications for doing so are evaporating 'as Japanese women distance themselves from the domestic track and the number of children declines' (169). The economic downturn may have convinced the majority of the population that it is no longer feasible to follow a division of labour based on the woman staying at home raising the kids and the man at work fending for their subsistence. Yet, neither religious institutions nor businesses have managed to update their structures to reflect those changes. This leads to a looping effect, whereby discriminatory assumptions and policies (re)produce the conditions used to justify such discrimination, leading women to believe that alternative scenarios are there to help them adapt to or cope with a status quo that is, in practice, increasingly unfeasible and yet still the normative ideal.

In his recent review of former prime minister Abe Shinzo's so-called womenomics policies, Mark Crawford (2021) discusses how this looping effect works in the case of corporations. Since promotion is based on seniority (i.e. length of service), Crawford argues that discrimination based on the 'putative probability' that women will temporarily quit their jobs to have children 'becomes a self-fulfilling prophecy, since women have often quit their jobs when raising children due to their smaller chance of developing their careers in their firms' (6–7). A similar dynamic can be found in the spiritual business, where assumptions about femininity, women's lives and what women feel, desire and seek have fed into an iterative process of the gendering of spiritual therapy, seeming to affirm the normative basis of the discrimination that brought women to the therapeutic salon in the first place.

The gendering of spiritual therapy

Although spiritual therapists first and foremost consider themselves therapists and operate in a milieu shared with biomedical therapeutic interventions (Chapters 1 and 4), on a popular level, spiritual therapies have been associated with women's magazines and, to a certain extent, conceived of as an extension of 'mainstream' aesthetic care and the beauty industry.[9] Often in connection with or as an extension of fortune-telling columns, spiritual therapies have been most significantly promoted in women's magazines, such as *anan*, which appeared in the 1970s and claimed to be offering young, urban, female readers 'guidance and support about how to express themselves and attain a certain freedom' (Sakamoto 1999: 183). Ehara Hiroyuki started his career in 1992 as a columnist in the fortune-telling section of *anan* (Horie 2008: 43). Another exemplar in this category is the quarterly magazine *Trinity*, launched in 2001, which deals with what the media industry commonly presents as 'women's interests', such as health, fashion, interior design and travel, through a spiritual lens. By the time the spiritual boom had reached its peak in 2007, *Trinity*, which advertised itself as the pioneer magazine to specifically target 'spiritual women',[10] was selling 4,000 copies.

This led spiritual therapists to adapt their services to a female clientele, gendering the promotion and practice of their work through explanations about alleged psycho-physiological differences between men and women and by appealing to what they considered to be women's aesthetic sensibilities. Ms Namihira, for example, advanced the oft theard argument that 'women like trying new things and generally have an open mind, but men are always very suspicious and don't like meeting us face-to-face'. Mr Ushimoto, a fifty-year-old man, former civil servant and father of two boys, had built his website, his therapist's identity and his menu of sessions according to what he thought would satisfy his clientele. 'Almost all my clients are women, so my website is appropriately built to appeal to them', he explained, showing me that he employed white and rose colours, and offered sessions called 'Venus rose healing', 'Aphrodite beauty ray healing' and 'lily healing for a beautiful skin'. This 'feminine' aspect of his practice, he added, stemmed from his guardian deity and channelling entity, the Goddess Aphrodite.

As we saw in the example of Ms Godai, the cosmetic was seen as an extension of spiritual therapeutic goals. But for some therapists, aesthetic practices and arguments were also clearly a marketing ploy, sometimes even a strategy of concealment, to capture consumers for the less mainstream therapies that they provided. Ms Michiko was very clear about the attractiveness of spiritual therapies that combine fortune telling, colours and aroma oils: '*Esute*-type techniques and particularly aromatherapy and aura-soma are excellent ways to get women to your salon and make them regular clients before introducing more "spiritual" techniques such as reiki or channelling.' Aura-soma, a therapy created by British channeler Vicky Wall in 1982, involves the client choosing four out of a selection of more than a hundred bottles (new ones are periodically introduced), each containing double-coloured aroma oils. In order to advise the client on her issues, the practitioner will then 'read' the message implied by the sequence in which the client chose the bottles, the colours of the oils and the paragraph of explanatory text accompanying every bottle. Ideally, the session is repeated on a regular basis to verify if the client's situation improves. Clients are also asked to apply the aroma oils where they experience bodily pain and also on other parts of the body instead of or in addition to cosmetic creams.

This association of spiritual therapy with gender stereotypes and assumptions about what women are about, desire or look for was compounded by the issues faced by clients and how therapists interpreted these issues against their own experiences of precarity and ensuing salvation through the discovery of spirituality. This seemed to create a pernicious cycle of perpetual failure in their efforts to overcome precarity and subdue gender discrimination, due to the precarious nature of the business of spiritual therapy itself and the difficulty of advising clients whose issues were deeply embedded within the status quo. As I have previously discussed (Gaitanidis 2012b: 282), spiritual therapists were unanimous in claiming that Japanese women clients were either worried about finding the right partner or their relationship with their current partner, issues that mapped on to the first two of what Yoshio Sugimoto (2003: 154) refers to as the four major life-changing stepping stones that are normatively expected of a Japanese woman in her life: quitting her job and getting married.[11] For example, when I first met Ms Ōtani, a successful career woman aged thirty-five, she had been seeing spiritual advisor Mr Suzuki on an occasional basis for six months. Her parents wished her to enter the highly gendered role of a Japanese wife but this worried her. She felt that, at her age, she wanted to marry, but she did not want to stop working nor to lose the carefree life that her salary level enabled, which included travel abroad and dinners at expensive restaurants.

The women spiritual therapists I interviewed were highly critically of the gender discrimination facing many of their clients and which many had themselves experienced.[12] As already noted, most women spiritual therapists were single at the time I interviewed them. Eight had divorced because they could not freely pursue their spiritual therapy interests, which often required them to travel to attend seminars in Japan and abroad. Both divorcees and those who had never been married felt that a man should respect his wife's interests and, moreover, support her in developing them, something that many of them had not experienced when they had been pursuing their previous careers. They were also candid about gender discrimination in the workplace; as the stories we have heard so far indicate, many had changed their lives to become spiritual entrepreneurs in order to transcend such problems. Mr Takahashi, a practitioner of theta healing, explained that his clients, who he described as mostly housewives, expressed the wish to become professional practitioners, since they could neither rely on their husband's income alone nor go back at their age (thirties to fifties) to full-time, stable employment. Ms Seiko was characteristically blunt: 'You graduate university, you get an O.L. [office lady] job, and they make you quit at twenty-six years old because you marry; then you have kids and that's it. No opportunities for skilling-up, no equality for women.'

Ms Seiko's criticism stemmed from her personal ordeal in trying to keep a job while being married; she said that she had eventually given up after her (male) supervisor at her third workplace convinced her that it was better to open a therapy salon (Figure 5.1). Like others, she had struggled. She is now using a small room inside her apartment to run her business, but the fourth time I met her, in 2018, she complained that her husband was at risk of losing his job and that would mean that she would not be able to afford to offer her therapeutic services. When I met her for the second time in April 2014, I asked her how the worries of her clients had changed since she had entered the business in the late 1990s. Again, she reflected on her own experience, narrating a perfect blend between the plight of women and unrealistic workforce expectations:

> People still worry about jobs and family, but what they worry about seems to have changed. It used to be the case that clients hesitated about what the best job

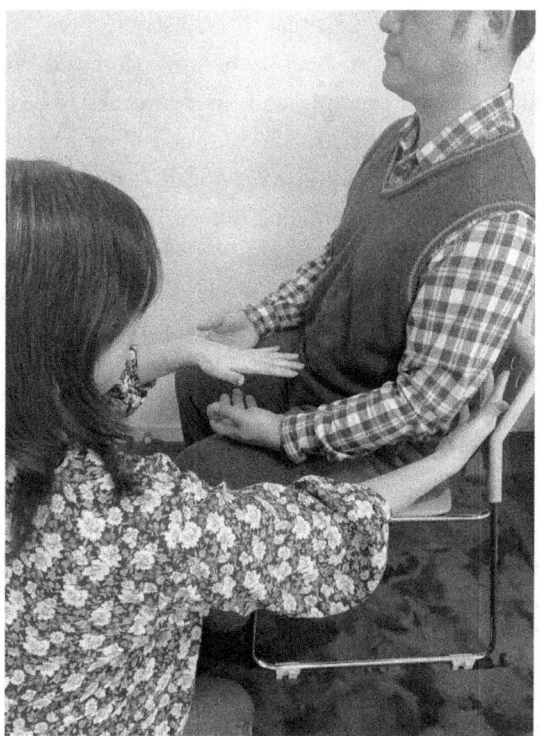

Figure 5.1 Ms Seiko treating a client with reiki. Photo used with the permission of the therapist.

was for them, but now, problems related to work are more about how failing yet another interview has snatched away from them their ideal future. But neither companies nor people are realistic! I mean hiring standards are crazy. You look at job adverts and you read that only people up to thirty-nine years old can apply for a permanent position. And, at the same time, you have women who want to have a permanent job, [and to be] married and having their first child in middle school by the time they reach forty. This is impossible today. It would mean that they would have had to give birth in their twenties. Who today gets married and has children just after graduating from university?

Other women, who were in a job that they were happy with, faced other kinds of discriminatory predicaments. Ms Iwato told me that she was subjected to sexual harassment at her workplace for three years before she ultimately quit her job, which she had really liked. She 'fled' to Hawaii, where she spent three months training in various spiritual therapies before returning to Tokyo to open her own salon.

At the same time, some spiritual therapists seemed to reinforce the stereotypes that had led them to open a therapy salon and brought clients to their door. Ms Kawasaki, for example, considered women to be burdened with a more physically and emotionally stressful life and referred particularly to issues related to marriage, childbirth, children's education and emancipation, which she explicitly associated with a woman's duties. In this and similar examples, issues stemming from the unequal status of women were interwoven with what women, both therapists and clients, still seemed to consider as one of their responsibilities in life: motherhood. Male therapists also simultaneously highlighted and reinforced these normative gender roles, as was evident when Mr Kobama explained the age span of his clients in relation to a period of change (*tenkai*) in women's lives: 'Except of course for the fact that the thirties is the decade when, for the professionally active individual, the body starts showing signs of tiredness in response to workload, for women, especially, it is the decade when most try to either bear or bring up a child.' In her recent analysis of popular literature linking pregnancy and childbirth to spirituality, Hashisako (2021: 188) notes how the emphasis on these life events as 'spiritual experiences' ends up strengthening the idea that pregnancy and childbirth are symbols of femininity. This creates a 'fictitious matriarchal family', from which the parents of the mother and the father of the child(ren) are virtually absent. 'The excessive emphasis on the female body ... and the recommendation of building up by oneself a "womanly" (*josei-rashii*) body that is beautiful, kind and positively cheerful', she argues, 'stands in sharp contrast to feminism's objective of liberating women from this [exact] situation' (197).

'Feminine' emotions and attitudes were considered as both appropriate traits for a spiritual therapist and common foundations of women clients' issues. I found recurrent tropes of men's stubbornness (*atagama ga katai*) and self-pride (*puraido*), contrasted with women's flexibility (*jūnansei*) and ability to look inwards (*jiko-seisatsu*), in therapists' responses to my frequently asked questions about why, in their opinion, the majority of their clients were women. Men were imagined as afraid to engage in the emotional work required by spiritual therapies, while women were deemed particularly fit for it. Emotional dispositions are the lynchpin that connects gender, spirituality and consumer capitalism. In her discussion of women's spiritual entrepreneurship, Kira Ganga Kieffer (2020) shows the gendering of capitalism in multilevel marketing companies, self-help and wellness guides, and spiritual business coaching, through four parameters: a rhetoric of New Age articulations of femininity; affirmations of 'women's intuition'; the expression of a selfless desire to help or teach customers rather than simply profit from them; and a narration of a personal spiritual transformation through capitalistic pursuits (81). Perhaps the most significant of Kieffer's arguments is that such articulations of femininity and altruistic consumerism coincided with the development of new business models in the 2000s, such as sustainable and social entrepreneurship (86). Spiritual entrepreneurship shares the same form as other twenty-first-century business ventures (McLaughlin et al. 2020). There are no -izations from religion to the market and vice-versa. Only common forms.

In her appraisal of Max Weber's theory of disenchantment, Courtney Bender (2015) argues that critics of spirituality have misunderstood it as something more related to religion than to secularity. She suggests that a closer reading of Weber helps us to align disenchantment with the apparently inescapable spirit of capitalism. From this perspective, the objectives of spiritual therapeutics as a practice offering people a way to cope with, rather than change the conditions that brought them to the salon in the first place seem to make more sense:[13]

> In a modern age filled with democratic promise, the expansion of scientific method and authority, and the norms of rational practice, spiritual therapeutics emerged as a new kind of discourse about the possibility of freedom within the limits posed by the 'felt' force of the universal spirit [of capitalism]. Put this way, the spirit is ever present, and its rules apply to all people. The spiritual writers agree with Weber: resistance is futile. But spiritual writers announce to their readers that accepting the truths of the spiritual laws of the universe and learning to work with them lead to a new kind of freedom. (Bender 2015: 52)

Conclusion

There is no doubt that spiritual therapists seek freedom: Freedom from a life of stress and exhaustion accompanying the rush to increase margins, profits and good prospects; freedom from pressures at work and at home where relationships seem to be as much a burden as a source of support; freedom from an inherently unequal system that continues to structurally disadvantage women. Recall the translator Yamakawa Akiko. Her story of constant self-discovery (Chapter 3) can also be read as a story of oppression by her husband Kōya. Her first crisis after failing to complete the workshop he had recommended ended up with her fleeing to her mother's home and blaming Kōya for fifteen years of a marriage that had basically been all about him. Later, it was she who became the breadwinner while he convalesced, yet both their names appeared on the two Shirley MacLaine books that she translated during those years. Twenty years later, she was still blaming herself for constantly comparing herself to her husband, a situation that was undoubtedly provoked by how Kōya constantly tried to take credit for work that both of them (or in some cases only Akiko) had contributed to. Many of Akiko's stories of self-emancipation are also trials to escape from Kōya's grip. If spirituality is gendered, that is because, to a great extent, it reflects the issues that its participants face in daily life.

Spiritual therapists' struggles to work within the system by finding coping mechanisms are as much a promise of spiritual therapy as they are a reflection of the neoliberal ideal of entrepreneurial innovation. Leaving the system entirely remains an option, but an option that means abandoning the chance to earn an income and spread the word. Yet, trying to subdue the system by playing it at its own game risks even less freedom. The spiritual business is not only replete with the normative gender expectations from which therapists were trying to escape when they joined; it also offers no guaranteed stability. As a service industry at the threshold between the welfare and cosmetics industry, it needs to remain competitive in the growing market of monetized experiences (Zuboff 2019: 7), while simultaneously answering to the ethics of consumer protection. In this chapter we have met spiritual therapists who have struggled to make a financial success of their business, but what happens when they fail on the ethical side and end up on trial for fraud? Where does the path to alternative ways of making a living by advising others cross that of criminal behaviour? How is the spiritual business connected to capitalism even in the ways in which it is outlawed? These are the questions I consider in the next and final chapter of this monograph.

6

Spirituality on trial

In April 2020, a woman going by the pseudonym 'Flower Garden' started a blog to share her new career as a therapist, providing 'healing' and 'counselling'. Despite the vague wording and the absence of a link to the website of her salon, her use of hashtags common to the blogs of spiritual therapists, such as 'law of attraction' (*hikiyose no hōsoku*) and good fortune (*kaiun*), signalled that she had just entered the spiritual business. Several entries followed in May that presented some moments from her life with her children, her likes and dislikes, and advice on how using the 'correct' toothbrush could bring success to her readers' lives. Then nothing until a new and surprising entry on 8 July: 'The magic was broken in an instant: ditching the spiritual!' Having invested 'a lot of money and time', she writes, she was ultimately left with nothing but the realization that everything she had been told in the seminar that she had been attending was 'fiction'; the seminars were all about making money.[1]

Flower Garden is by no means the only individual involved in the spiritual to have become disillusioned. The hashtag *datsu-supi* ('ditching the spiritual') first surfaced on Japanese Twitter in 2011 in a series of tweets by bloggers attacking the predatory marketing practices and extortionate prices of those who had become addicted to spirituality as a money-making business. There have also been an increasing number of court cases involving organizations and individuals offering spiritual services, who have been sued or prosecuted for breach of contract, fraud and financial misconduct. Consumer contract legislation has even been updated to include for the first time the category of 'spiritual sales' (*reikan shōhō*). This chapter turns to consider the terms of the criticism and moral judgement that spiritual business has attracted both from within its own ranks (the spirituality ditchers) and from the community of legal professionals involved in consumer fraud. Does spiritual fraud represent for them evidence of the commodification, hence corruption of spirituality, as scholarly critiques of spirituality tend to frame it? In other words, do non-scholarly critics of spirituality consider it primarily in relation to religion and ideas about what 'good' religion should be? Or do they view it within an alternative framework?

Spirituality as corrupt religiosity?

As the previous chapter has highlighted, while capitalist consumer society is inseparable from contemporary religiosity (Redden 2005), religion is not just economic activity. Religion and consumption inform one another, feed one another and rationalize one another. Consumption in spiritual therapy settings is a common experience that blends materialistic and spiritual elements. As such it often resembles other types of prosumption, a term first coined by Alvin Toffler ([1980] 2022) to reflect the 'progressive blurring of the line that separates producer from consumer' (Ritzer and Jurgenson 2010). The observations that I have made in the previous chapters about the central role played by the self in the practice and experience of spiritual therapies illustrate just how much consumption engulfs the totality of a person's life, not just the moments typified by commercial exchanges. If modern society is therefore in toto a consumer culture (Dawson 2013: 136), religious dynamics, self-transformation and monetary transactions are impossible to disentangle from one another.

Yet, in explicating what is 'modern' about the contemporary economics of religion, scholars have tended to reify a pejorative image of the 'sacred' being 'commercialized' for individual benefit. This argument is based on an implicit, nostalgic ideal of 'authentic' or 'good' religiosity, in which money is associated with donation for a public good or is a symbol of gratitude for time spent listening to and advising or treating the client. This is related to the normative assumption highlighted by Mitsutoshi Horii (2018: 204–5) that religion is supposed to provide public benefit. In cases of 'bad' religion or spirituality, money is associated with economic possession, personal fortune and assets that the client is hoaxed into giving away in exchange for false promises of cure and salvation. Shimazono Susumu, for example, has argued that oblation, is (and, implicitly, ought to be) an essentially communal activity, which 'continues to be further trampled by the stampede of mass media and efficiency-maximizing organizations' (Shimazono 1998: 187). He claims that Japan is 'a "superpower" when it comes to the ways of commercializing the sacred' (187).

Horie (2021) has criticized Shimazono and other scholars who seem to seek alternatives to capitalism in the act of oblation for the benefit of communal life, since their arguments sound no different to those of some religious groups that have been taken to court for emptying the pockets of their believers (118). He seems to acknowledge that spirituality should be judged on capitalist ethics. The temporary relationships built between spiritual service providers and consumers, based on constant mutual checking of the price and safety of those services, are, he considers, a better fit in today's capitalist societies where the negation of private property on religious grounds would be experienced as a sort of violence (139). Yet, he still seems to believe that spirituality ought to be embedded in public schemes not individual transactions.

Horie expands on Hashisako Mizuho's theory that the product selection and socializing among and between visitors and booth owners at mind-body-spirit fairs function as a 'safety device' against Aum-like escalations (Hashisako 2008: 25). Horie's (2021: 140–2) argument can be summarized as follows: if mainstream capitalism undermined the religious meaning and role of donations and created misunderstandings (and sometimes real issues) regarding the relation between money and religious organizations, individualized spirituality is so embedded in capitalism that the market's regulating functions have saved it from being associated with large-scale financial frauds. He nevertheless recognizes that there is risk that economic disparities might become legitimized as disparities between those who have invested enough in themselves and those who have not. Returning to the positive qualities that religious scholars associate with the publicness of religion, Horie ultimately concludes that spirituality ought to move away from the individual and enter public life, for example, the workplace (142). He thereby reiterates the idea that a 'good spirituality' is a 'publicly beneficial spirituality'.

Such criticisms of the commodification of individual spirituality, which are found in both popular and scholarly discourse, create the illusion that 'spiritual sales' and 'religious fraud' are essentially different from other (secular) types, as they are judged in relation to the domain of 'religion'. Predicated on a secularist distinction between for-profit work and altruistic or non-profit work, 'good' religion is positioned as being somehow above or separate from capitalism. This has been reinforced by both spirituality scholars and the media as they have increasingly tended to talk about religious organizations' 'social contributions' (Inaba and Sakurai 2012). Hence, religious fraud is viewed as a product or manifestation of religion's corruption by money, or more specifically capitalism. But to assume that fraudulence in the offering of spiritual services is related to the capitalist commodification of religion is as wrong as presuming that transactional exchanges between members and religious leaders or between therapists and clients are solely regulated by 'rational' capitalist behaviour. Upon what terms, then, have spirituality ditchers like Flower Garden come to judge spirituality?

Ditching the spiritual[2]

The hashtag *datsu-supi* ('ditching the spiritual') first appeared in three tweets criticizing an individual who was offering meditation sessions for a price that was deemed 'too high'. Online blog entries and anonymous replies that immediately followed expressed users' concerns about what they described as an addictive money-making business. 'The *datsu- supi* movement is basically a ditching-people-who-make-money-out-of-the-spiritual movement', one blogger announced (Nori 2018). 'The spiritual took the wrong direction when it started promising money to those who did not have it', argued another, drawing a direct comparison with self-development seminars, which had 'profited from Japan's economic downturn' (Tomotomoheaven 2019). A third blogger expressed a desire to 'raise the alarm against those who use the spiritual to make business' (Raku-hapi 2019). At first glance these attacks launched by insider cyber-critics of spiritual business seem to echo the 'capitalism corrupts religion' argument. But on closer examination we find that they are in fact arguing within the frame of market logic. They might critique predatory marketing, but nevertheless assume that spiritual striving and self-transformation will take place in a consumer capitalist frame.

Reflecting on more general online trends, most of the 504 blog posts that had used the 'ditching the spiritual' hashtag by July 2019 were authored by only a dozen or so individuals.[3] Their criticisms can be divided into three types of argument: critiques of the transformation of spirituality into a fashionable, income-earning market (Raku-hapi 2019); critiques of the conceptualization of the spiritual as mysterious (*fushigi-na*) or religious (*shūkyō-teki*) rather than ordinary (*nichijō-teki*) (Takizawa 2017); and critiques of those who choose to rely on gurus (*kyōso*) and spiritual leaders (*shidōsha*) rather than deciding on their lives by themselves (Takehisa 2018). None of the arguments found on *datsu-supi* blogs by former spirituality fans call for the disappearance of spiritual activities. Nor are all of them the kind of ubiquitous warning to be found both within and outside the spiritual business against overpriced sessions.[4] Instead, we find on these blogs calls for an interaction with spiritual therapies that is more 'normal', 'ordinary', 'responsible' and less 'dependent'.

One of the most expressive (and sometimes extreme) *datsu-supi* blogs ran from November 2015 to April 2019, when it was moved to a new website where all previous blog entries were effectively turned into a manual of why and how to get out of the spiritual (the website stopped being updated in April 2020). The blogger, who I will call K,[5] defines the spiritual as 'a behaviour principle (*kōdō genri*) that leads to the fulfilment of one's wishes and to happiness ... it is our life and energy and, like everyone else, I think that to polish our spiritual [selves] based on our own feelings without being disturbed by others is a wonderful thing'. The spiritual is here conceived as something essentially personal and private. That is why, according to K, 'it should not be turned into a business method [a networking business] by people to profit from those who are weak and end up being spiritual believers (*shinja*)'. But K's main target is not those profiteers but rather their clients, who have failed to understand what spirituality really is. For K, the spiritual is not something people ought to believe in; it is not an object of faith, since it corresponds to a part of every human being. As K puts it: 'The spiritual cannot become business, because the spiritual is something entirely individual.' To convince his readers, K gives an example:

> Imagine that we translate the spiritual as 'soul' (*tamashii*). In that case, it would mean that it is possible for the soul to become the object of a transaction (*tamashii ga shōbai ni naru*). Do you understand what this means? The soul cannot be sold. It is part of its owner. My soul is only mine. Your soul is only yours. It should not be handled by someone else.

For K, the spiritual business has lived off the social anxieties experienced by the Japanese in the post-war period. Using a graph summarizing key events of the second half of the twentieth century, especially those related to the United States and Japan such as the Vietnam War or the burst of Japan's economic bubble, K argues that social changes shake up human values. As a result, people seeking a way out of these anxieties are attracted to various currents of thought (*shisō*). Echoing scholarly analyses of the spiritual by figures such as Shimazono (Chapter 2), K argues that 'the spiritual boom is a symbol of the Heisei era'. K also blames the media, which 'should have been more cautious' in circulating vague messages about the possible existence of an 'invisible realm'. In the end, however, it all boils down to the fact that social changes and larger historical trends have prevented the fostering of self-esteem in the Japanese people, making them dependent on others: 'When your self-esteem is low, you cannot bear responsibility for your ideas, decisions and lifestyle. So, you end up clinging to others.'

This lack of self-esteem, K argues, draws people who are not yet sure (*kakuritsu sarete inai*) of their identity and who experience harsh lives (also due to their lack of self-esteem) to a message common among people making a business out of the spiritual: 'Be the way you are (*ari no mama no jibun de*).' 'But why would you pay money for such an obvious thing?' asks K:

> It is only your low self-esteem that is praised through such messages ... and, instead of touching your feet to the ground and getting on with your life, you are sucked into the spiritual shopping of 'self-searching' ... and like a wandering ghost, lose yourself. Then soon, you mistake your acts for doing something spiritually noble, and start craving for easy money. ... you become addicted to spiritual goods ... and travel around the country to acquire 'licenses' and, eventually, put up your own advertising sign: 'How about healing yourself?'

K's message is clear: this is a personal problem of the clients of spiritual therapists (who, on being sucked into the business, might then go on to become therapists themselves). As K writes in red letters in the prologue of his online manual: 'There should not exist a business living off the *kokoro* (heart, mind).' K does not criticize people engaging in self-improvement *per se*; only when they pay others to do it for them.

K and other spirituality ditchers do not associate consumerism with superficial religion as some religious studies scholars have done (Chapter 2). Spiritual therapies are consumed because they bear meaning and have a certain value, even if, according to K, the same can be achieved through one's own efforts of what I can only interpret as increased self-attention (see Chapter 4). As Véronique Altglas (2014b: 268) aptly demonstrates in her study of participants of spiritual courses and workshops in Europe, the imperative of self-improvement 'pre-exists the act of consumption itself and is not defined by "consumers" from their own self-authority, outside a framework of social norms about the self'. However, the most significant aspect of K's argument is the way that he conceives of the 'real' or 'orthodox' spiritual as a part of the individual that cannot be subjected to monetary transactions. K is an exception in claiming that ideally all spiritual seminars and sessions should be free. But even here the problem is not their commodification. It is the fact that one entrusts their 'spiritual' to someone else, who then makes a profit out of the disposition that has brought this client to their doorstep. Ultimately, it is that disposition (=low self-esteem) that K criticizes, not self-searching or the fact that one might pay for spiritual products.

Orthodox spirituality

Since the early twentieth century, the distinction between religious orthodoxy and religious heresy has frequently been read as a distinction between 'bad religion' and 'good religion' based on the abovementioned idea that religious corporations ought to contribute to public benefit. This allowed public authorities and the general populace to counter arguments of infringement of religious freedom advanced by so-called cults by simply labelling those groups as bad religion. In Japan, as in the United States, use of the word 'cult' expanded to cover other activities, including spiritual therapy salons and multilevel marketing businesses offering self-development seminars and workshops, which were attacked for their assumed association with bad religion, not because they were religious *per se*. Anti-cultists use a critique of capitalism to emphasize the essential purity of 'good religion' and point the finger at the essentially rationally structured (criminal and unethical) manipulation of innocent members by 'bad religion'.

The approach of spirituality ditchers is slightly different. Theirs is not a criticism of the commodification of the spiritual to draw attention to some 'traditional' (albeit, foregone) religiosity. After all, they themselves have participated in the twenty-first-century spiritualities that selectively reject established religions. Spirituality 'ditchers' instead point the finger at 'irresponsible' consumerism and at those who exploit people's naïve spiritual seeking to enrich their bank accounts. But their main targets are the consumers of the spiritual, who they criticize, not for being duped by 'bad religion', but for not understanding what this new spirituality is really about. It is not something you pay someone else to do. You do it yourself.

The narratives of those who leave 'the spiritual' express this change in their lives as an exit or passage from their role as a fan or avid reader of the spiritual or a regular client of its related therapies. They embrace 'a posture of confrontation' (Wright 2014: 710) through the public claims that they make about spirituality, as illustrated in the blog posts of individuals such as K. This kind of tactic, as an act of 'exclusive similarity' (Josephson 2012: 29–38), allows those leaving the spiritual to claim a distinction between 'real' or orthodox spirituality and consumer fraud spirituality or the heretical spiritual. I previously argued, that 'this would qualify them in scholarly terms as "apostates"', in the sense that they rhetorically position themselves as members of an authoritative community of consumers that they have now turned against (Gaitanidis 2020).

However, for them to be spirituality apostates in the theological sense, those 'ditching spirituality' would have had to negate *supirichuariti* – something that they did not do. Rather, the *datsu-supi* movement has been about imagining 'alternatives' within a spiritual business for which having no choice but to play the neoliberal game is constitutive of community membership.

K is very explicit in his critique of how the business works and attracts followers. His blog has an entire section on how every spiritual therapy seminar or workshop is, he argues, essentially multilevel marketing. In another section he critiques those who try to make a living by publishing personal information from other sources on their websites in order to amass 'likes' and earn a profit from the advertisements attached to their blogs. Although perhaps on the more extreme end, K's warnings fundamentally target how the spiritual is promoted to future clients, rather than the business of spiritual therapy itself: 'No fair human relationships can be created by people making a profit out of making recommendations to others.' Less vociferous ditchers locate the problem in how clients take what they are told at face value, and how therapists rely too much on the authority of their professional certificates. 'It is not about "do not make money out of the spiritual"; if you decide to make a living out of selling the spiritual then you ought to offer clients more than they have paid' writes one blogger.

In this sense, it is more productive to think of those leaving the spiritual as 'spiritual heretics'. In his call for a reappraisal of the analytic power of the category of 'heresy', Takashi Shogimen notes that its medieval meaning etymologically stemmed from the Greek term *hairesis* or 'the act of choosing' (Shogimen 2020). A heretic was a person who insisted on the truth of their claims even when confronted with the violent assertion of orthodoxy through the Inquisition. This conception of heresy has regained relevance in the contemporary world, where historical heretics are lauded as people who stood up against repressive regimes. Hence, while historians have pointed to the 'essentially authoritarian and institutional' nature of heresy as a category, Takashi argues that heresy is not primarily a matter of power, even in medieval accounts:

> What makes the suspect heretical is the individual's pertinacious dissent from the authority of the interrogator, not overt submission to it. The suspects' overt affirmation that they are losers by submitting to the interrogating authority saves them from the sentence of heresy. Heretics are those who insist on the truth of their claims, thus refusing to submit to the power of the interrogator. Heretics rather strip truth-claims from the institutional power of the interrogator,

thereby attempting to show the latter as naked power that is not backed by truth. In terms of subjective intentions, heretics in the mainstream medieval account also cannot be viewed entirely as losers because they consider themselves to be the guardians of truth, if not the winners of the power game. In the medieval accounts, domination was countered by truth claims, not by modern assertions of freedom. (Shogimen 2020: 742)

If K's rhetoric gives us a glimpse of what 'true' spirituality is supposed to be in practice, it seems to be related to good consuming practices, namely ethical, conscious and reasonable consumption that requires clients to assess the claims of the services they buy. K is a heretic because K considers themself to be a guardian of 'real' spirituality, not a loser who has submitted to the allure of the spiritual business as it currently operates. The 'spirituality' that K proclaims is often stripped word-for-word out of the pamphlets and blogs of the malevolent companies and individuals that, K claims, have misinterpreted it and are trying to make easy money by defrauding others. The system that K critiques is basically 'bad capitalism'. Ultimately, you are the producer of the best product for you. K's ideas are therefore an expression rather than a rejection of capitalist consumerism and neoliberal values. Within this system, the right of choice that is assumed in every act of consumption is automatically a moral act as individuals experience it as an exercise of their responsibility (Wuthnow 1989: 88). In that sense, 'neoliberalism represents a highly efficient, indeed an intelligent, system for exploiting freedom. Everything that belongs to practices and expressive forms of liberty – emotion, play and communication – comes to be exploited' (Han 2017: 3). Under these circumstances, the ethics regarding what is good or bad consumer behaviour take an insidious turn, and an economy of moral judgement arises that ultimately places all responsibility on the individual:

> When people are presumptively rational, behavioural failure comes primarily from the lack of sufficient information, from noise, poor signalling or limited information-processing abilities. But when information is plentiful, and the focus is on behaviour, all that is left are concrete, practical actions, often recast as good or bad 'choices' by the agentic perspective dominant in common sense and economic discourse. The vast amounts of concrete data about actual 'decisions' people make offer many possibilities of judgement, especially when the end product is an individual score or rating. Outcomes are thus likely to be experienced as morally deserved positions, based on one's prior good actions and good taste ... Everyone seems to get what they deserve. (Fourcade and Healy 2017: 24–5)

Spirituality ditchers exhibit more comfort with the explicit linkages between religious or spiritual striving and capitalist consumption than do anti-cult critics. They do not try to argue outside the logics of the capitalist consumerism in which our daily lives are embedded. If anti-cult rhetoric is framed as a critique of the commodification of religion, the spiritual ditchers seem to be positioned against unfair practices within the neoliberal economy of moral judgement. They seem to agree that the consumer should be responsible for their choices, but they believe that neoliberal capitalism should be empowering its consumers by offering them enough and relevant information to make moral choices. The problem is that, in reality, profit-chasing has become more important than fair transactions. Hence what the spiritual business promotes is often not what it actually manages to deliver (although it potentially could). Not all ditchers espouse such a message; many may go no further than to attack exorbitant prices. But those who do seem to be neither counter-materialist nor counter-religious; their concern is with the 'proper' way that the two, capitalism and religion, are and should be entangled.

This can be further illustrated if we return to the more recent blog of Flower Garden, whose moral critique of the spirituality that she professes to have ditched is ultimately grounded in issues of integrity and, more implicitly, the rights of consumers to be treated fairly. Although something is always lost in the process of translation, I cite several chunks from the blog so that readers can grasp for themselves something of its moral tone and affective power.

Flower Garden's blog

I'll be honest with you.

I used to call myself a 'therapist' on this blog.

But in reality, I was only doing it with my family, friends and colleagues at a [therapy] seminar. ...

It's true [however] that I used to be an aesthetician.

Last year, from 2019, I've been taking lessons as a therapist in a 'seminar'.

... By increasing your own energy, you can send energy remotely, making it easier to heal your loved ones and attract happiness. ...

With hindsight, it was a parade of all the common catchphrases [that seminars like these use]. But I just went there. ...

(By the way, it was not reiki!). ...

And then I found myself attending seminar after seminar and pouring money into it until I had spent as much as a million yen.

This opening to Flower Garden's 8 July 'ditching the spiritual' blog entry might suggest that it was the vast amount of money that she had been duped into spending that was at the heart of her complaints about the seminar she had been attending. What follows, however, reveals that her doubts and discomfort were precipitated by her moral response to how her teacher, 'a kind of "guru" at the top', had handled the Covid-19 pandemic. Flower Garden writes that 'even after March, when there were strong calls for restraint, she continued to give seminars in various cities', telling attendees: 'Thoughts and feelings become reality, so be positive' and 'there is no need for self-restraint'. Flower Garden continued to attend the seminar for an unspecified period of time, thinking: 'I have high energy, I'll be fine.' Feeling increasingly uncomfortable, she finally stopped going. But at that point, she writes, 'I hadn't yet questioned the "energy" or the "teachings" themselves. In fact, I started this blog and thought I wanted to heal people with energy'.

She 'started to wake up' as 'the world went into self-restraint' but her teacher carried on holding in-person rather than online seminars:

> It happened one day, out of the blue, like lightning. …
> I realized that everything about our 'teacher' was fiction.
> Our teacher's basic lesson was that, as Japanese, we ought to cooperate with each other. I could relate to that very well. …
> But what our teacher was actually doing during the Corona pandemic was the opposite. …
> It seemed to me that she was trying to force a lot of people to come to her face-to-face seminars.

It was at this point, she claims, that she made the decision to leave and to 'cut all ties with the organization'.

> I don't mean to denigrate all spirituality, but if you're into spirituality now.
> Just for a moment.
> Stop.
> Look at yourself.
> Look at your 'teacher'.
> You may find that you see a different landscape.

After this, Flower Garden's blog entries stop again until March 2021. Almost all of her subsequent posts consist of a critique of her former teacher, which she then extrapolates into all spiritual seminars that promise their participants success and money. In each post, Flower Garden re-narrates her experience in the same terms, warning people not to fall into the trap of liars like her 'teacher'.

Like K, Flower Garden is a spiritual heretic; she does not negate spirituality but rather speaks truth to the 'fiction' of those who would continue to make money out of the spiritual business even in the context of a global pandemic. Also, like K, her derisory comments towards her 'teacher' are punctuated by serious admonitions to others like her who have fallen into what she calls spiritual frauds (*supirichuaru sagi*). That she considers her former teacher's actions almost criminal is made evident when, in an entry posted in early April 2021, she includes a link to the website of a law firm which dedicates an entire page to 'the five tricks of spiritual frauds' and advises victims to contact the police and/or their local consumer affairs centre before seeking the help of a lawyer to get their money back. But the law firm also draws a distinction between an older kind of spiritual fraud and the dynamics of contemporary spiritual sales:

> Spiritual fraud is characterized by making you dependent on them and repeatedly cheating you out of your money. It is similar to spiritual sales, but instead of preying on people's anxieties and threatening them that they will die within a year if they don't buy the product, they [spiritual sales] do the opposite: they blow up your hopes by saying that 'buying this will make you happy'.

This distinction is reminiscent of the boundary work practiced by 'new' therapists like Ms Koyama (Chapter 1), who try to distance themselves from the 'obsolete' *reinōsha*. But in this case it is not based on an alleged difference between old and new religiosities, but between old and new fraudulent behaviour. The legal argument is essentially moral and targets the protection of consumers, just like the argument made by Flower Garden, who only started doubting the ethics of the spiritual seminar company when she began questioning the morality of her teacher's continuation of in-person seminars during the pandemic, which put her (paying) students at risk. Flower Garden ditched the spiritual for exactly the kind of behaviour that lawyers consider fraudulent. But what exactly is fraudulent about spiritual sales?

Spirituality sales and the law

In the April 2017 issue of *Consumer Law News*, a lawyer's report on a case related to spiritual therapies was published in the religion-related affairs section of the magazine (Imaizumi 2017). Permeating the piece is a sense of confusion about how to deal with what the author calls 'the increasing number of pseudo-religious or religious-like self-help seminars' (200). The case concerns a complaint made by an individual against Modern Mystery School (MMS), a company offering self-development and training seminars in various spiritual therapies. The complainant accused the school of having falsely led them to believe that they would be able to radically improve their fortune and meet a good partner. On the basis of this deception, the complainant claimed, they had been made to pay a total of at least 5,543,600 yen (roughly US$47,000) for channelling and other types of seminars over a period of seven years, from April 2007 to June 2014. As the complainant had no proof of payment for most of the seminar fees and wanted to settle the case as quickly as possible, the lawyer decided to focus on the most recent sum of money (1,188,000 yen) for which proof existed. The legal argument rested on Article 4(2) of the Consumer Contract Law, which obliges businesses to explain matters that are disadvantageous to their customers. It was argued that MMS had infringed this on the grounds that 'the specifics of the services provided by MMS (when and what is to be done) are unclear and ... a contract was not even drawn up' (Imaizumi 2017: 201). A settlement was reached out of court, and the full amount was refunded.

When I conducted the majority of my interviews in 2009, ten out of the approximately seventy spiritual therapists who I decided to focus on were graduates of MMS (then called RMMS). From their descriptions of that institution, I surmised that MMS resembled 'a spiritual business version of a pyramid scheme' (Gaitanidis 2011: 191), in that it was based on recruiting paying clients who, once captured, were then encouraged to become teachers (paying further fees), who could then recruit their own students on condition that they continued to pay into the scheme:

> All initiates must go through a two-day programme to understand the basics of the RMMS cosmology at a cost of ¥55,000. At that point everyone is strongly encouraged to become a teacher, after spending a total of ¥58,270 on preliminary classes, which will enable them to teach the adept programme to others, but, for every newly formed adept, they will have to pay ¥5,000 back to Gudni [Gudnason, the owner of MMS]. Of course, there are several types

of teacher certificates, each with the necessary preliminary classes, and each allowing the newly qualified/graduated teacher to hold identical classes at his own healing salon, but with the obligation to attend a monthly meeting at the Tokyo headquarters and pay royalties for some of the sessions owned by Gudni. Finally, once the rank of 'guide' is reached, the RMMS member will be able to teach any course figuring in the RMMS curriculum, which at the moment includes thirty, with new ones being introduced every year. (Gaitanidis 2011: 191)

This is perhaps not the only time that MMS has been accused of deception, financial misconduct or worse; a journalist recently reported on several cases of sexual coercion, financial fraud and risk to life during training seminars, based on testimonies coming mostly from branches of MMS outside of Japan (Wilding 2021). The schemes of such institutions often change over time in response to market trends and client reactions, but the experience of the complainant in the case cited in *Consumer Law News* sounds very credible.

During my fieldwork, I met several spiritual therapists who reimbursed clients for their sessions in response to claims of dissatisfaction and most therapists expressed a positive stance (at least to me) towards refunding clients in such contexts. I often heard them say: 'If a client asks for their money back, you have to give it. There is no reason not to.' However, none of the therapists I interviewed dealt with the relatively large sums of money handled by companies like MMS. The people I conversed with were those who, like the complainant in the case against MMS, had themselves paid large sums of money to such educational institutions in order to gain a variety of qualifications. Client complaints were therefore unlikely to develop into major incidents that ended up in court. Nevertheless, given that the media and scholars tend to focus on prosecutions that involve religious organizations rather than private persons, cases like that of MMS might only be the tip of the iceberg of those in which spiritual therapists are prosecuted like any other type of professional in the service industry. Where does 'religion' fit into that?

Religion is not defined in the Japanese Constitution, but trials involving religious matters can be grouped into three general types. These include the two categories described by Ernils Larsson (2020): trials relating to 'freedom of religion' (Article 20 of the Constitution), such as when family members assert their right to have their Christian relatives enshrined in Shinto shrines; and trials relating to the 'separation of religion and state' (Article 89 of the Constitution), which often involve financial exchanges between public officials and representatives of religious institutions.[6] There is also a third category of cases, namely trials like that of MMS that deal with illegal acts (murder, violence, fraud, etc.) committed by religious organizations or individuals, whether or not they are officially registered as religious corporations.

Studies of the first two types of trial abound (see, e.g. Ehrhardt et al. 2014; Larsson 2020) and seem to confirm Winifred F. Sullivan's claim that 'the more the government protects free exercise, the more it tends to recognize and arguably establish religion; the more the government seeks to sequester religion in the name of disestablishment, the more it tends to diminish the space for religious observance' (Sullivan [2005] 2018: xxi). A recent example was the ruling made by Japan's Supreme Court on 24 February 2021 that the Naha city government had 'violated the constitutional separation of politics and religion' when it had granted a Confucian temple, rebuilt in a public park, an exemption on paying any land rent (Abe 2021). The court did not address the question of whether Confucianism is a religion, only whether the facilities and activities of the temple were 'of religious nature' (Tsukada 2021: 13). Given that the temple is registered as a general incorporated association (*ippan shadan hōjin*) and not as a religious corporation (*shūkyō hōjin*), this ruling effectively broadened the scope of what could be legally designated a religious activity.

The Confucian temple case reflects an anxiety about how to define and deal with religion that is embedded in Japan's construction as a modern secular state. As Jolyon Baraka Thomas (2019: 26) points out in his discussion on the Meiji constitutional regime as a 'secularist system', secularity is not a mere absence, diminution or ideological subordination of religion. Rather, it is 'the state of being uncertain about what counts as religion and what does not' (26). According to Thomas, 'utter anxiety about the relationship between religion and not-religion dominated the [Meiji] period' (45). The regime attempted to distinguish between them, and then, sometimes quite arbitrarily, acted on such a distinction to dictate social, legal and political life. But the question of how to define religion remained unresolved, a situation that made the Meiji regime repressive towards marginal movements labelled 'heresies', but supportive, for example, of shrine rites described as non-religious civic duties (28).

Nearly 100 years later, the same kind of anxiety can be seen in how scholars, journalists and lawyers have tried to trace the limits of where the freedom of religion ends and illegal activity starts. Hence, cases related to what have been popularly known as 'spiritual sales' (*reikan shōhō*) are considered special. In the MMS case, the argument that the complainant's lawyer made was based on the (secular) entrepreneurial misconduct of the company, but it alluded to the specifically religious character of the organization's services: 'MMS denies that it is a religious organization and even though it confesses that it conducts seminars as a commercial activity, it forces people to pay large sums of money by imposing deceptive and vague contracts.' The language in the original text is ambiguous, but my reading of the lawyer's argument is that the religious character of the services provided by MMS was taken as the (or at least a key) source of the organization's insincerity and lack of integrity. The intangible claims upon which such spiritual sales are made – hence their 'religious' nature – makes them difficult to deal with. As the claimant's lawyer in the MMS case writes, the effects of their channelling course (taken by the complainant) as explained by an MMS manager in terms of 'awakening the sixth sense … were all abstract and utterly impossible to verify' (Imaizumi 2017: 201).

At the same time, such cases do not fit the idea that religion should contribute to public benefit, so even though the services offered might be of a religious rather than secular nature, scholars like Sakurai Yoshihide – who bemoans the complete absence of guaranty and quality control in the therapy sessions offered by spiritual counsellors, channelers and other types of holistic practitioners (Sakurai 2009a: 173–4) – consider that the spiritual business cannot be treated as religion; it is commercial. Moreover, its commercial activities have nothing to do with providing efficacious services. They are about tricking clients into handing over cash by making them believe that they will get a quick fix for a problem:

> The spiritual business is characterized by the fact that it has ceased to be a religious organization, which requires ethical codes of conduct and social relations, and has become a commercial entity that sells spiritual goods and services … [Its] commercial practices are based not on satisfying the clients with the efficacy of the spiritual goods and services themselves, but on manipulating their perception of risk so as to make them willing to lose money in order to gain the benefit of solving a specific problem. (Sakurai 2009a: 236, 238)

Lawyers make a similar argument, although they focus more on the question of freedom of religious belief, which is guaranteed by the Constitution. Lawyers specializing in problems related to spiritual sales have, since the late 1990s, argued that 'freedom of religion does not mean that you can threaten or deceive citizens' (Itō, Kitō and Yamaguchi 1999: 99). Hence, despite the distinct label of 'spiritual sales', the majority of cases of fraud and other problematic activities committed by religious organizations are, like the MMS case, treated like any other case involving similar illegalities. Yamaguchi Hiroshi, one of the most renowned lawyers to have established experience in such cases, has explicitly argued that 'there is no need to consider different criteria for determining illegality between commercial activities subject to regulations such as door-to-door sales and consumer protection ordinances in Tokyo and other prefectures, and religious organizations soliciting donations and selling goods' (Yamaguchi 2003: 52–3). How has this worked in practice?

Fictitious billings in the era of consumer protection

In December 2020, I used the LEX/DB database[7] to identify 306 legal court rulings (both civil and criminal) in which the following keywords, commonly used by spiritual therapists, appeared in the text: *reinō* or spiritual powers (80 cases), *uranai* or fortune telling (217 cases) and *supirichuaru* (9 cases).[8] While this cannot be considered an exhaustive search of cases involving spiritual sales, it provides a sufficient body of rulings from which to gain insights into the kinds of cases brought to court and the grounds upon which they are judged. As is to be expected, a chronological breakdown of these entries (Graph 6.1) shows clearly that there was a short time lag between the popularization of *supirichuaru* as a term and its appearance in legal judgments. We can infer that the sudden increase of *reinō* and *uranai* cases in, respectively, the early and late 1990s date back to issues occurring in the late 1980s and early 1990s. In the late 1980s, several civil cases of fraud and criminal cases of extortion were brought to trial that involved the Unification Church and Hō No Hana Sanpōgyō, both new religious movements, resulting in the award of what amounted to several billions of yen in damages. These cases attracted media attention and led to the

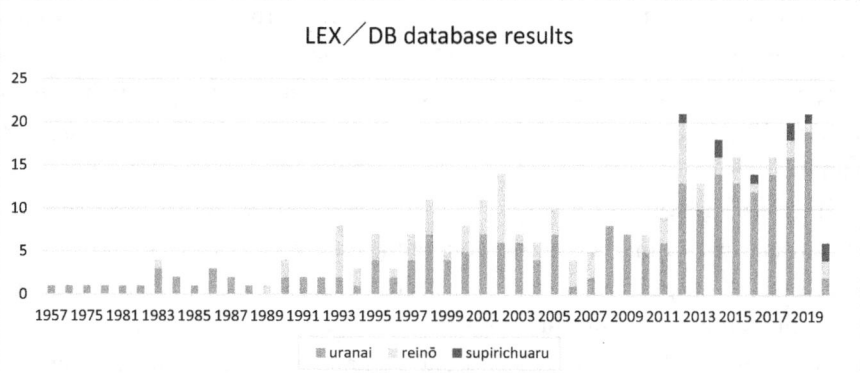

Graph 6.1 Number of entries corresponding to the keywords *reinō*, *uranai* and *supirichuaru* in the LEX/DB database. Compiled by the author.

formation in 1987 of the National Network of Lawyers against Spiritual Sales (Kanō 2003), a group of approximately 300 lawyers who continue to deal with and raise concerns about such issues. As of September 2021, the network had calculated that the claims for cases related to 'spiritual sales' from 1987 to 2020 amounted to more than 123 billion yen.[9]

Many of these cases, notably those involving Aum Shinrikyō and Kōfuku no Kagaku, are famous and have attracted a considerable amount of media attention (Baffelli 2016). Cases that focus on some sort of therapeutic practice, which tend not to make the news, typically involve individuals who are accused of claiming supernatural powers that allow them to cure diseases for what end up being exorbitant prices. To cite an illustrative example: In 1996, the Toyama district court in north-western Japan sentenced a local Buddhist priest to two years' imprisonment and a four-year suspended sentence for having defrauded a family of 4 million yen.[10] The priest had claimed that he had inherited spiritual powers in the esoteric Buddhist tradition of his parent temple (then located in Wakayama prefecture) and that he could cure the illness of the family's eldest daughter by appeasing the spirit of a miscarried foetus who was bringing them misfortune. The court's findings against the priest were based on two key pieces of evidence. First, another priest who had trained at the same parent temple testified to the accused's lack of any training in or possession of supernatural powers. Second, the accused was discovered to have devised manuals and guidelines that he had used to extract personal information from people visiting his temple, so as to systematically make them believe that their issues could be cured by appeasing the spirits of dead relatives. It was this systematization of religious practice that the court condemned, although no religious organization could ever fulfil the ideal of spontaneity that this judge and the lawyers for the prosecution seemed to associate with 'good religion'. The court did not discuss the ontological status of spiritual powers *per se*, but based its decision on testimonials and documents that proved that the accused purposefully sought to dupe his clients. This inferred that the accused did not believe that he, himself, had such powers.

This case reflects a more general pattern in court trials involving both organizations and individuals offering therapeutic services based on beliefs in the existence of spiritual powers: the actions of the accused are basically judged (and condemned) as false promises made to customers. The civil case of the company Earth Heart, which has occupied prefectural courts in the south of Japan for most of the second decade of this century, remains paradigmatic. Earth Heart, like the Confucian temple in Naha, is registered as a general incorporated association rather than as a religious corporation. The latest class action lawsuit, reported in the news in late September 2021, involves a group of twenty-seven plaintiffs who used to be paying members of Earth Heart, which offered lessons on 'hand power' to allegedly cure ills. The plaintiffs have sued Earth Heart and one of its branches at Fukuoka's district court for damages exceeding 21 million yen, the amount that they claim to have spent on lesson fees and Earth Heart products since 2009 (Hiratsuka 2021). In 2015, the Supreme Court condemned Earth Heart for promotion of therapeutic services with no scientific or medical basis, concluding that 'the content of the advertisements must be said to be fraudulent and contain false contents'. The court did not concern itself with the verity of the alleged existence of 'hand power', only with the advertisement of such a therapeutic method as having guaranteed effects, holding that this constituted a lie.

Regardless of the significance and high visibility of some of these trials, the majority of the 306 court rulings that use the keywords *reinō*, *uranai* and/or *supirichuaru* are not concerned with false promises directly related to spiritual services. These unrelated cases can be divided into two groups. The first testifies to the ubiquity of spirituality practitioners in contemporary life. It consists of judgements that either refer to advice given to the plaintiff or defendant by a fortune teller or psychic as a contextual factor in the case, or that mention the practice of spirituality in describing a defendant's or complainant's status, such as 'self-proclaimed psychic' or 'used to read palms as a hobby'. Take, for example, one of the many cases of adultery in this group of court rulings. The defendant was accused of having an affair with the plaintiff's wife, and, as a result, of causing the breakdown of their marriage and emotional distress to the plaintiff, who was seeking payment of damages. The court dismissed the claim on the grounds that the evidence presented, which consisted of entries in the wife's diary, was not sufficient proof that the adultery had occurred: 'Although the plaintiff claims that there was an act of infidelity, the diary merely contains proof that the wife had imagined, based on the result of fortune-telling, that she had a one-sided crush on the defendant.'[11]

The second group of cases illustrates the prosaic character of spiritual therapy and fortune-telling services, showing them to be regular businesses that face the same issues as any other business and are subject to the same legislative framework. It consists of cases of defamation and fictitious claims, copyright issues, trademark-related issues, sexual harassment and power harassment within companies employing fortune tellers, and the like. For example, two books published in 2011, *The Miraculous Spiritual Doctor* and *Spiritual Healing of a*

Medical Doctor, were the subject of a contractual dispute, in which the defendant-author was found guilty by a court in 2016 for unpaid contract fees and delay damages caused to the publisher.[12] Such court rulings, although unrelated to the services provided by spirituality practitioners, present a fascinating picture of ordinary Japanese lives and the degree to which the spiritual business is deeply embedded within many of them.

It is therefore not surprising to see that cases in which spiritual and fortune-telling services are themselves the object of contention, are judged within the same legislative framework. Rather than revealing any peculiarly 'religious character' to the services that spirituality practitioners provide, these cases reflect the changing nature of consumer issues during the last thirty years. We know that the problems confronting consumers have changed as a result of the proliferation of luxury goods, the exponential growth of the financial services industry and the development of e-commerce, among other factors. Whereas most complaints made to local consumer centres in Japan in 1971 had to do with product safety and quality, by 1997, the majority related to issues arising from unfair business practices and consumer contracts (Ikemoto 1999: 29, cited in McLachlan 2002: 243). According to data collected since 1984 by the National Consumer Affairs Centre of Japan (*Kokumin Seikatsu Sentā*), the number of consumer affairs consultations peaked in 2004 at 1,920,000. In 2021, it stood at around 900,000 a year, with about a third of these consultations being about fictitious claims (National Consumer Centre 2021: 21).

To give just one illustrative example: in a case brought to trial in 2018, which is typical of the kind of damage claims related to spiritual therapy, two plaintiffs accused the defendant and the company he was associated with of making them believe that their lives would be ruined if they did not pay 14.2 and 4.8 million yen, respectively, for a session called *kotodama* (lit. spirits of words). The court dismissed the case as follows:

> The court ruled that the plaintiff had sensed that the defendant had 'psychic powers' merely based on observation of the defendant's behaviour. The defendant did not flaunt his psychic abilities; and the plaintiff was not in a 'closed space' and could not be said to have been mind-controlled; furthermore the psychic sessions, which were designed to help relieve clients from anxiety and realize their desires, were not outside the range of services provided by the defendant's company.[13]

In other words, the court held that the provider of the *kotodama* session had neither lied about the purpose of his business nor claimed to possess any

Figure 6.1 A typical illustration found on posters and websites warning against spiritual sales. Printed with permission from Irasutoya.

supernatural powers. Like the other cases I have discussed, the case did not rest on whether or not the defendant had psychic powers, but on whether or not the services he had provided were fictitious (Figure 6.1). In this case, the judge found the defendant to have been sincere in his business transaction and the clients to have been unrealistic in their expectations of what they were buying with their money.

Despite the common legislative framework under which spiritual and other types of consumer fraud are judged, recent legislative developments highlight the resurgence of ongoing anxiety about how to deal with cases involving spiritual businesses, which appear to be at risk of being pushed into illegality purely as a result of the intangible character of their services. A new addition to the Consumer Contract Act illustrates this problem perfectly. Its latest amendment (June 2019) is designed to protect consumers from various disparities in the quality and quantity of information between consumers and businesses. Several new clauses are added, expanding the list of acts that can form the basis for revoking a contract. One specifically addresses spiritual sales (*reikan shōhō*) – for the first time in post-Second World War legal history. The official translation reads as follows:

> The trader indicates to the consumer that psychic sense (*reikan*) or other special abilities that are difficult to be reasonably verified have shown that a serious disadvantage would occur to the consumer unless the consumer takes certain measures to fuel their fear, and then, the trader informs the consumer that the

serious disorders can be completely avoided if the consumer enters into the contract. (Consumer Contract Act 2019, Chapter 2, Section 1, Article 4(3)(vi))[14]

According to this new provision, and under the general rules of rescission (Article 7(1)), an individual who believes that they have been the victim of spiritual sales and wishes to revoke the contract has to place a complaint within one year from the moment they noticed a problem or within five years from the moment they signed the contract.

The Japanese government's Consumer Affairs Agency (CAA) rationalizes the addition of this new provision by noting that there have been a high number of related consumer complaints and that this type of business belongs to the category of contracts 'forged under circumstances that make it impossible to reach a rational decision' (CAA 2018: 2). Two examples of prosecutable cases are brought forward to illustrate what they mean: 1) 'I can see spirits. An evil spirit has possessed you and your condition will worsen if you do not do anything. If you buy this rosary, the evil spirit will go away', 2) 'I can see the future. If you do not do anything, your child will run away from home in three years. If you take this vase (*tsubo*), your child's rebellious days will end, and they won't run away from home' (2).

Miyashita Shūichi, a scholar of the civic code and consumer-related laws, praises the inclusion of spiritual sales in the law as 'ground-breaking' (*kakkiteki*). He notes that the adjective 'serious', used twice in the new clause, ought to be interpreted qualitatively so that any scale of disadvantage or disorder experienced by the consumer can be considered fraudulent, not just what the lawyers think is 'serious' (Miyashita 2018: 40). Other scholars, who approach the issue from the perspective of business owners, have been less positive about the general changes that consumer laws have undergone recently, commenting that 'the new contract law is far more subjective in its assumptions about who is strong and who is weak in various types of transactions and allows the weak an escape from oppressive terms' (Jones 2017). The new provision regarding spiritual sales is an illustration of that change of tone. It is a welcome aid for the dozens of lawyers who have been dealing specifically with such cases since at least the end of the 1980s. But what are its broader implications for 'the spiritual' as an imagined alternative based on the hope offered by unverifiable claims?

The law now seems to require sellers of spiritual services to tone down their advice to clients and lower their prices, but it also seems to imply that fuelling a client's fears about their future and offering an 'alternative' (=the spiritual) is illegal, since it is impossible to provide proof to substantiate such warnings or to guarantee the realization of clients' hopes. This makes this type of service particularly prone to potential litigation. While the law only regulates *how* services are sold, the evidentiary basis for assessing the fairness of a transaction puts into question the legitimacy and even legality of these services altogether. After all, the spiritual business relies on the client trusting or believing that the practitioner can see, hear or feel things that the client cannot. If a plaintiff was to win a reimbursement based on a claim that a spiritual therapist's services breached the new provision of the contract law, would the court decision not effectively outlaw spiritual abilities?

Fictitious billings or fictitious selves?

Like every consumer, clients in the spiritual business are free to choose, but the moral decisions they make depend on how the value of what they buy is mirrored back to them by the seller. Spiritual 'fraud' therefore rests in unmet expectations, not in the rationality or soundness of the therapies themselves. As Mr Yogino put it, he knows that a client has been successfully hypnotized when the customer is satisfied. At the same time, a spiritual salon as a business is required to comply to certain ethical standards of common sense, fairness and integrity,[15] which effectively push the spiritual therapist to either guarantee the quality of their services or to make public disclaimers. This is, of course, by no means unique to Japan.

Charles McCrary (2018) shows that, since 1944, fortune tellers and other practitioners offering similar services in the United States have been subject in court to a 'sincerity test'. In the absence of a method to prove the truth of religious belief, this test seeks to prove that the person offering the services is sincere in holding that belief. McCrary notes that this test has been problematic from the outset: 'When one is being insincere, he or she knows the belief isn't true. But, doesn't then the law, at least implicitly, also assume it is false?' (270). Jeremy Patrick (2020) finds the same paradox in secular governance of religion by courts in other English-speaking countries, such as the UK, Canada and Australia. In an international comparison of cases of fraud involving fortune tellers and spiritual counsellors, Patrick observes that 'prohibitions on fortune-telling, when justified by the prevention of fraud, represent a legislative determination of epistemological truth: that there is no such thing as psychic or supernatural means to foretell the future' (139). Patrick does not dismiss the need for state intervention, even if paternalistic, in cases where lonely individuals are driven into bankruptcy through their involvement in the spiritual business. But he argues that 'routine fortune-telling should be unabashedly legal' (140).

It is very difficult to test the sincerity of a fortune teller or spiritual counsellor based on testimonies from people sharing the same beliefs. Although not expressly noted by Patrick, the enduring popularity of particular spiritual therapists relies on their distinction from other practitioners in the business (Chapter 5). Hence, it might be difficult to find someone willing to claim that they practice spiritual counselling in exactly the same way as a defendant and are therefore able to speak to the sincerity of a defendant's beliefs. Moreover, the idea that the defendant's sincerity in their beliefs should be tested to determine their innocence is predicated on the mistaken assumption that the customer 'really care[s] whether the promised supernatural or psychic powers are real' (Patrick 2020: 27). As I have pointed out throughout this book, clients do not need to believe in the existence of angels or guardian spirits to gain a certain emotional relief from speaking to spiritual therapists. Trying to gauge the sincerity of a therapist in what they do or believe in cannot account for the perceived quality of the service provided. Sincerity is interactional. Hence, clients seek legal advice when they start believing that the spiritual therapist or fortune teller did not frame the value of the services that the client paid for in an appropriate way.

In a discussion on the rise of 'sincerity' in the modern period, Webb Keane (2002) notes that the normative ideal of sincerity in speech is always attached to some kind of moral and interactive judgement: 'In being sincere, I am not only producing words that are transparent to my interior states but am producing them *for you* … sincerity is a certain kind of public accountability to others for one's words with reference to one's self' (75). More importantly, Keane finds a common form in the ways that Protestant Christianity and the projects of modernity and capitalism sought to shape the 'authentic' consumer subject, who is constantly accountable to others and to themself and, thus, morally responsible for making free and authentic choices: 'Protestantism and modernity (and, one might add, capitalism) *alike*, even *conjointly*, seek to abstract the subject from its material and social entanglements in the name of freedom and authenticity' (83).

Authenticity and the freedom of choice were ethical concerns central to the rise of consumer claims about the quality of services in the 1990s, which coincided with the rise of self-help groups that many sociologists of spirituality equated with the so-called rise of spirituality (Chapter 2). Many of those self-help groups have themselves served as claimants' groups. Koike (2009) links this phenomenon to the rise of 'therapy culture', noting the use of psychotherapeutic language (such as 'trauma') in such groups to explain the effects of damages inflicted on victims of harassers, rapists and violent religious organizations. Partly echoing Kitanaka's (2012) concept of socializing medicalization (Chapter 4), Koike (2009: 232) thereby points to the invasion of public and legal management further into the private lives of individuals, for whom spirituality functions as a sort of safety net against the rising number of traumatic experiences of what he perceives as the contemporary 'weak self'.

From K's 'lack of self-esteem' to Koike's 'weak self', good spirituality is always imagined as a world apart, a solution to a needy self that transcends society and the market. But what if the contemporary problem of 'fictitious billing' (=bad spirituality) is symbolic of the constant battle that spirituality, therapy and the market are engaged in to attribute a material and moral value to our fictitious selves?

Conclusion

Scholars critical of unequal and unproductive capitalist exchanges occurring in religious settings seem to share an 'impossible wish' that religion or spirituality 'be separated from the "rational" mistakes/crimes perpetrated by either the providers of religious services … or their client-members' (Gaitanidis 2020: 57). More specifically, academic critiques of spirituality and spiritual business have been framed in relation to nostalgic ideas of what religion, in essence, is or should be. But cyber-critiques launched by spirituality ditchers and legal cases involving 'fraudulent' spiritual sales demonstrate that spirituality in practice is more often judged in relation to ideals that cut across what are frequently conceptualized as distinct fields of religion and economy or 'the market'. These ideals – of fairness, integrity, sincerity, common sense – reflect the ethics of consumer protection laws as much as they do the hopes of believers like the blogger K that 'true' or 'real' spirituality can help people help themselves.

Although the grounds of their criticisms of the spiritual business are not the same, scholars, spirituality ditchers and lawyers all seem to share a perception of individuals who have become involved in this particular 'game' as losers – losers who have failed to understand what 'good' spirituality (or religion) is really about and who have been duped and exploited as a result of a weak self or lack of self-esteem. Yet, regardless of their predicaments, none of the nearly 100 people involved in some way in the spiritual business who I have met since 2008 ever admitted to having lost to the game of life. If there are any 'losers' in this business, these are only the 'losers' who misused or were produced by the uncertainties of the common form shared by spirituality and neoliberalism: 'Uncertainty is essential to religion, but also to markets and money' (Van der Veer 2014: 131). I concluded the previous chapter by suggesting that clients-turned-practitioners like Akiko Yamakawa, Ms Kawasaki and Ms Jinnai were seeking freedom within (rather than from) a precarious system. But I doubt that they would accept any pity from others. Like the 'heretical' stance of the spirituality ditchers, spirituality for these practitioners is about pertinacious dissent against being considered a 'loser'. Some may have shown bitterness towards more successful therapists and anger towards apparently inherent social inequalities, but none ever admitted defeat. To the contrary, they all believed that they knew what they were doing and why they may have failed in the past. Being true and sincere to oneself was, after all, what they valued the most. Borrowing from Durkheim's sociological theories on religion and modernity, scholars of the New Age and holistic spirituality have tended to interpret this disposition as a sacralization of the self or the individual. But, as we have seen, paying attention to the self and valuing sincerity, fairness and common sense are not unique features of spirituality or religion; they are ubiquitous requirements of capitalist consumer life.

Conclusion: Spirituality and the 'alternative'

'Spirituality' is one of those words that cannot be uttered without an affective undertone. In some cases, it might conjure a deep feeling of respect for the text or experience that it is being associated with. It often expresses the will of the individual to capture in a single word a kind of essence, an existential matter that is difficult to explain. When used in that positive sense, we might hear an accompanying tone of relief, for there is a high probability that spirituality was the term that the speaker had been looking for in the last few minutes of their conversation. It is one of those words that conveniently summarizes complex ideas without necessarily explaining them. In many cases, spirituality announces a turning point in the conversation; it marks a certain depth after which the dialogue, if it does not move on to something else, will probably only revolve around illustrations of that term.

In other contexts, it may be accompanied by a feeling of contemporaneity. Spirituality is a term with a strong sense of temporality as part of the catch-copy for a new product, the benefit promised by a new service, or the one aspect of our health that others have so far ignored. Signalling the 'alternative', the 'complementary' or simply everything that we had not thought about with our *materialist* minds, the spiritual in its adjectival form is a buzzword that guarantees a novelty in our lives that is supposed to simultaneously express our unchanging essence. In this sense, spirituality is, perhaps paradoxically, constantly 'new' and *en vogue*. It might therefore be uttered with feelings of scepticism, disdain, derision or even caution. Spirituality can be a fad, a consumer scam, a fake religion. Like many concepts subdued by their temporality, it can represent everything that is wrong *and* good with our times.

The most basic definitions of spirituality approach both the timeless and timely aspects of spirituality to account for its 'chameleon-like' features (Sheldrake 2012: 1). Spirituality means ..., but it originally meant .... Although I have discussed how scholars have chosen to define 'spirituality', I offer no new definition. My concern instead has been to connect this chameleon-like phenomenon back to the various surroundings that it reflects and to explore what spirituality in contemporary Japan *did* for those involved in the spirituality-making process, rather than what spirituality *is*. The brief appearance of a field of *supirichuariti* studies in Japan at the turn of the twenty-first century was, in this respect, a missed opportunity; in practice, it failed to challenge an institutional- or tradition-based idea of 'religion' by showing how so-called spiritual experiences were not reducible to novel expressions of a timeless popular and moral essence resurfacing in times of crisis. It is partly in response to this that I have contextualized these experiences without assuming that they are first and foremost 'spiritual'. My only assumption has been that the affective undertones and feeling of contemporaneity connected to this timeless–timely concept masked actual human hopes, fears, aspirations and experiences. In the end, if there is a central concept running through this book, it is alternativity, not spirituality. Alternativity is the thread that holds together the various concerns, interests and imaginaries that have fed the chameleon of contemporary spirituality.

Spirituality-making

The context in which spirituality became a scholarly sub-discipline in Japan was shaped by sociological debates about the perennial existence, salvific essence and public function of 'popular religion'. The convenient threshold that the Aum affair has offered for exegeses on contemporary religion has had less of an impact on how scholars think about religion than has previously been assumed. Indeed, the study of 'spirituality', lauded at the time as the next best 'thing', was plagued with pre-Aum assumptions. In seeking an alternative for the once highly popular field of the study of new religious movements, the editors of *A Sociology of Spirituality* pushed a frame that resembled that of the post-Second World War scholars who thought they had found an alternative to State Shintō in new religious groups. It was the study of precisely those groups that sociologists like Yumiyama Tatsuya considered worn out at the end of the twentieth century (Yumiyama 2015: 146); for them, spirituality became the new alternative. The point here is not that scholars have continued to talk about religion under the cover of spirituality, but that they have continued to look for (different) alternatives for religion, which in practice always fails to live up to what they hope it can do for them and for society. *Supirichuariti* was the latest in a line of scholarly alternatives. Others, such as the academic study of popular spiritual therapies (*minkan seishin ryōhō*; see Kurita, Tsukada and Yoshinaga 2019) or 'esotericism' (see Asprem and Strube 2021), have shown greater promise in rehabilitating 'alternative' scenarios and integrating them into the study of religion without always reiterating the hopes of those who research them.

Scholars are perhaps not to be blamed for thinking that something new was happening at the end of the twentieth century. From the 1980s, the media, and particularly the publishing industry, had been selling *seishin sekai* products as new alternatives to conservative, traditional and organized religion. But, as illustrated in the case of two significant publishers of New Age bestsellers, Jiyūsha and Tama Shuppan (Chapter 3), the editors of *seishin sekai* books did not consider them alternative to religion. For Jiyūsha's founder, Shirley MacLaine's *Out on a Limb* was the story of a successful woman; readers were supposed to glean from it insights into how to conduct their own lives. For Tama Shuppan's founder, his professed aim of 'ditching religion' did not mean that he was rejecting it for an alternative (just as the spirituality ditchers were not negating spirituality). We might even say that his establishment of a publishing house was a religious deed in itself. His engagements with religion had left him with a sense of 'mission' that made him part of a much longer history among publishers of the promotion of stories meant to discipline and cultivate (*shūyō*) younger generations. This, coupled with the market conditions of the 1970s and structure of the book market, was what propelled the continued growth in self-development literature. The 'alternative to religion'-spin that was attached to some of this self-development literature was a marketing strategy reinforced by specialized publishers, editors and, not least, translators like the Yamakawas, whose lives became enmeshed with the New Age literature that they introduced into the Japanese market.

For the spiritual therapists, who were deeply embedded in these discourses of alternativity at the start of the new millennium, the mainstream that they seemed to be challenging through their use of the adjective 'spiritual' was not religion at all. Spirituality was 'the alternative' *tout court* or the alternative of [fill the blank]. The adjective 'spiritual' carried the nuance that their services did not belong to the legalized practice of medicine, but also that they did not require any kind of 'religious' belief or commitment. If for some therapists this meant that the therapy sessions they offered were an alternative to biomedical treatments, their shared vocabulary with Rogerian counselling, which has been highly influential in Japan, effectively qualifies them as complementary and not alternative to mainstream treatments.

That spiritual therapy needs to be placed back into a therapeutic context becomes even clearer when we turn to consider its practice – that is, what the most representative individuals of the so-called spiritual boom have been doing over the last twenty years. Placing spiritual therapists within their therapeutic milieu allows us to understand the mainstream concerns and therapeutic culture that their practice emulates and shares (Chapter 4). Similarly it is only when we situate spiritual business within the broader economic and ethical frameworks of which it is a part (Chapters 5 and 6) that we see clearly how the alternative messages of hope attached to spirituality have concealed how much it is associated with the mainstream that it rejects.

Looping effects in the rise of spirituality

As I have emphasized throughout, this monograph is not intended as another critique of spirituality as 'fake alternativity' (just as it is not a critique of spirituality as 'corrupt religiosity'). It instead fleshes out the potential that alternative discourse surrounding religion *still* offers for questioning what we mean by 'religion' in a particular context. There is a subversive potential in the act of seriously engaging with discourse and practices thought of as 'alternative'. As the breadth of scholarly literature referred to in this monograph illustrates, the study of religion needs to extend beyond what we used to consider the subject of religious studies. This is not merely a reflection of the recent, loud calls for interdisciplinary or transdisciplinary research; it is a recognition that what we mean by 'religion' in a certain context is co-constituted by other domains in that same context, such as, in this monograph, therapy and precarity.

By drawing on Ian Hacking's notion of 'looping effect' to reconnect spirituality to its contexts, as I have done in Chapters 4–6, it is possible to harness the alternativity discursively associated with spirituality in order to challenge the status quo that spirituality claims but fails to counter. To reiterate Hacking's basic premise: 'People classified in a certain way tend to conform to or grow into the ways that they are described; but they also evolve in their own ways, so that the classifications and descriptions have to be constantly revised' (Hacking 1995: 21). One of Hacking's most important arguments is that looping effects are solidified by a common moralizing causation (13), that is, they need something to support them, often moral in nature, which presumes the ability to act and *mal*-act and assumes responsibilities.

Such a looping effect was responsible for the exponential increase of the market for alternative therapies, which was driven by both marketing strategies and media exegeses of *iyashi* products, and also by late-twentieth-century psychiatric and national warnings of a depression 'epidemic' (Chapter 4). The example of hypnotherapy shows that the common moralizing causation supporting this looping effect has been a contemporary ubiquitous emphasis on self-attention, which subdues and often effaces any explanation of malaise or disease that lies beyond the individual, and which burgeons into an assumed ability to change oneself and an accompanying responsibility to positively influence others. Therapists who felt cured by experiencing spiritual therapies and who then went on to open their own salons *acted on* this newfound ability, which they thought enabled them to teach clients how to express their ailments so as to maximize the effects of their therapeutic self.

Through another looping effect, we find that the instabilities of the spiritual business (re)produced the conditions of precarity that led individuals to enter it in the first place (Chapter 5). Supporting this looping effect were normative assumptions about women's abilities, desires, emotions and life stages, which have gendered the non-permanent workforce (Crawford 2021) as much as the domain of spiritual therapy itself. Again, my point is that the therapists I interviewed have *acted upon* genuine hopes for emancipation from the life of stress and exhaustion that accompanies the rush to increase margins, profits and good prospects, and from pressures at work and at home where relationships seem to be as much a burden as a source of support. But, in the end, they often fall back into similar difficulties. The spiritual business is a business after all, structured by the same entrepreneurial form as any other business. Globalized late capitalist culture and counter-cultural narratives feed on each other's alternativity, meeting at the nexus of an audience constantly needing healing and growth.

Operating within contemporary regimes of attention and gender (among others) spiritual therapists have been acting upon their therapeutic hopes as a result of the same moral imperatives upon which many others in the contemporary world base their judgements and act on a daily basis (to pay attention, to be a good woman, to be a good capitalist). That spiritual therapy is as regular a business as any other in the service industry becomes even more obvious when it comes to the criticism and moral judgement that it has attracted both from within its ranks and from the community of legal professionals involved in consumer fraud (Chapter 6). In both cases, we find criticisms that echo standard calls for more fair market practices. If 'spirituality ditchers' attack consumers of the *supirichuaru* for their naiveness in believing any spiritual entrepreneur's promises, 'spiritual sales' lawyers accuse the same entrepreneurs of breaching the Consumer Contract Act on the basis that they exaggerate the quality of their services.

The spiritual business reproduces the structure of the neoliberal market as much as its problems. A third looping effect thus appears in the form of the ethical standards of neoliberal economies. Contemporary spirituality, originally conceived as something intangible and beyond monetization, mirrors these standards back onto those perceived to have failed to 'properly' uphold them. The common moralizing causation supporting this loop, I suggest, consists of the constant battle that spirituality, therapy and the market seem to be engaged in to attribute a material and moral value to our fictitious selves. If self-attention has exaggerated our fictitious selves and if various precarities (economic, gendered, health-related) have pushed us into the monetization of those same 'selves' as our very last possessions, the so-called rise of spirituality has highlighted how much we still struggle to attach a moral value to the process of *self*-(re)making. Where does this all lead us?

Spirituality as an alternative imaginary

In the introduction, I made reference to Jonathan Z. Smith's (1990) statement about comparisons being triadic rather than dyadic processes. It is not X that is compared to Y, but X to Y with respect to Z. As an alternative imaginary, spirituality conjured different kinds of Zs for different people. For the *supirichuariti* scholars of Chapter 2, spirituality was the *alternative for* religion with respect to what religion (as an assumed good) can and should do for society. As reflected in the calls for wider public acknowledgement of the therapeutic functions of religion in post-3.11 Japan, the Z here was about the hope that religion continues to function as a bond-forming power that can save us from disasters, whether natural or social. This is why the notion of salvation was inherited by and placed at the core of spirituality studies. The Z of the publishers, editors and translators who we met in Chapter 3 may appear similar to that of *supirichuariti* scholars, but there is a radical difference in how the comparison is framed. Spirituality is presented as a choice, an *alternative to* religion, as one of two (or more) things that can do the same, that is, empower us to achieve individual happiness and success. Of course, not all choices are considered on an equal footing, but they are contained (understood, evaluated, experienced) within the same frame, which in this case is self-cultivation and self-development.

Paradoxically, the foremost representatives of spirituality, who seemed to be deeply embedded in this 'alternative' imaginary, do not make the same comparison as either publishers or scholars. Their Z is much more difficult to pin down. There is no question that many, if not all of the spiritual therapists whom I met have been aiming for self-development, but the *alternative of* spirituality that they promote exceeds the frame of what religion can do for them and for their clients. Their spirituality appeals to a larger audience that is assumed to be looking for alternative ways of life, alternative lifestyles, alternative worldviews and the like, from a position of precarity, exclusion and a need for healing. The Z here is varied and depends on the individual experiences of the therapists. Precisely what spirituality offers an alternative from differs according to what the therapist has identified as the central concern of their therapy, which in turn will depend in part on the concerns and interests of the client. This is why the practice of counselling is central; without listening to the client's Z, the spiritual therapist cannot properly do their job.

There are thus at least three distinct associations between alternativity and spirituality in contemporary Japan: It can be an *alternative for* religion, an *alternative to* religion or an *alternative of* [fill the blank]. The discourses framed around these three kinds of comparisons reveal a common foundation for their different Zs. This foundation imagines religion and its alternatives to have a 'therapeutic' function, in the widest possible sense of the term. Spirituality is therapeutic for the nation, therapeutic for society, therapeutic for the individual; it is therapeutic with transcendental or salvific, ameliorative or healing nuances. In short, spirituality is about therapeutic imaginations identified implicitly or explicitly with religion. Cross-pollination between the three kinds of comparisons is how the existence of a new epistemic field of 'spirituality' was imagined into being and then used as a label for what had become newly associated with it. Spirituality became a new phenomenon that was both explained and explainable by the existence of its homonymous media 'boom' and what came to be considered the new spiritual needs and wants of the (Japanese) people. The looping between and mutual reinforcement of the three – originally distinct – comparisons created the illusion of an actual 'alternative', which was then essentialized and (falsely) described as countercultural, counter-institutional and holistic.

In other words, the rider of alternativity seems to acquire value by erasing the concerns, hopes and interests that originally connected the alternative to its context and by building its own cross-contextual frame. While this monograph has focused on the rise of spirituality in contemporary Japan, I hypothesize that the same is likely true of the making of 'alternative' religion across different regional contexts and historical periods, and that the framework I have outlined here can therefore be productively applied more broadly. But what are the implications for the study of religion more generally of this kind of critical engagement with alternativity?

Studying the 'alternative'

A group of scholars, who primarily work on Japanese cases, have recently called for religious studies scholars to study the corporate form, arguing that, as a tool of analysis, it 'enables investigations of how realms often considered separately – politics and economics, state and corporations, law and religion, economics and religion, morality and finance, the private and the public – have always been intertwined' (McLaughlin et al. 2020: 696). This monograph highlights that another (alternative) tool of analysis through which this can be achieved is alternativity. By examining discourse and practice framed as alternative religion, this book has reconfirmed how religion, nation, law, corporations, economics, medicine *and* academia continue to be engaged in (re)forming the self, from the publishing industry's continuous fascination with shifting formats of *self*-cultivation literature and the counselling profession's emphasis on *self*-discovery, to the growing market centred on *self*-attention, the structural problems of a work ethic and entrepreneurial ideals that ask for *self*-emancipation, and the ethical standards of consumption that ask for *self*-restraint and for us to control the monetization of the fictitious *self*.

The lives, thoughts and practices of the scholars, therapists, clients, translators, editors and publishers who we have met in the pages of this book also provide some broader insights into how our constant search for alternatives influences our life choices and, by extent, broader societal shifts. In this sense, this monograph has perhaps been less about religion *per se*, than it has been about alternativity as an essential aspect of contemporary daily life. What remains to be considered in greater depth are the moral dilemmas and challenges that the creation of such alternatives and their accompanying fictitious selves entail. Scholars, for example, have been challenged by the moral judgements implicated in decisions to keep some phenomena and experiences out of the scope of the study of religion. Post-pluralism has attempted to attend to these dilemmas by reintegrating scenarios once excluded as alternative into a pluralist canvas, but it does not, as we have seen in this book, necessarily negate the value judgements of the old pluralist paradigm. It just rescues once rejected concepts (such as 'esoteric', 'occult' or 'spiritual'), and positively integrates them into a continuously growing pluralist picture that looks more interactive and dynamic but remains two-dimensional. We are aware now of the politics that led to the rejection of certain epistemic fields throughout history, but what should we do after we reintegrate such fields into our current knowledge of the world?

This monograph suggests that one answer to this question resides in exploring the role played by 'alternativity', the *point de capiton*, the upholstery button that holds things together by sustaining its supporting moralizing causations – and hope – through the illusion of a zero-mainstream and alternative fields. Alternativity is, I propose, a way into studying contemporary religion and society *tout court*. We might start with the reflexive question: What are the moral imperatives upon which our hopes for alternative analytical or descriptive concepts feed?

Japanese terms and names

Terms

aku	悪
atagama ga katai	頭が固い
ayashii	怪しい
bunkō	文庫
chōetsusei	超越性
chōetsu shikō	超越志向
chōnōryoku	超能力
chōrō	長老
datsu-supi	脱スピ
gaiken wo naosu	外見をなおす
genjitsuteki	現実的
fuhenteki	普遍的
fukashisei	不可視性
fukoku kyōhei	富国強兵
fukyō	布教
fushigi-na	不思議な
futsū no hito	普通の人
gendaijin	現代人
genshi shūkyō	原始宗教
gyaku kōsu	逆コース
hadō	波動
hakkōmoto	発行元
hamachatta	ハマちゃった
hiden	秘伝
hikiyose no hōsoku	引き寄せの法則
hisōsasei	非操作性
inochi	命
ippan shadan hōjin	一般社団法人
iryō	医療

itami	痛み
iyashi	癒し
jibun	自分
jikaku no jidai	自覚の時代
jiko-seisatsu	自己省察
jinsei-ron	人生論
jitsuzai-sei	実在性
jōikatasu	上意下達
josei-rashisa	女性らしさ
jūnansei	柔軟性
kaiun	開運
kakkiteki	画期的
kakuritsu	確立
kanpō	漢方
kanshinka suru	関心化する
katei kyōiku	家庭教育
keiken-teki	経験的
kentōkai	検討会
kōdō genri	行動原理
kokoro	心
kōnin shinrishi	公認心理士
kotodama	言霊
kyōso	教祖
kyōyōshugi	教養主義
kyūsai shūkyō	救済宗教
minkan fusha	民間巫者
minkan ryōhō	民間療法
minshū shūkyō	民衆宗教
naniwa-bushi	浪花節
nichijō-teki	日常的
nijū no jikansei	二重の時間性
ningen kojin	人間個人
ōbei	欧米
odoroodoroshii	おどろおどろしい
omajinai	おまじない
omikuji	おみくじ

puraido	プライド
rakugo	落語
reikan shōhō	霊感商法
reikon	霊魂
reinōryoku	霊能力
reisei	霊性
sagi	詐欺
seijiteki kachi no yūetsu	政治的価値の優越
seijitsusei	誠実性
seirei	精霊
seiri-teki	生理的
seishin ryōhō	精神療法
seishin sekai	精神世界
seitai	整体
seiyō	西洋
sekai kankyō	世界環境
shakyō	写経
shiatsu	指圧
shidōsha	指導者
shingai	侵害
shinja	信者
shinki	新奇
shinrei	心霊
shin-reisei undō	新霊性運動
shisō	思想
shōbai	商売
shōjo-rashisa	少女らしさ
shominteki	庶民的
shūdan rikōshugi	集団利功主義
shugenja	修験者
shūgō shūkyō	集合宗教
shūkyō	宗教
shūyō	修養
supirichuaru	スピリチュアル
supirichuariti	スピリチュアリティ
tamashii	魂

tayōna dentō no hibikiai	多様な伝統の響き合い
tebanasu	手放す
tōgō iryō	統合医療
toritsugi	取次
tsubo	壺
uchū no ki	宇宙の気
uranai	占い
yonaoshi	世直し

Names

Akiyama Makoto	秋山眞人
Anaguchi Keiko	穴口恵子
Araki Michio	荒木美智雄
Asano Makoto	浅野信
Bungeisha	文芸社
Daiwa-shobō	大和書房
Fukui Tatsū	福井達雨
Fukuoka Masanobu	福岡正信
Hakujusha	柏樹社
Harukawa Seisen	春川栖仙
Hirakawa Shuppan	平河出版
Hirauchi Yoshio	平内嘉雄
Honda Seiroku	本多静六
Hori Ichirō	堀一郎
Hotsuma Tsutaye	ホツマツタヱ
Ishii Takeshi	石井健資
Itō Hiroshi	伊東博
Itoga Kazuo	糸賀一雄
Jinbunshoin	人文書院
Kadokawa Haruki	角川春樹
Kan Enkichi	菅円吉
Kinjo Hiroshi	金城寛
Kobayashi Takakazu	小林敬和
Kōdansha	講談社
Koizumi Yoshihito	小泉義仁
Kubotera Toshiyuki	窪寺俊之

Masuda Masao	増田正雄
Matsunaga Taro	松永太郎
Matsushita Kōnosuke	松下幸之助
Mikasa-shobō	三笠書房
Misawa Yutaka	三澤豊
Miura Sekizō	三浦関造
Nanatsumori-shokan	七つ森書館
Nieda Rokusaburō	仁戸田六三郎
Nihonkyōbunsha	日本教文社
Nihon Shinrei Gakkai	日本心霊学会
Nirasawa Jun'ichiro	韮澤潤一郎
Noma Seiji	野間清治
Okada Kotama	岡田光玉
Oshikane Fujio	押鐘冨士雄
Ōtsuki Yoshihiko	大槻義彦
Sano Miyoko	佐野美代子
Satō Hatsume	佐藤初女
Seiunsha	星雲社
Sekai Mahikari Bunmei Kyōdan	世界真光文明教団
Sekiguchi Sakae	関口榮
Sunmark Shuppan	サンマーク出版
Tama Shuppan	たま出版
Taniguchi Masaharu	谷口雅春
Tenmyōdō Shinkyōkai	天明道心教会
Toda Yoshio	戸田義雄
Tōhan	トーハン
Tokuma-shoten	徳間書店
Tokuma Yasushi	徳間康快
Tomoda Fujio	友田不二男
Uchiyama Kōshō	内山興正
Umesao Tadao	梅棹忠夫
Uozumi Akira	魚住昭
Uritani Tsunanobu	瓜谷綱延
Uritani Yūkō	瓜谷侑広
Wada Shigemasa	和田重正

Yamakawa Akiko　　山川亜希子
Yamakawa Kōya　　山川紘矢
Yamazaki Yoshinobu　　山崎芳伸

Notes

Introduction

1. I am not suggesting that scholars using such qualifications necessarily abide by an essentialist idea of 'pure' religion versus the diluted version they seem to be describing. Yamanaka Hiroshi, who proposed the concept of 'light (*karui*) religion', makes it very clear that this is not what he is doing (Yamanaka 2020: 21), although there might have been a better term to express the same arguments without inviting the reader to assume an implicit contrast with 'heavy religion', whatever that might be. The problem is not essentialism; everyone is conscious of that today. It is the separate realm *(ryōiki)* in which scholars have to first place 'religion' if they want to develop arguments regarding its contemporary 'forms'.
2. The use of *reisei* to translate 'spirituality' has been attributed to the work of D. T. Suzuki (1972; originally published in Japanese in 1944), who discusses *reisei* as something of a universal essence that transcends the duality of mind and body, and whose institutionalized form gives birth to religion. This discussion can often be found in texts about the concept, especially those that follow Suzuki's idea that, despite its universal presence, it is possible to identify a typically 'Japanese' spirituality (Suzuki 1972). Andō Reiji (2020: 67–8) notes that Suzuki probably borrowed the compound *reisei* from the work of Guifeng Zongmi (780–841), the fifth patriarch of the Huayan (Kegon) school of Buddhism, known for his comparisons between Chan (Zen) and Huayan (Kegon). However, the first time he employed *reisei* for 'spirituality' was in his Japanese translations of Emanuel Swedenborg's work, most notably, *Heaven and Hell* (1785) (Yoshinaga 2014). Andō argues that Suzuki's understanding of 'spirituality' was influenced by the work of the American zoologist Edward Drinker Cope (1840–1897) who had claimed that the energy behind the evolution of species connects mind and matter and originates from a sort of universal and transcendental consciousness. Cope's texts on this idea (as well as Henri Bergson's texts on the *élan vital*, also inspired by Cope) and some of Suzuki's texts were published by Open Court Press (La Salle, Illinois), where Suzuki worked for eleven years as a translator and interpreter. For more on the influence of publishers and translators in the process of spirituality-making, see Chapter 3.
3. For a general introduction to the use of the word *okaruto* in this context, see Gaitanidis and Stein (2021).

4 While I have cited Shimazono's (2004) monograph here, note that the same content was previously published as a journal article (Shimazono 1999), which was itself a summary of the third chapter of an earlier book (Shimazono 1996). It then subsequently reappeared as the second chapter of a book published over a decade after its first appearance (Shimazono 2007), meaning that this particular argument remained among 'new publications' for at least a decade. Although beyond the scope of this book, this practice of constant reiteration (and sometimes partial updating) of essentially the same content through numerous publications spanning several years, if not decades, is a significant and so far understudied element in the propagation of ideas in academic discourse. I am not necessarily critical of it, but the way it works to allow certain ideas to survive and influence succeeding generations is worthy of further consideration.

5 Polls seldom define their terms and also create new meanings and sometimes new categories, a good example being the 'religious nones', a recently adopted label for those who do not identify with any religion. While this category is new, the numbers of people selecting 'none of the above' in survey questions about religious affiliation/identity (from which the term label 'religious nones' is derived') do not seem to have significantly changed in quantity since polling began at the start of the twentieth century (Wuthnow 2015: 200–1). To give another example of the typical ambiguity of polls, an editorial in the British edition of *The Guardian* on 28 March 2021, framed around the upcoming publication of the most recent census data, talked of a spiritual enigma: while the number of Britons identifying themselves as Christian was predicted to drop for the first time to below 50 per cent, the majority of the remainder of the population did not seem to be 'militantly secular' and the public's interest in Christian media culture appeared to be on the rise. The editor expressed puzzlement, asking: 'Could Britain become post-secular as well as post-Christian?' This of course depends on how terms such as 'secular' or even 'Christian' are defined and how those definitions are then fed back to a public being asked to identify with them.

6 The most common reason given for the impossible number of religious memberships is that the figures are reported by the religious organizations themselves, which are sometimes lax in tracking down changes and updating their lists. Also, people tend to check more than one box if they are asked to choose among several religious faiths.

7 On 15 December 1954, one the largest national newspapers, the *Yomiuri Shinbun*, published a roundtable discussion among five leading scholars of religion or philosophy (Kan Enkichi, Nieda Rokusaburō, Oguchi Iichi, Hori Ichirō, Toda Yoshio) about what they saw as the characteristics of Japanese religiosity (*shūkyō-shin*). Despite their differences in opinion regarding, for example, the importance

of Buddhism or Shinto in Japanese daily life, all seemed to agree that from a 'European' god-centred perspective the Japanese were non-religious.
8 The term 'religiousness' is often used to avoid the definitional issues associated with the term religion, but it has its own problems. Nagatani Chiyoko (2021: 16–17) distinguishes between at least three meanings: (1) religiousness as the essence of religion, the kind of instinct that makes people construct religion according to George Simmel, (2) religiousness as the degree or extent to which someone exhibits religious behaviour or holds religious knowledge; a quantifier found in psychological tests, (3) religiousness as religion-likeness, which is a nuance often found in post-1970s research on non-institutional religions. I use 'religiousness' in its second sense, although most spirituality scholars use it in its third sense.
9 Shimazono notes that he could confirm earlier usage of the word in periodicals published by a company affiliated with the new religious movement Agonshū. For more on this group, see Baffelli and Reader (2018).
10 One should not assume that these three disciplinary fields adopted *supirichuariti* independently. There must have been significant exchanges, especially in the following direction: transpersonal psychology→hospice care→sociology of religion. In his explanations of the meaning of *supirichuariti*, Shimazono, for example, often refers to the writings of Kubotera Toshiyuki, a chaplain of the spiritual care programme at Yodogawa Christian Hospital (Shimazono and Graf 2012: 478–9).
11 Here, one may find parallels with the English terms psychic and psychical, which 'possess elite intellectual roots and were born in the professional academy' (Kripal 2010: 8) of late-nineteenth-century England and America.
12 To understand and analyse the role of media in the 'rise of spirituality' without falling into the trap of looking for (and, by default, homogenizing) spiritual narratives across different platforms, it is necessary to examine the distinct features of different forms of media and how audiences engage with them in what are often very different ways. In this monograph, I focus on the influences of the structure of the book market and translation on the rise of the *seishin sekai* literature that inspired the spiritual therapists who I interviewed. While it is beyond the scope of this monograph to expand my analysis beyond printed matter, see Gaitanidis (forthcoming) for a discussion on paranormal television programmes in Japan that examines the entanglements between the particular medium of television and religion. There, I link the popularity of these programmes, including Ehara Hiroyuki's televised appearances, to the changing structures of television production and to shifts in relations between the small screen and its audiences at the turn of the twentieth-first century.
13 Reflecting the tendency towards triads, in his critique of McCutcheon, Fong calls for a third, psychoanalytic approach that lies outside the constructionist/essentialist

divide and ties experiences 'back to more everyday occurrences and their relation to their individual histories' (Fong 2014: 1138).

1 Spiritual therapists

1. I provide an example of this scholarly accusation that spirituality is 'superficial' towards the end of Chapter 2.
2. The association is still listed as a member group on shintotaikyo.org (accessed 25 March 2021).
3. On aura reading and aura photography, see Gaitanidis (2019).
4. For a brief overview of the development of the anthropology of religion in Japan, see Tanaka (2021). For a critical analysis of studies of shamanism in Japan see Gaitanidis and Murakami (2014).
5. Perhaps the 'royal touch' scene in Macbeth, act IV, Scene 3 remains the most famous historical example.
6. *Setai* (lit: tuning the body) is a form of bone manipulation that originated in the 1920s from a mixture of Chinese and American chiropractic theories and techniques regarding the 'correct' position of the body. On the history of *seitai*, see Tanojiri (2019).
7. Miura Sekizō (1883–1960) was a translator of English modern metaphysical literature through which he popularized modern yoga and the ideas of the Theosophical Society in Japan. Yoshinaga (2010) considers him to have been a source of inspiration for many authors and fervent followers of the *seishin sekai*.
8. The 'law of attraction' refers to the idea that positive thoughts attract those things about which we have positive thoughts. It originates in the nineteenth century New Thought movement (Horowitz 2014) but became widely popular again at the start of the twenty-first century with the publication of Rhonda Byrne's *The Secret*.
9. Indicatively, popular CAM treatments were *a priori* targeting physical ailments: one hundred visited a judo therapist, eighty-four an acupuncture/moxibustion practitioner, sixty-three a yoga instructor, thirty-three a chiropractor, twenty-nine an aromatherapist and two a homeopathist. The number of survey participants who said that they had not visited any type of health service during the preceding twelve months was 1,030.
10. At the time of writing, the list had last been updated on 16 December 2019. See https://jupa.jp/category2/ (accessed 1 August 2021).
11. Counselling had been practiced in Japanese schools on an informal and *ad hoc* basis since the 1950s, when teachers were introduced to the counselling theories of Carl Rogers (Kanazawa 2007).

12 Despite the introduction of national certification, the scientific quality of psychological counselling might not significantly change in the near future. The recommended curriculum has been criticized for being too accommodating to non-evidence-based counselling techniques, such as the Rorschach test (Harada 2019). Moreover, to take the MHLW examination it is necessary to have first successfully completed an undergraduate or postgraduate course in a related field, whereas a spiritual counsellor certificate can be obtained from the Spiritual Master Academy for the price of 600,000 yen and a maximum of three months of study. See https://japan-spiritual.jp/shikaku/ (accessed 1 August 2021).

13 A feasibility study on the integration of medical psychologists and clinical psychologists into one national certification programme was conducted, but the proposal was suspended in 2005 due to opposition from medical associations (Yagi 2008: 151).

14 A relatively recent review of coaching in Japan suggests an intriguing link to Carlos Ghosn, the former Chairman and CEO of Nissan who, after being charged with financial fraud, caused an international incident when he fled from Japan to Lebanon on 30 December 2019 while released on bail (Greimel and Sposato 2021). Nishigaki Etsuyo claims that Ghosn helped introduce coaching into Japan's corporate culture as a type of staff training in around the year 2000 while conducting restructuring within Nissan (Nishigaki 2018: 539).

15 Itō was a recipient of the Government Appropriation for Relief in Occupied Areas (GARIOA) Fund scholarship from the Supreme Commander for the Allied Powers' Institute for Educational Leadership (IFEL), which Brian J. McVeigh (2017: 174) credits with playing a role in disseminating post-war psychology in Japan. Indeed, between 1949 (when GARIOA started) and the early 1990s, clinical psychology was the most popular field among Japanese using GARIOA and later the Fullbright scheme to study in the United States; at least 140 psychologists in Japan were supported by these American scholarship programmes during this period (Fumino 1997: 354).

2 Spiritual academia

1 My account here is based on a summary of his presentation subsequently published in the JASRS' journal *Religion and Society*. See Terada (2015: 130–1).
2 The Japanese character used is 代わる.
3 In his paper for the same panel, Tsukada Hotaka demonstrates that 83 per cent of papers published in *Religion and Society* dealt with post-war phenomena. For a summary of his paper see Tsukada (2015).

4 This paper is largely based on a chapter originally written in Japanese (Horie 2007), which begins with a review of the literature that employs the concept of *supirichuariti*, which is itself based on an earlier publication (Horie 2003).

5 The *Nihon Supirichuarisuto Kyōkai* was founded in 1959 by restarting the Tokyo Spiritualist Association (*Tokyo Shinrei Kagaku Kyōkai*), originally opened in 1930 as the executive branch of the Society for Scientific Research on Spiritual Phenomena (*Shinrei Kagaku Kenkyūkai*), established by the 'father of Japanese spiritualism', Asano Wasaburō (1874–1937) in 1922 (for more on Wasaburō in English, see Hardacre 1998). The *Nihon Supirichuarisuto Kyōkai* is not to be confused with either the Spiritualism Association of Japan (*Nihon Supirichuarizumu Kyōkai*) founded by Ehara Hiroyuki in 2011 or the Japan Psychic Science Association (*Nihon Shinrei Kagaku Kyōkai*), another offshoot of Wasaburō's association, founded in 1946. For more on spiritualist associations in the postwar period, see Tsushima (1999).

6 Lifespace (a company offering self-development seminars) and Pana Wave (a new religious movement) were both involved in incidents that attracted media attention. The founder and leader of Lifespace, Takahashi Kōji (1938–2015), was sentenced to prison for the murder of 66-year-old Shinichi Kobayashi, whose mummified body was found at a hotel in Chiba prefecture in November 1999. That July, Kobayashi, who had suffered a cerebral haemorrhage, had been taken out of hospital and brought by his son to be cured by Takahashi. Despite his failure to treat Kobayashi, who died one day after leaving the hospital, for several weeks Takahashi had continued to claim that Kobayashi remained alive. For more on this case, see Koike (2004). Pana Wave was a small religious movement, whose members had toured Japan from April to May 2003 to look for a location free from the electromagnetic radiation that they believed was harming people and the environment. They attracted media attention when they refused to move their white vans from an area where they had been parked for several months. What Dorman (2005) calls a 'moral panic' ensued, stemming from public perception of the similarities between the group and Aum Shinrikyō, as well as the police's willingness to show that (this time) they were going to react quickly. A raid of the group's facilities led to nothing more than charges for possession of three falsely registered vehicles, and the media soon lost interest. See Dorman (2005).

7 In an earlier publication, Shimazono (1997: 175, 182) explains that these youth had been looking for a transcendence (*chōetsu shikō*) that the this-worldliness of Japanese religiosity had been unable to offer; this had eventually led them to reject the world around them.

8 Here, I have been inspired by a similar fallacy observed by Egil Asprem (2014: 18) in the use of the concept of 'esotericism'.

9 As mentioned in the Introduction, the concept has of course been used and possibly first drew attention in other scholarly fields, but since this monograph is focused on the study of religion, I discuss academic debates within that discipline only.
10 The collection edited by Kashio (2002) is mostly based on presentations given at these workshops.
11 Yoshinaga (1998: 39) emphasizes that Japan's 1960s counter-culture may not have been a counter-culture of the North American kind, but simply the substitution of a culture of economic ethos for a culture that started looking inward.
12 For Shimazono's earlier review of Araki's *Shūkyō no sōzō*, see Shimazono 1989.
13 Fujiwara Satoko (2021: 143) notes that Araki Michio was known as 'a wholehearted Eliadean', but also points out that many scholars of his generation would probably not have called themselves phenomenologists: 'These scholars are not necessarily "religionists" or apologists for the sui generis nature of religion, even though they generally sympathize with religions … [They] were primarily interested in what human beings are; as a result, they could be called "human essentialists" rather than "religious essentialists". The same can probably be said of many of the *supirichuariti* scholars, although Fujiwara does not discuss this.
14 Euro-America (*ōbei*) has become something of a replacement for the 'West' (*seiyō*) in scholarly writings, but remains strongly limited to examples from the United States or the UK. It is thus fair to say that this replacement has done nothing to resolve the problematic use of vague world dichotomies.
15 Bellah had come across the term 'American Shinto' in Harvey Cox's (1965) treatise on American secularization, *The Secular City*, but it was originally used by Lutheran pastor and historian Martin E. Marty to talk of the mid-twentieth-century American 'religion-in-general' (Gaston 2019: 210).
16 Shimazono's engagement with Yasumaru's work is extensive. For a short summary of his critique of Yasumaru's ideas in English, see Shimazono (2004): 42–5.
17 Horie is alluding here to Bellah's original argument that 'neither religious man nor the structure of man's ultimate religious situation evolves, then, but rather religion as symbol system' (Bellah 1964: 359).
18 This book is based on Horie's doctoral dissertation, submitted at the University of Tokyo, with Shimazono Susumu as his principal examiner.
19 There is an interesting parallel between how Yasumaru, Shimazono and others conceptualized 'the popular' that they imagined to be supporting popular religion and providing resources for world transformation and renewal, and Habermas's distinction between the level of life-world, where human beings communicate on a taken-for-granted basis and reproduce social institutions and practices, and the level of social system, which is dominated by money and power.

3 Print spirituality

1 'Ms Uehara' is a pseudonym.
2 Shimazono Susumu's argument for the rise of a new spirituality culture relies mostly on 'the spiritual intellectuals' (Shimazono 1993), a term he uses to refer to eight or nine key popular authors and academics who from the 1970s to the start of the 1980s 'embodied and produced an early form of what nowadays in Japan is called "spirituality"' (Shimazono and Graf 2012: 464). Exactly who is defined as belonging to this category varies among scholars writing on the topic and has changed as Shimazono and other researchers expanded it to identify what they saw as a common trend in modern Japanese intellectual history (Shimazono 1992, 2007; Prohl 2000; Gebhardt 2001, 2013). I do not engage in debates about these figures or delve into their ideas in this book. While they have undoubtedly produced influential works, the spiritual therapists with whom I conversed almost always referred to North American New Age authors when asked about the ideas that had influenced their practice; those who read Japanese authors mostly mentioned Ehara's publications. While these tendencies partly reflect the timing of my fieldwork, I think they also illustrate the degree to which scholarly interpretations of literary phenomena do not always take into account readerships beyond elite intellectual circles. Moreover, as I go on to discuss, my primary concern in this chapter is to shift the focus away from the authors of literature that came to be labelled as spiritual (on whom there is already a substantial body of research) towards the role of actors within the publishing industry in spirituality-making.
3 See the category occultism/psychology on the publisher's website: http://www.hirakawa-shuppan.co.jp/pickup/index.html?action=genre&genre=psychology (accessed 7 December 2020).
4 I return to a discussion of this process of creative translation in my discussion on the Yamakawas in the second part of this chapter.
5 Although it is beyond the objectives of this book, there is a significant need for further research on the development of cheap didactic literature that aimed to teach people to adapt to the fast-changing capitalist times and on its nineteenth-century globalization (Hsiung 2018).
6 This did not prevent New Thought from having influence on the religious front. It is well known that Taniguchi Masaharu (1893–1985), who founded the religious group Seichō no Ie in 1930, was influenced by New Thought literature (Ono 1995).
7 Members of the 'elite' who managed to pass through this narrow corridor to success had their own 'self-cultivation' boom during the same period, which scholars have called *kyōyōshugi* (lit. 'culturism'). This boom was almost exclusively supported by another famous publisher, Iwanami-shoten (Ōmi 2020: 43).

8   His most popular monograph, published in 1967, is *Michi wo hiraku: Hibi no kotoba*, a collection of essays that had previously appeared in the magazine PHP. It has sold more than 5 million copies and was translated into English and published by McGraw Hill in 2010 as *The Path: Find Fulfillment through Prosperity from Japan's Father of Management*.

9   *Publishing News* (*Shuppan Nyūsu*) was a periodical informing the public of the trends of the publishing industry every ten days. It was printed for the final time in March 2019, when the company behind it closed its doors, blaming the constant decline of the print market in Japan (since 1988 for books and since 1995 for magazines) (Katō 2018).

10 There was a similar stimulation of paperback sales in the American publishing market in the late 1960s and 1970s due to the entry of mall store chains into the book market (Thompson 2012: 36).

11 There are some interesting cross references within the system that highlight the arbitrariness of this division between religion and not-religion. For example, the latest version of the NDC (Mori 2014), suggests to users who consult cat. 148 (divination) to also check the Shinto festivals sub-cat. 176.8 dedicated to fortune lots (*omikuji*) and spells (*omajinai*). Similarly, cat. 147 is linked to cat. 387, 'popular beliefs', while sub-cat. 147.3 'automating writing / spirit possession' is linked to 163.9, 'shamanism'. There are also interesting divisions, such as the note at the end of all sub-categories of 147 that books related to UFOs could alternatively be collected under 440.9, which is a separate label for UFOs created under 440, 'astronomy and space sciences'. In another note, under the cat. 169 'other religions, new religions', Sōka Gakkai-related entries are specifically singled out as needing to be categorized under 188.98, a sub-category of 188.9, Nichiren Buddhism.

12 Librarians in Japan are free to classify their own books using the NDC categories, but since they generally start by consulting an online database where they can see how other libraries have categorized the same books, they tend to make their classifications based on that information and on how the book has been classified in systems other than the NDC. According to a librarian at my institution, who I thank for spending thirty minutes explaining her work, no new categories can be suggested. If a librarian feels that a book does not fit under an existing label, they can suggest on the system alternatives to how the majority of other libraries may have classified it. The librarian also mentioned that library users occasionally ask for NDC classification changes based on their expertise, although this remains rare.

13 The fortune-telling industry has possibly benefitted the most from internet technologies and the digitalization of information, with an exponential growth observed in web-based services (Martin 2009). Its lack of growth as a book industry market is also indicative of the *supirichuaru* not necessarily covering everything that normative and secularist notions of 'superstition' or 'quasi-religion' tend to include.

14 See notes 30, 32, 33.
15 On Honda Seiroku's influence on modern Japanese shrine scenery see Imaizumi (2013: 34); Rots (2017a: 174).
16 https://nendai-ryuukou.com/article/025.html (accessed 12 November 2020).
17 Most book and convenience stores in Japan work with one of two *toritsugi*: Tōhan or Nippon Shuppan Hanbai.
18 This system has also impacted the speed of growth of the digital print market. Since publishers can rely on the established networks and efficient distribution systems of the *toritsugi*, the book's design, acquirement of ISBN and other type of data are only completed a few days before it goes on sale. This means that the majority of stores cannot advertise upcoming titles, and, even more importantly in today's e-book market, cannot sell digital prints of the book before it comes out on paper (Hoshino 2012: 240).
19 Kiyota (2019) also mentions the introduction of a consumption tax of 3 per cent in 1987 as another possible cause (this was gradually increased to reach 10 per cent in 2019).
20 Makino (2012: 200) offers an example with the concept of 'power' (*chikara*) in self-help books, based on a published interview with a magazine editor.
21 Anka claims to have had an encounter with a UFO in 1973, which launched him into reading about fringe science and the New Age, before attending a channeling school that led him to start communicating with Bashar. See https://www.bashar.org/about-darryl/ (accessed 14 December 2018).
22 http://www.seishin-sekai.com/category3/category3-1/ (accessed 14 December 2020).
23 See the company's profile: http://jiyusha.co.jp/top/ (accessed 5 November 2020).
24 See http://jiyusha.co.jp/top/地湧社設立趣意書より (accessed 5 November 2020).
25 While still at Hakujusha, Masuda worked as the editor on the first edition of Fukuoka Masanobu (1913–2008)'s *Shizen Nōhō: Wara Ippon no Kakumei*, which later became one of the most famous texts of the alternative food movement, translated into at least twenty-seven languages, including English (Fukuoka 1978). For an interview with Masuda on the reasons for establishing his publishing house, including his views on the role of women see Chiwaki no Mori (2015a).
26 Uritani mentions that the first religion he joined had twenty-one provisions for conducting one's life and that originally the headquarters were in Shimizu city in Shizuoka, but they moved to the surroundings of Habikino-city, in Osaka, in around 1953 (Uritani 1990: 57–8). Both pieces of information crosscheck perfectly against the teachings and history of P. L. Kyōdan.
27 Details that give the identity of the organization away include his description of the founder as a 'Master O', who at 05.00 am, on 27 November 1959, after five days of high fever, received a divine revelation (Uritani 1990: 83); he also writes that the group took the name Sekai XXXXX Bunmei Kyōdan (89).

28 This echoes my detailed critique of such -izations of religion in Chapter 1.
29 One of Tama Shuppan's long-sellers has been the Japanese translation of Gina Cerminara's *Many Mansions* (New York: Sloane, 1950), a hagiography of Edgar Cayce, which announces the late twentieth-century renewed interest in reincarnation and hypnotherapy (Bender 2010: 131 and Chapter 4).
30 http://www2.gol.com/users/angel/index.htm (accessed 17 December 2020).
31 *Out on a Limb* (1983, trans. 1986), *Dancing in the Light* (1986, trans. 1987), *It's All in the Playing* (1987, trans. 1988), *Don't Fall Off the Mountain* (1975, trans. 1989), *Going Within: A Guide to Inner Transformation* (1990, trans. 1990), *Dance While You Can* (1991, trans. 1992), *The Camino: A Journey of the Spirit* (2000, trans. 2001), *Out on a Leash: Exploring the Nature of Reality and Love* (2003, trans. 2004). Except for the last two, all translations were originally published by Jiyūsha and five have been published in pocketsize editions by Kadokawa-shoten.
32 *Many Lives, Many Masters* (1988, trans. 1991), *Through Time into Healing* (1992, trans. 1997), *Only Love Is Real: A Story of Soulmates Reunited* (1997, trans. 1999), *Messages from the Masters: Tapping into the Power of Love* (2001, trans. 2001, paperback with different title 2004), *Meditation: Achieving Inner Peace and Tranquility in Your Life* (2002, trans. 2007), *Mirrors of Time: Using Regression for Physical, Emotional, and Spiritual Healing* (2002, trans. 2006), *Eliminating Stress, Finding Inner Peace* (2003, trans. 2005), *Same Soul, Many Bodies* (2005, trans. 2005), *Miracles Happen: The Transformational Healing Power of Past Life Memories* (2012, trans. 2012, pocket edition 2015). All Japanese editions have been published by PHP Kenkyūsho.
33 *The Pilgrimage* (1987, trans. 1995 published by Jiyūsha, pocket edition 1998 by Kadokawa-shoten), *The Alchemist* (1988, trans. 1994, pocket edition 1997, with illustrations 2001, twentieth anniversary edition 2014; first translation published by Jiyūsha, all others by Kadokawa-shoten), *The Valkyries* (1992, trans. 2013 published by Kadokawa-shoten), *By the River Piedra I Sat Down and Wept* (1994, trans. 1997 published by Jiyūsha, pocket edition 2000 by Kadokawa-shoten), *The Fifth Mountain* (1996, trans. 1998, pocket edition 2001, all Japanese editions published by Kadokawa-shoten), *The Magical Moment* (2013, trans. 2014 published by Diamond-sha).
34 *The Celestine Prophecy* (1993, trans. 1994, pocket edition 1996), *The Celestine Prophecy: An Experiential Guide* (1995, trans. 1995, new edition with different title 1999), *The Celestine Prophecy: A Pocket Guide to the Nine Insights* (1996, trans. 1996), *The Tenth Insight: Holding the Vision* (1996, trans. 1996, pocket edition 1997, pocket guide 1997), *The Tenth Insight: Holding the Vision: An Experiential Guide* (1996, trans. 1997, pocket edition 2011), *The Celestine Vision: Living the New Spiritual Awareness* (1997, trans. 1998, pocket edition 2001), *The Secret of Shambhala: In Search of the Eleventh Insight* (1999, trans. 2001), *God and the*

Evolving Universe: The Next Step in Personal Evolution (2002, trans. 2004), *The Twelfth Insight: The Hour of Decision* (2011, trans. 2011). All Japanese editions have been published by Kadokawa-shoten.

35 *The Secret* (2006, trans. 2007), *The Power* (2010, trans. 2011), *The Magic* (2012, trans. 2013), *The Secret Daily Teachings* (2013, trans. 2014). All Japanese editions have been published by Kadokawa-shoten.

36 *Flight into Freedom* (1988, trans. 1994); the translation was published by Nipponkyōbunsha.

37 *Joy* (2004, trans. 2013), *Courage* (1999, trans. 2013), *Intuition* (2001, trans. 2016), and *Creativity* (1999, trans. 2017). All Japanese editions have been published by Kadokawa-shoten.

38 *Bibs* (2009, trans. 2011); the translation was published by PHP Kenkyūsho.

39 This observation is based on an analysis of the yearly catalogues of publications compiled between 1994 and 2007 by one of the few dedicated *seishin sekai* bookstores in Japan, Book Club Kai (https://www.bookclubkai.jp/).

40 Albeit without the normative gloss that Faure (1993) gives to the term 'Suzuki effect'.

41 It is hard to believe that Kōya paid 75,000 yen (half of his salary at the time) to participate in a three-day seminar without confirming its purpose, as he claims (Yamakawa, Yamakawa and Kokusai 2015: 40). This claim, and the fact that most of the Yamakawas' accounts describe this seminar as 'strange' (*kimyō-na*), are perhaps a way to distance themselves from the problems with which these seminars later became associated in Japan. Kōya claims that it was not the ideas of the seminar that were problematic but the management style, which 'was exactly the same as a new religion' (39). They asked for exorbitant fees (the course at the next level up cost 280,000 yen at the time) and forced people who wanted to continue their classes to find new participants. See note 6 in Chapter 2 on the incident associated with Life Space, a company established by a former student of Life Dynamics.

42 Trainers in these seminars were known to be quite strict (some say on purpose) with complaints varying from bullying to physical violence. For a first-person account of a trainer humiliating participants unable to find a partner, see Futazawa and Shimada [1991] 2009: 29–30.

43 For an interview that the Yamakawas gave about Jiyūsha, see https://www.youtube.com/watch?v=coQVf3CV2Uc (accessed 15 December 2020).

44 The Yamakawas would later complain that at that time there was only one other publisher who would have accepted their offer: Tama Shuppan (Yamakawa, Yamakawa and Kokusai 2015: 51).

45 Asano Makoto (b.1954) is the son of an educator in the Non-Church Movement, who founded the International Association of the New Age (later renamed Asano Research Institute) in 1985. He has been instrumental in introducing to Japan the

thought and practice of the American seer Paul Solomon (1939–1994). Asano claims to have conducted more than 16,000 readings and his son, Hikari, still conducts private hourly sessions for 5,000 yen. See https://asanosouken.co/ari/pg199.html (accessed 24 November 2020). Paul Solomon has been compared to Edgar Cayce, perhaps explaining why many of Asano's books have been published with Tama Shuppan.

46 Akiko even claims to have been possessed by the spirit of Jesus Christ, from whom she continued to receive messages later in her life.

4 Alternative therapies in the age of attention

1 Melody came into prominence from 1991 onwards through her publication of a series of nine books titled *Love Is in the Earth*, in which she developed what she called 'crystal healing'. By the start of the new millennium, her workshops in the United States and Canada were already forming the first generation of crystal healing teachers, with two levels of certification; see https://taomchi.com/. According to a post on Ms Kawasaki's blog, Melody passed away in 2019.
2 According to Lindsey B. Yates (2016), Coué may have been inspired by Eastern Orthodox Christian contemplative prayers (Hesychasm) dating back to at least the fourteenth century.
3 Both the Japan Hypno-management Association and Aura Reiki Academy had already disappeared or would do so shortly after I interviewed Ms Kawasaki in 2009, while the Japan Spiritual Association reappeared in 2010 under new management and with a different curriculum. Aside from organizations like these ones, courses were also offered by individuals who later switched to other endeavours. As I will discuss in the next chapter, the characteristic precariousness of the spiritual business is also characteristic of the society in which the therapists live.
4 According to Fujioka, the first upsurge seems to have mostly been driven by a rising consciousness about daily hygiene and, for example, the dangers of smoking tobacco (Fujioka 2015: 238).
5 The first SSRI (fluvoxamine) was introduced in May 1999; paroxetine was released one year later. Various reasons are suggested for such a delay, including the tendency of Japanese psychiatrists to prescribe anti-anxiety drugs instead of anti-depressants (Kirmayer 2004) and the protectionism of the Japanese pharmaceutical market which, until recently, made it difficult for non-Japanese drugs to enter (Umemura 2011).
6 The very first issue, published in 1997, is not available. However, the catalogue published in 1999 covered the years 1998 and 1999 and is described by the editors as being the same as the one published in 1997, with the addition of five healers and

seventeen techniques (TAG 1999: 3). I have therefore used the 1999 catalogue as my starting point.
7 These catalogues titled *Kokoro to karada o iyasu serapii ōru gaido* (*Therapy All Guide to Heal Mind and Body*) were published by BAB Japan in Tokyo. Where I cite from a particular volume, I use the acronym TAG and provide the year and page number(s) of the volume in brackets.
8 The dialogue reproduced here is based on notes that I took immediately after the session.
9 https://sites.google.com/site/hanstendamhsi/about-hans- (accessed 17 February 2022).
10 The other hypnotherapist often mentioned by my interviewees was Trisha Caetano (also Amsterdam-based), a self-proclaimed 'pioneer in integration and regression therapies' (https://www.trishacaetano.com/; accessed 18 November 2021) who also runs courses in Japan.
11 Weiss (1988) recounts that, when in a hypnotic state, one of his patients (Catherine) started remembering traumatic experiences of previous lives and how these explained her current anxiety problems. Since then, other hypnotherapists have appeared with their own regression methods, including Hans Tendam and Trisha Caetano.

5 Precarities in the spiritual business

1 That there is a bifurcation between religion and economy in scholarly studies of spirituality was originally suggested by Taira (2009) and later repeated, in Japanese, by Koike (2013), but their analyses do not extend such polarization to a broader critique of research on religion and economy.
2 Hanegraaff ([1996] 1998: 17) had previously argued that such 'battering', as Heelas qualifies this criticism, caused the term 'New Age' to lose its appeal as 'many people no longer want[ed] to be associated with it'.
3 On recalling her marriage, Ms Jinnai narrated a visit to a *reinōsha* with her mother who did not agree with her daughter's decision. But the *reinōsha*'s advice was that if Ms Jinnai had made up her mind no one should oppose her. 'A good *reinōsha*', she explained, 'is like a good spiritual therapist. They would give you a choice between A and B but would let you decide by yourself. Most *reinōsha* however are dangerous, because they push you to take A over B or B over A. They do not let you find *your* answer.' This reflects the criticism and 'othering' of *reinōsha* among spiritual therapists discussed in Chapter 1.
4 For a more detailed description of the workings of setting up a spiritual therapy salon, see Gaitanidis (2011).

5 See https://www.meti.go.jp/press/2021/06/20210630004/20210630004.html (accessed 13 September 2021).
6 See https://survey.gov-online.go.jp/index-ko.html (accessed 10 September 2021).
7 Based on statistical data, Roemer (2009: 304) argues that, in Japan, 'women are much more likely than men to claim affiliation with new religions or Christianity'.
8 For a more extended discussion on the simultaneous legitimization and subversion of gender norms afforded by new or alternative religious movements see Gaitanidis (2012b): 269–73, on which this paragraph draws.
9 For an extended discussion of this argument see Gaitanidis (2012b): 276–80, on which this and the following two paragraphs draw.
10 See https://www.el-aura.com/about/ (accessed 15 September 2021).
11 In the latest edition of this textbook, Sugimoto (2021: 176) has revised the wording and now states that, in regards to the entrance of women to the job market: 'From a life-cycling perspective, women must generally make decisions at three different times; at marriage, following childbirth, and when their child commences schooling.'
12 This is a point I have previously rehearsed in a discussion of the subversive potential of spiritual therapies, where I use some of the same empirical examples that I draw on in this and the next paragraph. See Gaitanidis (2012b): 280–4.
13 Here I have borrowed from Linda Woodhead's (2007: 576) analysis of religion and gender in contemporary western societies, specifically her discussion on holistic therapies as a primarily 'questing' rather than counter-cultural type of religion, since they allow women to construct modes of selfhood that help them to cope with rather than change 'the contradictions and costs of the unequal distribution of power and unpaid care work' (Gaitanidis 2012b: 271–2).

6 Spirituality on trial

1 In this chapter, I will refer to several internet blogs by individuals who criticize the spiritual business. Some of them, like Flower Garden's, are very personal and only followed by what one can assume are people who know their authors. Flower Garden's blog has ten followers. Others are more popular (see endnotes 3 and 5), but it is difficult to gauge the extent of their influence based on these numbers alone. What interests me most here is how these 'insiders' frame their critique of *supirichuariti*.
2 This section draws on materials previously published in Gaitanidis (2020).
3 I traced these blog posts through the popular Japanese blog platform *ameba*. Although I do not have access to the number of readers, Nori's blog is by far the most popular, since the author writes mostly about this topic and possesses a

YouTube channel where each of his videos have gathered several hundred viewers. Many of the other posts are essentially one-off updates to blogs otherwise dedicated to a variety of subjects that interest their authors.

4 American channelers of the early 1990s showed similarly pragmatic attitudes towards money (Brown 1997: 144–52). However, the spiritual ditchers' critique, embedded as it is in debates of what ethical consumerism ought to be about, is a new development.

5 As of February 2022, K's original blog had gathered 233 likes. The author has been posting about their blog on Twitter since 2015, but they have only forty followers on that platform.

6 In practice, many cases cannot be so clearly divided, the Confucius Temple litigation that I will go on to examine being one example. One could also divide these categorizations into further subtypes, as Hotaka Tsukada (2018: 33) does when he proposes that cases arising out of relations between politics and religion relate to one of four issues: the Yasukuni shrine, the separation of religion and state, religious education and the political activities of religious organizations.

7 LEX/DB Internet is owned by a private firm (TKC) and employed for educational purposes by 97 per cent of schools offering a university law degree in Japan (https://lex.lawlibrary.jp/). Holding approximately 290,000 court decisions, as well as laws, regulations, ordinances and legal periodicals, LEX/DB is the largest database of its kind in Japan, with the oldest entries going back to 1875.

8 Cases using two or more of these keywords were counted only once, but I have counted retrials as separate cases as the rulings are sometimes different. While other keywords such as *kitō* (prayer) could have been used for a more extensive search, I chose to employ those terms more frequently employed by spiritual therapists. The timespan of the 306 cases collected therefore reflects the period in which these keywords have been employed; any future research on historical trends going back to the nineteenth century would need to take this into account. Note that the terms 'cult', 'mind control' and 'brain washing' rarely appear in court decisions in Japan, even though they have been frequently used in media discourse since the Aum affair of 1995, spurred by an active import of ideas and theories from American authors (Ushiyama 2019). Only eight out of the 306 cases collected contained the word 'cult'; of those, four concerned Aum Shinrikyō and Kōfuku no Kagaku. Of 204 entries in the LEX/DB database to use the word 'cult', only twenty-two contain the term 'mind control', but even then this is not a term employed by the court, only by those giving testimonies in the trials. The first instance where 'mind control' appears is in a trial held on 13 December 1995 for a robbery and murder case that had nothing to do with Aum or any other religious organization.

9 https://www.stopreikan.com/madoguchi_higai.htm (accessed 29 October 2021).

10 Toyama district court, 19 June 1998. Case number: heisei 8 nen (wa) dai 121 gō.

11 Tokyo district court, 19 January 2017. Case number: heisei 27 nen (u) dai 27774 gō.
12 Tokyo district court, 26 August 2016. Case number: heisei 28 nen (u) dai 20167 gō.
13 Tokyo district court, 8 October 2019. Case number: heisei 30 nen (u) dai 28288 gō.
14 See http://www.japaneselawtranslation.go.jp/law/detail/?id=3578&vm=04&re=02 (accessed 27 February 2022).
15 Integrity (*seijitsusei*) has even become a quantifiable marker of quality. This is evident in its recent inclusion as a category in the annual business rankings published in Nikkei ESG, a periodical that publishes information on best business practices related to environmental and social friendliness as well as governance skills. Toyota was at the top of the integrity ranking, when it was added for the first time in 2020, followed by Suntory and Apple, prompting a journalist to announce that the age of sustainability will be soon replaced by the age of integrity (Kimura 2021).

References

Abe, Shunsuke (2021), 'Top Court: Free Rent to Confucian Temple in Naha is Unconstitutional', *The Asahi Shimbun*, 25 February. https://www.asahi.com/ajw/articles/14219626 (accessed 18 November 2021).
Allison, Anne (2013), *Precarious Japan*, Durham, NC: Duke University Press.
Altglas, Véronique (2014a), '"Bricolage": Reclaiming a Conceptual Tool', *Culture & Religion* 15 (4): 474–93. doi: 10.1080/14755610.2014.984235.
Altglas, Véronique (2014b), *From Yoga to Kabbalah: Religious Exoticism and the Logics of Bricolage*, New York: Oxford University Press.
Ama, Toshimaro (2004), *Why Are the Japanese Non-Religious?* New York: University Press of America.
Ammerman, Nancy T. (ed.) (2007), *Everyday Religion: Observing Modern Religious Lives*, Oxford: Oxford University Press.
Andō Reiji (2020), 'Seimei to reisei', in Nishimura Akira, Ōtani Eichi, Sueki Fumihiko and Shimazono Susumu (eds), *Kindai Nihon shūkyō-shi vol. 3: Kyōyō to seimei*, 60–70, Tokyo: Shunjūsha.
Araki Michio (1987), *Shūkyō no sōzō*, Kyoto: Hōzōkan.
Aramaki Hiroshi (2019), *45-nen de Nihonjin wa dō kawattaka (1): Dai 10-kai 'Nihonjin no ishiki' chōsakara*, Tokyo: NHK Hōsōbunkakenkyūsho.
Araya Hidehiko, Tanabe Shintarō, Shimazono Susumu and Yumiyama Tatsuya (eds) (1995), *Iyashi to wakai: Gendai ni okeru care no shosō*, Tokyo: Hābesuto-sha.
Arimoto Yumiko (2011), *Supirichuaru shijō no kenkyū: dēta de yomu kyū-kakudai māketto no shinjitsu*, Tokyo: Tōyō Keizai Shinpōsha.
Asprem, Egil (2014), 'Beyond the West: Towards a New Comparativism in the Study of Esotericism', *Correspondences* 2 (1): 3–33.
Asprem, Egil, and Julian Strube (eds) (2021), *New Approaches to the Study of Esotericism*, Leiden: Brill.
Aubry, Timothy, and Trysh Travis (eds) (2015). *Rethinking Therapeutic Culture*, Chicago: University of Chicago Press.
Aupers, Stef, and Dick Houtman (2010), 'Religions of Modernity: Relocating the Sacred to the Self and the Digital', in Stef Aupers and Dick Houtman (eds), *Religions of Modernity: Relocating the Sacred to the Self and the Digital*, 1–30, Leiden: Brill.
Baffelli, Erica (2016), *Media and New Religions in Japan*, London: Routledge.
Baffelli, Erica (2017), 'Contested Positioning: "New Religions" and Secular Spheres', *Japan Review* 30: 129–52. doi: 10.15055/00006736.

Baffelli, Erica, and Ian Reader (2012), 'Editors' Introduction: Impact and Ramifications: The Aftermath of the Aum Affair in the Japanese Religious Context', *Japanese Journal of Religious Studies* 39 (1): 1–28.

Baffelli, Erica, and Ian Reader (2018), *Dynamism and the Ageing of a Japanese 'New' Religion: Transformations and the Founder*, London: Bloomsbury Academic.

Bailey, Edward (1998), *Implicit Religion: An Introduction*, London: Middlesex University Press.

Barshay, Andrew E. (2019), 'The Protestant Imagination: Robert Bellah, Maruyama Masao and the Study of Japanese Thought', in Matteo Bortolini (ed.), *The Anthem Companion to Robert N. Bellah*, 191–213, New York: Anthem Press.

Becker, Carl, and Yumiyama Tatsuya (2009), *Inochi kyōiku to supirichuariti*, Tokyo: Taishō University Press.

Beckford, James (1989), *Religion and Advanced Industrial Society*, Boston: Unwin Hyman.

Bellah, Robert N. (1964), 'Religious Evolution', *American Sociological Review* 29 (3): 358–74.

Bellah, Robert N. ([1957] 1985), *Tokugawa Religion: The Values of Pre-Industrial Japan*, London: Collier MacMillan.

Bellah, Robert N., Richard Madsen, William M. Sullivan, Ann Swidler and Steven M. Tipton (1985), *Habits of the Heart: Individualism and Commitment in American Life*, Berkeley: University of California Press.

Bender, Courtney (2010), *The New Metaphysicals: Spirituality and the American Religious Imagination*, Chicago: University of Chicago Press.

Bender, Courtney (2015), 'Spirit', in Timothy Aubry and Trysh Travis (eds), *Rethinking Therapeutic Culture*, 46–57, Chicago: University of Chicago Press.

Benedict, Ruth (1947), *The Chrysanthemum and the Sword: Patterns of Japanese Culture*, London: Secker & Warburg.

Benesch, Oleg (2014), *Inventing the Way of the Samurai: Nationalism, Internationalism, and Bushido in Modern Japan*, Oxford: Oxford University Press.

Berlant, Lauren (2011), *Cruel Optimism*, Durham, NC: Duke University Press.

Blacker, Carmen (1999), *The Catalpa Bow: A Study of Shamanistic Practices in Japan*, 3rd edn, Surrey: Routledge Curzon.

Borovoy, Amy (2016), 'Robert Bellah's Search for Community and Ethical Modernity in Japan Studies', *Journal of Asian Studies* 75 (2): 467–94.

Braun, Erik (2017), 'Mindful but Not Religious: Meditation and Enchantment in the Work of Jon Kabat-Zinn', in David L. McMahan and Erik Braun (eds), *Meditation, Buddhism, and Science*, 173–97, Oxford: Oxford University Press.

Brown, Michael F. (1997), *The Channeling Zone: American Spirituality in an Anxious Age*, Cambridge, MA: Harvard University Press.

Bunting, Madeleine (1997), 'The Dark Side of Enlightenment', *The Guardian*, 27 October. http://www.ex-cult.org/fwbo/Guardian.htm (accessed 18 November 2021).

Butler, Judith (2004), *Precarious Life: The Powers of Mourning and Violence*, London: Verso.

Butler, Judith (2009), *Frames of War: When Is Life Grievable?* London: Verso.

CAA (Consumer Affairs Agency) (2018), 'Shōhishakeiyakuhō no ichibu o kaisei suru hōritsu (heisei 30 nen hōritsu dau 54 gō) kaku kaisei jikō no gaiyō', *CAA*, 15 June. https://www.caa.go.jp/policies/policy/consumer_system/consumer_contract_act/amendment/2018/pdf/consumer_system_cms101_200826_02.pdf (accessed 8 November 2021).

Carrette, Jeremy, and Richard King (2004), *Selling Spirituality: The Silent Takeover of Religion*, New York: Routledge.

Cassidy, Claire Monod (1996), 'Cultural Context of Complementary and Alternative Medicine Systems', in Mark S. Micozzi (ed.), *Fundamentals of Complementary and Alternative Medicine*, 9–34, London: Churchill Livingstone.

Chartier, Roger (1991), *The Cultural Origins of the French Revolution*, trans. Lydia G. Cochrane, Durham, NC: Duke University Press.

Chiwaki no Mori (2015a), 'Jiyūsha no yūrai', *YouTube*, 4 April. https://www.youtube.com/watch?app=desktop&v=5mln8w3SAvU (accessed 18 November 2021).

Chiwaki no Mori (2015b), 'Chiwaki no Mori intabyū: Yamakawa Kōya, Akiko go fusai', *YouTube*, 7 April. https://www.youtube.com/watch?v=coQVf3CV2Uc (accessed 18 November 2021).

Clark, Herbert H., and Susan E. Brennan (1991), 'Grounding in Communication', in Lauren B. Resnick, John M. Levine and Stephanie D. Teasley (eds), *Perspectives on Socially Shared Cognition*, 127–49, Washington: American Psychological Association.

Clements, Rebekah (2015), *A Cultural History of Translation in Early Modern Japan*, Cambridge: Cambridge University Press.

Cook, Joanna (2018), 'Paying Attention to Attention', *Anthropology of This Century* 22. http://aotcpress.com/articles/paying-attention-attention/ (accessed 18 November 2021).

Cox, Harvey (1965), *The Secular City*, Springfield, OH: Collier Books.

Crawford, Mark (2021), 'Abe's Womenomics Policy, 2013–2020: Tokenism, Gradualism, or Failed Strategy?', *Asia-Pacific Journal* 19 (4), 15 February. https://apjjf.org/2021/4/Crawford.html (accessed 18 November 2021).

Crockford, Susannah (2021a), *Ripples of the Universe: Spirituality in Sedona, Arizona*, Chicago: University of Chicago Press.

Crockford, Susannah (2021b), 'What Do Jade Eggs Tell Us about the Category "Esotericism"? Spirituality, Neoliberalism, Secrecy, and Commodities', in Egil Asprem and Julian Strube (eds), *New Approaches to the Study of Esotericism*, 201–16, Leiden: Brill.

Dake Mitsuya, Ōmi Toshihiro and Yoshinaga Shin'ichi (2020), *Nihon bukkyō to seiyō sekai*, Kyoto: Hōzōkan.

Dawson, Andrew (2013), 'Entangled Modernity and Commodified Religion: Alternative Spirituality and the "New Middle Class"', in François Gauthier and Tuomas Martikainen (eds), *Religion in Consumer Society: Brands, Consumers and Markets*, 127–42, London: Routledge.

DeJonge, P. Michael, and Christiane Tietz (2015), 'Introduction: Translating Religion', in P. Michael, DeJonge and Christiane Tietz (eds), *Translating Religion: What Is Lost and Gained?* 1–12, London: Routledge.

Dorman, Benjamin (2005), 'Pana Wave: The New Aum Shinrikyô or Another Moral Panic?', *Nova Religio* 8 (3): 83–103.

Dorman, Benjamin (2007), 'Representing Ancestor Worship as "Non-Religious": Hosoki Kazuko's Divination in the Post-Aum Era', *Nova Religio* 10 (3): 32–53.

Dorman, Benjamin (2012), "Scholarly Reactions to the Aum and Waco Incidents," *Japanese Journal of Religious Studies* 39 (1): 153–77.

Doward, Jamie (2019), 'Buddhist, Teacher, Predator: Dark Secrets of the Triratna Guru', *The Observer*, 21 July. https://www.theguardian.com/world/2019/jul/21/sangharakshita-guru-triratna-buddhist-dark-secrets (accessed 18 November 2021).

Ehrhardt, George, Axel Klein, Levi McLaughlin and Steven S. Reed (eds) (2014), *Kōmeitō: Religion and Politics in Japan*, Berkeley: Institute of East Asian Studies, University of California.

Eichel, Steve K. D. (2010), 'Lay Hypnotherapy and the Credentialing of Zoe the Cat', in Deirdre Barrett (ed.), *Hypnosis and Hypnotherapy: Neuroscience, Personality and Cultural Factors*, 1, 125–44, London: Praeger.

Erickson, Milton H. (1980), *The Nature of Hypnosis and Suggestion*. New York: Irvington.

Farrelly, Paul J. (2019), 'Terry Hu: Writing Her Transition from Actor to New Age Authority in Taiwan', *Asian Ethnology* 78 (1): 53–73.

Faure, Bernard (1993), *Chan Insights and Oversights: An Epistemological Critique of the Chan Tradition*, Princeton: Princeton University Press.

Ferguson, Marilyn (1980), *The Aquarian Conspiracy: Personal and Social Transformation in the 1980s*, Los Angeles: J. P. Tarcher.

Fingarette, Herbert (1972), *Confucius: The Secular as Sacred*, New York: Harper Torchbook.

Fong, Benjamin Y. (2014), 'On Critics and What's Real: Russel McCutcheon on Religious Experience', *Journal of the American Academy of Religion* 82 (4): 1127–48.

Fourcade, Marion, and Kieran Healy (2017), 'Seeing Like a Market', *Socio-Economic Review* 15 (1): 9–29. doi: 10.1093/ser/mww033.

Frank, W. Arthur (2002), 'What's Wrong with Medical Consumerism?' in Saras Henderson and Alan Petersen (eds), *Consuming Health: The Commodification of Health Care*, 13–30, London: Routledge.

Fujioka Masayuki (2015), *Shōhi shakai no henyō to kenkō shikō: Datsu-busshitsushugi to aimaisa-taisei*, Tokyo: Hābesuto-sha.

Fujiwara, Satoko (1996), '"Kagami" to "ōgo": Ōmu Shinrikyō jiken ni yotte shūkyōgaku wa ikani kawatta ka', *Bulletin of the Department of Religious Studies at the University of Tokyo* 13: 17–31.

Fujiwara, Satoko (2016), 'Why the Concept of "World Religion" Has Survived in Japan: On the Japanese Reception of Max Weber's Comparative Religion', in Peter Antes, Armin W. Geertz and Mikael Rothstein (eds), *Essays on Comparative Religion*, 193–205, Sheffield: Equinox.

Fujiwara, Satoko (2019), 'Practicing Belonging? Non-Religiousness in Twenty-First Century Japan', *Journal of Religion in Japan* 8 (1–3): 123–50.

Fujiwara, Satoko (2021), '"What's Wrong with Philosophy?": Interviews with Toshimaro Hanazono and Yoshiko Oda (Japan)', in Fujiwara Satoko, David Thurfjell and Steven Engler (eds), *Global Phenomenologies of Religion: An Oral History in Interviews*, 123–45, Sheffield: Equinox.

Fukuoka, Masanobu (1978), *The One-Straw Revolution: An Introduction to Natural Farming*, trans. Chris Pearce, Tsune Kurosawa and Larry Korn, Emmaus, PA: Rodale Press.

Fuller, Overton Jean (2006), 'Saint-Germain, Le Comte de', in Wouter J. Hanegraaff, Antoine Faivre, Roelof van den Broek and Jean-Pierre Brach (eds), *Dictionary of Gnosis and Western Esotericism*, 1022–4, Leiden: Brill.

Fuller, Robert C. (1982), 'Carl Rogers, Religion, and the Role of Psychology in American Culture', *Journal of Humanistic Psychology* 22 (4): 21–32.

Fuller, Robert C. (2001), *Spiritual, but Not Religious: Understanding Unchurched America*, Oxford: Oxford University Press.

Fuller, Robert C., and William B. Parsons (2018), 'Spiritual but Not Religious: A Brief Introduction', in William B. Parsons (ed.), *Being Spiritual but Not Religious: Past, Present, Future(s)*, 15–28, London: Routledge.

Fumino Yō (1997), 'Shinsei daigaku no secchi to ryōteki kakudai no kiban', in Satō Tatsuya and Mizoguchi Hajime (eds), *Tsūshi: Nihon no shinrigaku*, 339–65, Kyoto: Kitaoji-shobō.

Funabashi, Yoichi and Barak Kushner (eds) (2015), *Examining Japan's Lost Decades*, London: Routledge.

Futazawa Masaki and Shimada Hiromi ([1991] 2009), *Sennō taiken*, 2nd edn, Tokyo: Takarajimasha.

Gaitanidis, Ioannis (2010), 'Socio-Economic Aspects of the "Spiritual Business" in Japan: A Survey Among Professional Spiritual Therapists', *Shūkyō to shakai (Religion and Society)* 16: 143–60.

Gaitanidis, Ioannis (2011), 'At the Forefront of a "Spiritual Business": Independent Professional Spiritual Therapists in Japan', *Japan Forum* 23 (2): 185–206. doi: 10.1080/09555803.2011.598015.

Gaitanidis, Ioannis (2012a), 'Spiritual Therapies in Japan', *Japanese Journal of Religious Studies* 39 (2): 353–85.

Gaitanidis, Ioannis (2012b), 'Gender and Spiritual Therapy in Japan', *International Journal for the Study of New Religions* 3 (2): 269–88. doi: 10.1558/ijsnr.v3i2.269.

Gaitanidis, Ioannis (2019), 'More Than Just a Photo? Aura Photography in Digital Japan', *Asian Ethnology* 78 (1): 101–25.

Gaitanidis, Ioannis (2020), '"Spiritual Apostasy" in Contemporary Japan: Religion, Taboos and The Ethics of Capitalism', *Silva Iaponicarum* 60/61: 41–65. doi: 10.12775/sijp.2019.60-61.3.

Gaitanidis, Ioannis (2021), 'Economy and Spirituality', in Erica Baffelli, Andrea Castiglioni and Fabio Rambelli (eds), *The Bloomsbury Handbook of Japanese Religions*, 35–41, London: Bloomsbury Academic.

Gaitanidis, Ioannis (forthcoming), 'The Supernatural Is Not Religion: *Okaruto* TV Programs in Japan', in Carole M. Cusack and Venetia Robertson (eds), *Handbook of Contemporary Religion, Film and Television*, Leiden: Brill.

Gaitanidis, Ioannis, and Aki Murakami (2014), 'From Miko to Spiritual Therapist: Shamanistic Initiations in Contemporary Japan', *Journal of Religion in Japan* 3 (1): 1–35. doi: 10.1163/22118349-00301001.

Gaitanidis, Ioannis, and Aike P. Rots (2021), 'The Corporate Nature of "Alternative" Practices', *The Immanent Frame*, 9 April. https://tif.ssrc.org/2021/04/09/the-corporate-nature-of-alternative-practices/ (accessed 18 November 2021).

Gaitanidis, Ioannis, and Justin Stein (2021), 'Japanese Religions and the Global Occult: An Introduction and Literature Review', *Japanese Religions* 44: 1–32.

Gaston, K. Healan (2019), *Imagining Judeo-Christian America: Religion, Secularism, and the Redefinition of Democracy*, Chicago: University of Chicago Press.

Gebhardt, Lisette (2001), *Japans Neue Spiritualität (Japan's New Spirituality)*, Wiesbaden: Harrassowitz.

Gebhardt, Lisette (2013), *Gendai Nihon no supirichuariti: Bungaku, shisō ni miru shinreisei bunga*, trans. Hidetaka Fukazawa and Asukai Masatomo, Tokyo: Iwanami-shoten.

Greimel, Hans, and William Sposato (2021), *Collision Course: Carlos Ghosn and the Culture Wars that Upended an Auto Empire*, Boston: Harvard Business Review Press.

Hacking, Ian (1995), *Rewriting the Soul: Multiple Personality and the Sciences of Memory*, Princeton: Princeton University Press.

Haga Manabu (1995), 'Self-Development Seminars in Japan', *Japanese Journal of Religious Studies* 22 (3/4): 283–99.

Haga Manabu (2004), 'Tokumei-teki de, katsu'shinmitsu'na kakawari', in Itō Masayuki, Kashio Naoki and Yumiyama Tatsuya (eds), *Supirichuariti no shakaigaku*, 34–55, Tokyo: Sekai-shisōsha.

Haga Manabu and Yumiyama Tatsuya (1994), *Inoru, fureau, kanjiru: Jibun sagashi no odessee*, Tokyo: Inter Press Corporation.

Hall, David D. (ed.) (1997), *Lived Religion in America: Toward a History of Practice*, Princeton: Princeton University Press.

Hammer, Olav (2010), 'I Did It My Way? Individual Choice and Social Conformity in New Age Religion', in Stef Aupers and Dick Houtman (eds), *Religions of Modernity: Relocating the Sacred to the Self and the Digital*, 49–68, Leiden: Brill.

Han, Byung-Chul (2017), *Psychopolitics: Neoliberalism and New Technologies of Power*, trans. Erik Butler, London: Verso.

Hanegraaff, Wouter J. ([1996] 1998), *New Age Religion and Western Culture: Esotericism in the Mirror of Secular Thought*, Albany: State University of New York Press.

Harada Takayuki (2019), 'Kono kuni de "jishō shinri kaunseraa" ga ranritsu suru genjō wa yōyaku kawaruka: "kōnin shinrishi" o gozonjidesuka', *Gendai Media*, 31 March. https://gendai.ismedia.jp/articles/-/63818?imp=0 (accessed 18 November 2021).

Hardacre, Helen (1984), *Lay Buddhism in Contemporary Japan: Reiyukai Kyodan*, Princeton: Princeton University Press.

Hardacre, Helen (1998), 'Asano Wasaburō and Japanese Spiritualism in Early Twentieth-Century Japan', in Sharon A. Minichiello (ed.), *Japan's Competing Modernities: Issues in Culture and Democracy 1900–1930*, 133–53, Honolulu: University of Hawai'i Press.

Hardacre, Helen (2017), *Shinto: A History*, Oxford: Oxford University Press.

Haruyama Shigeo (1995), *Nōnai Kakumei*, Tokyo: Sunmark-shuppan.

Hashisako Mizuho (2008), '"Seinaru mono" no anzen sōchi: "Supicon" no jirei kara', *Nenpō shakaigaku ronshū* 21: 25–36.

Hashisako Mizuho (2019), *Uranai o matou shōjo: Zasshi 'My Birthday' to supirichuariti*, Tokyo: Seikyūsha.

Hashisako Mizuho (2021), *Ninpu, shussan o meguru supirichuariti*, Tokyo: Shūeishashinsho.

Hatoyama Yukio (2010), 'Dai-174-kai kokkai ni okeru Hatoyama naikaku sōri daijin shisei hōshin enzetsu', *Cabinet Public Affair's Office*. http://www.kantei.go.jp/jp/hatoyama/statement/201001/29siseihousin.html (accessed 18 November 2021).

Hayashi, Makoto (2006), 'Religion in the Modern Period', in Paul L. Swanson and Clark Chilson (eds), *The Nanzan Guide to Japanese Religions*, 202–19, Honolulu: University of Hawai'i Press.

Heelas, Paul (1996), *The New Age Movement: The Celebration of the Self and the Sacralization of Modernity*, Cambridge: Blackwell.

Heelas, Paul (2008), *Spiritualities of Life: New Age Romanticism and Consumptive Capitalism*, Oxford: Blackwell.

Heelas, Paul, and Linda Woodhead (2005), *The Spiritual Revolution: Why Religion Is Giving Way to Spirituality*, Oxford: Blackwell.

Hirano Naoko (2006), '"Taishū supirichuariti" no genzai', *Bulletin of the Graduate Division of Literature of Waseda University* 52: 69–78.

Hirano Naoko (2019), 'Taishō-ki no Usui reiki ryōhō: Sono kigen to hoka no seishin ryōhō to no kankei', in Kurita Hidehiko, Tsukada Hotaka and Yoshinaga Shin'ichi (eds), *Kingendai Nihon no minkan seishin ryōhō: Fukashina/okaruto enerugii no shosō*, 217–40, Tokyo: Kokushokankōkai.

Hiratsuka, Yuta (2021), 'Damages Suit Launched in Southwest Japan Over "Healing Hand" Seminar Fees', *The Maichini*, 23 September. https://mainichi.jp/english/articles/20210923/p2a/00m/0na/009000c (accessed 18 November 2021).

Hommerich, Carola, Naoki Sudo and Toru Kikkawa (2021), *Social Change in Japan 1989–2019: Social Status, Social Consciousness, Attitudes and Values*, London: Routledge.

Hong, Soo Kyeong (2017), 'Food as Medicine: The Cultural Politics of "Eating Right" in Modern Japan, 1905–1945', PhD diss., Cornell University, Ithaca.

Horie Norichika (2000), 'Shinrigakuteki jikojitsugenron no keifu to shūkyō: Kyūsai, jikojitsugen, iyashi', *Bulletin of the Department of Religious Studies, University of Tokyo* 27: 57–73.

Horie Norichika (2003), 'Reisei kara supirichuariti e', *Kokusai shūkyō kenkyūsho newsletter* 38: 14–22.

Horie Norichika (2004), 'Shūkyō no yukue', in Ikegami Yoshimasa, Shimazono Susumu, Fumihiko Sueki, Oda Yoshiko, Tsuruoka Yoshio and Seki Kazutoshi (eds), *Iwanami kōza: shūkyō no yukue*, 270–91, Tokyo: Iwanami-shoten.

Horie Norichika (2006), 'Media no naka no "supirichuaru"', *Sekai* 759: 242–50.

Horie Norichika (2007), 'Nihon no supirichuariti gensetsu no jōkyō', Japan Association for Transpersonal Psychology/Psychiatry (ed.), *Supirichuariti no shinrigaku*, 35–54, Osaka: Seseragi-shuppan.

Horie Norichika (2008), 'Media no naka no karisuma – Ehara Hiroyuki to media kankyō', in Kokusai Shūkyō Kenkyūsho (ed.), *Media ga umidasu kamigami*, 41–64, Tokyo: Akiyama Shoten.

Horie Norichika (2009), *Rekishi no naka no shūkyō shinrigaku*, Tokyo: Iwanami-shoten.

Horie Norichika (2009–11), 'Spirituality and the Spiritual in Japan: Translation and Transformation', *Journal of Alternative Spiritualities and New Age Studies* 5: 66–81.

Horie Norichika (2010), 'Supirichuaru to sono anchi: Ehara bangumi to sono juyō wo megutte', in Kenji Ishii (ed.), *Baraeti-ka suru shūkyō*, 50–74, Tokyo: Seikyūsha.

Horie Norichika (2013), 'Narrow New Age and Broad Spirituality: A Comprehensive Schema and a Comparative Analysis', in Steven J. Sutcliffe and Ingvild Sælid Gilhus (eds), *New Age Spirituality: Rethinking Religion*, 99–116, Durham: Acumen.

Horie Norichika (ed.) (2019a), *Shūkyō to shakai no sengo-shi*, Tokyo: University of Tokyo Press.

Horie Norichika (2019b), *Poppu-supirichuariti: Media-ka sareta shūkyōsei*, Tokyo: Iwanami-shoten.

Horie Norichika (2021), 'Shōhi shakai to shūkyō no henyō: Sei naru mono e no hōken kara jiko e no hōken/tōshi', in Shimazono Susumu, Sueki Fumihiko, Ōtani Eichi and Nishimura Akira (eds), *Kingendai shūkyō vol. 6: Mosaku suru gendai*, 111–43, Tokyo: Shunjusha.

Horii, Mitsutoshi (2018), *The Category of 'Religion' in Contemporary Japan: Shūkyō and Temple Buddhism*, Cham, Switzerland: Palgrave Macmillan.

Horowitz, Mitch (2014), *One Simple Idea: How Positive Thinking Reshaped Modern Life*, New York: Crown.
Hoshino Eiki and Yumiyama Tatsuya (2019), *Higashi Nihon dai shinsai go no shūkyō to komyuniti*, Tokyo: Hābesuto-sha.
Hoshino Wataru (2012), 'Denshi shoseki to shuppan sangyō', *Jōhō no kagaku to gijutsu* 62 (6): 236–41.
Houtman, Dick, and Stef Aupers (2007), 'The Spiritual Turn and the Decline of Tradition: The Spread of Post-Christian Spirituality in 14 Western Countries, 1981–2000', *Journal for the Scientific Study of Religion* 46 (3): 305–20. doi: 10.1111/j.1468-5906.2007.00360.x.
Hsiung, Hansun (2018), 'Timing the Textbook: Capitalism, Development, and Western Knowledge in the Nineteenth-Century', *History of Knowledge*, 23 May. https://historyofknowledge.net/2018/05/23/timing-the-textbook/ (accessed 18 November 2021).
Huss, Boaz (2014), 'Spirituality: The Emergence of a New Cultural Category and Its Challenge to the Religious and the Secular', *Journal of Contemporary Religion* 29 (1): 47–60. doi: 10.1080/13537903.2014.864803.
Ikegami Yoshimasa (2020), ' "Kyūsai" moderu no ekkyō: "Shisha kuyō" kenkyū no shiten kara', in Kubota Hiroshi, Tsuruoka Yoshio, Hayashi Jun, Fukusawa Hidetaka, Hosoda Ayako and Watanabe Kazuko (eds), *Ekkyō suru shūkyōshi* 1, 365–87, Tokyo: Liton.
Imaizumi Masashi (2017), 'MMS (modan misuterī sukūru) to no kōshō jiken nitsuite', *Consumer Law News* 111: 200–1.
Imaizumi, Yoshiko (2013), *Sacred Space in the Modern City: The Fractured Pasts of Meiji Shrine, 1912–1958*, Leiden: Brill.
Inaba Keishin (2004a), *Altruism in New Religious Movements: The Jesus Army and the Friends of the Western Buddhist Order in Britain*, Okayama: Daigaku kyōiku shuppan.
Inaba Keishin (2004b), 'Shea sareru supirichuariti to ishiki henyō', in Itō Masayuki, Kashio Naoki and Yumiyama Tatsuya (eds), *Supirichuariti no shakaigaku*, 122–42, Tokyo: Sekai-shisōsha.
Inaba Keishin and Sakurai Yoshihide (eds) (2012), *Shakai kōken suru shūkyō*, Kyoto: Sekaishisōsha.
Inoue Nobutaka, Kōmoto Mitsugi, Tsushima Michihito, Nakamaki Hirochika and Nishiyama Shigeru (eds) (1990), *Shinshūkyō jiten*, Tokyo: Kōbundō.
Inoue Uimara, and Ōtani Akira (2018), *Maindofurunesu to saimin: Meisō to shinri ryōhō ga hokan shiau kanōsei*, Tokyo: Sanga.
Ishihashi Yoshiki, Horiguchi Itsuko, Kawaminami Kimiyo, Kigawa Mika and Marui Eiji (2016), 'Nihon no tōgō iryō no riyō jōkyō', *Kōsei no Shihyō* 63 (13): 25–30.
Ishii Kenji (2008), *Terebi to shūkyō: Oumu igo o toinaousu*, Tokyo: Chūō Kōron-shinsha.
Isomae Jun'ichi (2019a), 'Oumu Shinrikyō jiken, soshite Higashi Nihon daishinsai to no sōgū', in Shimazono Susumu, Yasumaru Yoshio and Isomae Jun'ichi (eds),

Minshū shūkyōron: Shūkyōteki shutaika to wa nani ka, 1–14, Tokyo: University of Tokyo Press.

Isomae Jun'ichi (2019b), 'Shūkyōteki shutaika to ten'ironteki kaishin', in Shimazono Susumu, Yasumaru Yoshio and Isomae Jun'ichi (eds), *Minshū shūkyōron: Shūkyōteki shutaika to wa nani ka*, 21–72, Tokyo: University of Tokyo Press.

Isomura Kentarō (2007), *Supirichuaru wa naze hayaru no ka*, Tokyo: PHP Shinsho.

Itō Masayuki (1999), 'Zentai tōgi no gaiyō (Wākushoppu (1) Seishin sekai no kōzu (2): Seishin sekai no "shakaisei" o tōshi suru)', *Shūkyō to shakai (Religion and Society)* 4 (Suppl.): 33–9.

Itō Masayuki (2003), *Gendai shakai to supirichuariti*, Hiroshima: Keisuisha.

Itō Masayuki (2004a), 'Atarashii supirichuariti bunka no seisei to hatten', in Itō Masayuki, Kashio Naoki and Yumiyama Tatsuya (eds) (2004), *Supirichuariti no shakaigaku*, 22–33, Tokyo: Sekai-shisōsha.

Itō Masayuki (2004b), 'Gurōbaru bunka no rōkaru-sei no "aida"', in Itō Masayuki, Kashio Naoki and Yumiyama Tatsuya (eds.) (2004), *Supirichuariti no shakaigaku*, 80–104, Tokyo: Sekai-shisōsha.

Itō Masayuki (2004c), 'Oumu Shinrikyō to sore igo: Gendai shūkyō kenkyū no shomondai', in Ikegami Yoshimasa, Shimazono Susumu, Sueki Fumihiko, Oda Yoshiko, Tsuruoka Yoshio and Seki Kazutoshi (eds), *Iwanami Kōza: Shūkyō, vol. 2, Shūkyō e no shiza*, 253–79, Tokyo: Iwanami-shoten.

Itō Masayuki (2021), *Gendai supirichuariti bunkaron: Yōga, maindofurunesu kara pojitibu shinrigaku made*, Tokyo: Akashi-shoten.

Itō Masayuki, Kashio Naoki and Yumiyama Tatsuya (eds) (2004), *Supirichuariti no shakaigaku*, Tokyo: Sekai-shisōsha.

Itō Yoshinori, Masaki Kitō and Yamaguchi Hiroshi (1999), *Shōhisha toraburu Q&A*, Tokyo: Yūhikaku-sensho.

Jain, Andrea R. (2014), *Selling Yoga: From Counterculture to Pop Culture*, Oxford: Oxford University Press.

Jain, Andrea R. (2020), *Peace, Love, Yoga: The Politics of Global Spirituality*, Oxford: Oxford University Press.

Jones, Colin P. A. (2017), 'How Japan Got New Contract Law It Neither Wants Nor Needs', *Asahi Newspaper*, 3 September. https://www.japantimes.co.jp/community/2017/09/03/issues/japan-got-new-contract-law-neither-wants-needs/ (accessed 18 November 2021).

Josephson, Jason A. (2012), *The Invention of Religion in Japan*, Chicago: University of Chicago Press.

Josephson-Storm, Jason A. (2017), *The Myth of Disenchantment: Magic, Modernity and the Birth of the Human Sciences*, Chicago: Chicago University Press.

Kanazawa Masumi (2007), 'Wa ga kuni no sukūru sōsharu wāku ni okeru kadai: "Gakkō" to "Sōsharu wāku" "Kaunseringu" no kankeishi kara', *Journal of the Japanese Society for the Study of Social Welfare* 48 (3): 66–78.

Kanō Yūji (2003), 'Shūkyō hanrei no shinten: Kono shihanseiki o furikaette', *Consumer Law News* (September Special Issue): 3–4.

Kasai Kenta (1998), 'Hajimeni (Wākushoppu (1) "Seishin sekai" no kōzō: Gendai shakai to gendaijin no ishiki o rikai suru tegakari toshite)', *Shūkyō to shakai (Religion and Society)* 3 (Suppl.): 6–8.

Kasai Kenta (2004), 'Sekai hyōjun no danshuhō', in Itō Masayuki, Kashio Naoki and Yumiyama Tatsuya (eds) (2004), *Supirichuariti no shakaigaku*, 57–79, Tokyo: Sekai-shisōsha.

Kasai Kenta (2007), *Danshu ga tsukuridasu kyōdōsei: Arukōru izon kara no kaifuku o shinji*, Tokyo: Sekai-shisōsha.

Kasai Kenta (2010), *Gendai meiseiron: Hensei ishiki ga hiraku sekai*, Tokyo: Shunjusha.

Kasai Kenta (2016), 'Introducing Chaplaincy to Japanese Society: A Religious Practice in Public Space', *Journal of Religion in Japan* 5 (2–3): 246–62. doi: 10.1163/22118349-00502009.

Kashio Naoki (2000), 'Komento (IV. Zentai tōron, gendai sekai no shūkyōsei/reisei, wāshoppu (2), 1999 nendo wāshoppu kiroku)', *Shūkyō to shakai (Religion and Society)* 6: 161–7.

Kashio Naoki (ed.) (2002), *Supirichuariti o ikiru*, Tokyo: Serika-shobō.

Kashio Naoki (2004a), 'Shūkyō-teki kyōdōsei ga seisei suru ba', in Itō Masayuki, Kashio Naoki and Yumiyama Tatsuya (2004), *Supirichuariti no shakaigaku*, 110–21, Tokyo: Sekai-shisōsha.

Kashio Naoki (2004b), 'Supirichuariti, aru "tsunagari" no kankaku no sōshutsu', in Itō Masayuki, Kashio Naoki and Yumiyama Tatsuya (eds), *Supirichuariti no shakaigaku*, 165–85, Tokyo: Sekai-shisōsha.

Kashio Naoki (2009), 'Gendai supirichuariti genshō no fuhensei to tokushusei: Nyūeiji to no kankeisei kara', *Star People* 29: 16–19.

Kashio Naoki (2010), *Supirichuariti no kakumei*, Tokyo: Shunjusha.

Kashio Naoki (2016), *Keio daigaku maindofurunesu kyōshitsu e yōkoso*, Kyoto: Kokushokankōkai.

Kashio Naoki (2019), *Maindofurunesu ga yoku wakaru hon*, Tokyo: Shuwa system.

Katō Yukiharu (2000), '"New Age" to "Local Religion": Chiiki shakai ni okeru shūkyōteki sekaikan no hendō ni tsuite', *Komazawa University's Journal of Buddhist Studies* 31: 45–58.

Katō Yūsuke (2018), 'Zasshi "Shuppan Nyūsu" ga kyūkan e: 75nen no rekishi ni maku', *Asahi Newspaper*, 10 October. https://www.asahi.com/articles/ASLBB5X2YLBB UCVL02R.html (accessed 18 November 2021).

Kawakami Tsuneo (2012), *'Bijinesu-sho' to Nihonjin*, Tokyo: PHP Kenkyūsho.

Kayama Rika (2006), *Supirichuaru ni hamaru hito, hamaranai hito*, Tokyo: Gentōsha.

Keane, Webb (2002), 'Sincerity, "Modernity", and the Protestants', *Cultural Anthropology* 17 (1): 65–92.

Kelner, Merrijoy, and Beverly Wellman (2000), *Complementary and Alternative Medicine: Challenge and Change*, Amsterdam: Harwood Academic Publishers.

Kieffer, Kira Ganga (2020), 'Manifesting Millions: How Women's Spiritual Entrepreneurship Genders Capitalism', *Nova Religio* 24 (2): 80–104. doi: 10.1525/nr.2020.24.2.80.

Kikuchi Hiroo (2004), 'Kotoba ga ikirare, shinkō ga katachizukurareru toki', in Itō Masayuki, Kashio Naoki and Yumiyama Tatsuya (eds), *Supirichuariti no shakaigaku*, 143–64, Tokyo: Sekai-shisōsha.

Kimura Maki (2021), 'Jidai wa "jizoku kanō na (sustainable)" kara 'seijitsusa (integrity) e', *Yahoo News*, 6 August. https://news.yahoo.co.jp/byline/kimuramaki/20210806-00251812 (accessed 18 November 2021).

Kinmonth, Earl H. (1981), *The Self-Made Man in Meiji Japanese Thought: From Samurai to Salary Man*, Berkeley: University of California Press.

Kinoshita Shūsui (2008), 'Shūkyōshin Shizuka ni iki tzuku', *Yomiuri Shinbun*, 30 May.

Kirmayer, Laurence J. (2004), 'The Sound of One Hand Clapping: Listening to Prozac in Japan', in Carl Elliott and Tod Chambers (eds), *Prozac as a Way of Life*, 164–93, London: The University of North Carolina Press.

Kisala, Robert (1999), *Prophets of Peace: Pacifism and Cultural Identity in Japan's New Religions*, Honolulu: University of Hawai'i Press.

Kitanaka, Junko (2008), 'Diagnosing Suicides of Resolve: Psychiatric Practice in Contemporary Japan', *Culture, Medicine and Psychiatry* 32 (2): 152–76. doi: 10.1007/s11013-008-9087-1.

Kitanaka, Junko (2012), *Depression in Japan: Psychiatric Cures for a Society in Distress*, Princeton: Princeton University Press.

Kitanaka, Junko (2015), 'The Rebirth of Secrets and the New Care of the Self in Depressed Japan', *Current Anthropology* 56 (12): 251–62, doi: 10.1086/683273.

Kiyota Yoshiaki (2019), 'Shuppan gyōkai no dōkō wo tadoru', *Eureka* 51 (10): 148–56.

Kobayashi Takakazu (1985), 'Seishin sekai no tabi 2', *Yomiuri*, 6 March (evening edn): 11.

Koch, Gabriele (2020), *Healing Labor: Japanese Sex Work in the Gendered Economy*, Stanford: Stanford University Press.

Koike Jun'ichi (2015), 'Shobutsu to jujutsu, hiden', in Shimazono Susumu, Takano Toshihiko, Hayashi Makoto and Wakao Masaki (eds), *Shobutsu, media to shakai (Nihonjin to shūkyō): Kinsei kara Kindai e*, 5, 125–47, Tokyo: Shunjūsha.

Koike Yasushi (1998), 'Pojitivu shinkingu kara nyūeiji made: Nettowāku dairekuto seringu to jiko keihatsu seminā no shūkyō shakaigaku', *Shūkyō to shakai (Religion and Society)* 4: 49–77.

Koike Yasushi (2004), 'Seishinsekai ni okeru okaruto-ka: Lifespace wo jirei ni', in Itō Masayuki, Kashio Naoki and Yumiyama Tatsuya (eds), *Supirichuariti no shakaigaku*, 225–48, Tokyo: Sekaishisō-sha.

Koike Yasushi (2007), *Serapī bunka no shakaigaku*, Tokyo: Keisō-shobō.

Koike Yasushi (2009), 'Higaisha no kureimu to supirichuariti', in Sakurai Yoshihide (ed.), *Karuto to supirichuariti: Gendai Nihon ni okeru 'sukui' to 'iyashi' no yukue*, 213–44, Tokyo: Minerva-shobō.

Koike Yasushi (2013), 'Gurōbarisēshon to serufu-supirichuariti', in Kubota Hirshi (ed.), *Bunka sesshoku no sōzōryoku*, 207–20, Tokyo: Lithon.

Kokugakuin University, Institute for Japanese Culture and Classics (IJCC) and Inoue Nobutaka (eds) (2017), *Gakusei shūkyō ishiki chōsa sōgō hōkokusho 1995–2015*. Tokyo: Kokugakuin University, IJCC.

Koyano Kuniko (1995), 'Nihon ni okeru shinrigaku no sengo no shuppatsu: 1945nen 8gatsu 15nichi kara 1950nendai ni kakete', *Bulletin of Ibaraki Christian University* 29: 201–20.

Krasner, A. M. (2002), *The Wizard Within: The Krasner Method of Clinical Hypnotherapy*, 3rd edn, Santa Ana, CA: American Board of Hypnotherapy Press.

Kripal, Jeffrey. J. (2010), *Authors of the Impossible: The Paranormal and the Sacred*, Chicago: Chicago University Press.

Kudo Grabosky, Tomoko, Harue Ishii and Shizuno Mase (2012), 'The Development of the Counseling Profession in Japan: Past, Present and Future', *Journal of Counseling and Development* 90: 221–6. doi: 10.1111/j.1556-6676.2012.00027.x.

Kumamoto Masaki (2018), *Ryōjutsu kara shūkyō e: Sekaikyūsei-kyō no kyōdan soshikiteki kenkyū*, Tokyo: Hābesuto-sha.

Kurita Hidehiko (2018), 'The Notion of *Shūyō* and Conceptualizing the Future of Religion at the Turn of the Twentieth Century', *Religious Studies in Japan* 4: 65–90.

Kurita Hidehiko (2020), 'Nihon shinrei chōsa, ākaibu-ka no igi', *Jinbunshoin*, 1 December. https://note.com/jimbunshoin/n/n0bd7bf55afa7 (accessed 18 November 2021).

Kurita Hidehiko, Tsukada Hotaka and Yoshinaga Shin'ichi (eds) (2019), *Kingendai Nihon no minkan seishin ryōhō: Fukashina/okaruto enerugii no shosō*, Tokyo: Kokushokankōkai.

Larsson, Ernils (2020), 'Rituals of a Secular Nation: Shinto Normativity and the Separation of Religion and State in Postwar Japan', PhD diss., Uppsala: Uppsala Universitet.

Laycock, Joseph (2014), 'Zen Meets New Thought: The Erhard Seminars Training and Changing Ideas about Zen', *Contemporary Buddhism* 15 (2): 332–55. doi: 10.1080/14639947.2014.932490.

Lewis, David (2017), *Religion in Japanese Daily Life*, London: Routledge.

Lock, Margaret M., and Vinh-Kim Nguyen (2010), *An Anthropology of Biomedicine*, Oxford: Wiley-Blackwell.

Long, Nicholas J. (2018), 'Suggestions of Power: Searching for Efficacy in Indonesia's Hypnosis Boom', *Ethos* 46 (1): 70–94. doi: 10.1111/etho.12190.

Luhrmann, Tanya (1989), *Persuasions of the Witch's Craft*, Cambridge, MA: Harvard University Press.

MacLaine, Shirley (1983), *Out on a Limb*, New York: Bantam Doubleday Dell Publishing Group.

MacLaine, Shirley (1986), *Auto on a rimu*, trans. Kōya Yamakawa and Akiko Yamakawa, Tokyo: Jiyūsha.
Makino Tomokazu (2012), *Jiko keihatsu no jidai: 'Jiko' no bunka shakai-gakuteki tankyū*, Tokyo: Keisō-shobō.
Makino, Tomokazu (2015), *Nichijō ni shin'yū jiko keihatsu: Ikikata, techōjutsu, katazuke*, Tokyo: Keisō-shobō.
Martin, Alex K. T. (2009), 'The Past, Present and Future of Fortunetelling', *The Japan Times*, 21 April. https://www.japantimes.co.jp/news/2009/04/21/reference/the-past-present-and-future-of-fortunetelling/ (accessed 18 November 2021).
Martin, Craig (2014), *Capitalizing Religion: Ideology and the Opiate of the Bourgeoisie*. London: Bloomsbury.
Maruyama Kazuaki (2008), 'Nihon ni okeru "kaunseringu" senmonshoku no hattatsu katei: Sangyō kaunserā o jirei toshite', *Bulletin of the Japan Society for the Study of Vocational and Technical Education* 38 (2): 1–8.
Matsui Takeshi (2013). *Kotoba to māketingu: 'Iyashi būmu' no shōhishakai-shi*, Tokyo: Sekigakusha.
Mayer, Andreas (2013), *Sites of the Unconscious: Hypnosis and the Emergence of the Psychoanalytic Setting*, Chicago: University of Chicago Press.
McCloud, Sean (2004), *Making the American Religious Fringe: Exotics, Subversives, and Journalists, 1955–1993*, Chapel Hill: The University of North Carolina Press.
McCrary, Charles (2018), 'Fortune Telling and American Religious Freedom', *Religion and American Culture: A Journal of Interpretation* 28 (2): 269–306. doi: 10.1525/rac.2018.28.2.269.
McCutcheon, Russell T. (1997), *Manufacturing Religion: The Discourse on Sui Generis Religion and the Politics of Nostalgia*, Oxford: Oxford University Press.
McCutcheon, Russell T. (2016), 'Fanfare for the Common e.g.: On the Strategic Use of the Mundane in the Study of Religion', in Peter Antes, Armin W. Geertz and Mikael Rothstein (eds), *Essays on Comparative Religion*, 153–64, Sheffield: Equinox.
McGuire, Meredith B. (2008), *Lived Religion: Faith and Practice in Everyday Life*, Oxford: Oxford University Press.
McLachlan, Patricia (2002), *Consumer Politics in Postwar Japan: The Institutional Boundaries of Citizen Activism*, New York: Columbia University Press.
McLaughlin, Levi (2019), *Soka Gakkai's Human Revolution: The Rise of a Mimetic Nation in Modern Japan*, Honolulu: University of Hawai'i Press.
McLaughlin, Levi, Aike P. Rots, Jolyon B. Thomas and Chika Watanabe (2020), 'Why Scholars of Religion Must Investigate the Corporate Form', *Journal of the American Academy of Religion* 88 (3): 693–725. doi: 10.1093/jaarel/lfaa041.
McVeigh, Brian J. (2017), *The History of Japanese Psychology: Global Perspectives, 1875–1950*. London: Bloomsbury.

MHLW (Ministry of Health, Labour and Welfare) (2013), 'Tōgō iryō' no arikata ni kansuru kentō-kai', *Koremade no giron no seiri*. https://www.mhlw.go.jp/stf/shingi/2r9852000002vsub.html (accessed 20 May 2021).

Millar, Kathleen K. (2017), 'Toward a Critical Politics of Precarity', *Sociology Compass* 11 (6): e12483. doi: 10.1111/soc4.12483.

Minowa Kenryō, Inaba Keishin, Kurosaki Hiroyuki and Kasai Kenta (2016), *Saigai shien handobukku: Shūkyōsha no jissen to sono kyōdō*, Tokyo: Shunjusha.

Miura Sekizō ([1929] 2005), *Reisei no taiken to ninshiki: Nihon yori zenjinrui e*, Kyoto: Ryūō-bunkō.

Miura, Takashi (2019), *Agents of World Renewal: The Rise of Yonaoshi Gods in Japan*, Honolulu: University of Hawai'i Press.

Miyashita Shūichi (2018), 'Kaisei shōhisha keiyaku-hō no seiritsu', *Kokumin Seikatsu* (July): 38–41.

Moretti, Laura (2020), *Pleasure in Profit: Popular Prose in Seventeenth-Century Japan*, New York: Columbia University Press.

Mori Kiyoshi (2014), *Nihon jisshin bunruihō*, Tokyo: Nihon toshokan kyōkai.

Morrow, Avery (2014), *The Sacred Science of Ancient Japan: Lost Chronicles of the Age of the Gods*, Rochester, VT: Bear & Company.

Murakami Shigeyoshi (1957), *Kindai minshū shūkyō-shi no kenkyū*, Kyoto: Hozōkan.

My Geisha (1962), [Film] Dir. Jack Cardiff, USA: Paramount Pictures.

Nagaoka Takashi (2015), *Shin shūkyō to sōryokusen: Kyōso igo o ikiru*, Nagoya: Nagoya University Press.

Nagaoka Takashi (2020), *Shūkyō bunka wa dare no mono ka*, Nagoya: Nagoya University Press.

Nagatani Chiyoko (2021), 'Ima, shūkyō o meguru naniga mondai na no ka', in Nagatani Chiyoko, Bessho Yūsuke, Kawaguchi Yukihiro and Fujimoto Toko (eds), *Shūkyōsei no jinruigaku*, 7–30, Kyoto: Hōzōkan.

Nakano, Tsuyoshi (1990), 'New Religions and Politics in Post-War Japan', *Sociologica* 14 (2): 1–29.

National Consumer Centre of Japan (2021), *White Paper on Consumer Affairs FY 2020*, Tokyo: Consumer Affairs Agency.

Nehring, Daniel, Ole Jacob Madsen, Edgar Cabanas, China Mills and Dylan Kerrigan (2020), *The Routledge International Handbook of Global Therapeutic Cultures*, London: Routledge.

Nishigaki Etsuyo (2018), 'Iryō, kenkō bunya ni okeru kōchingu no gakujutsuteki shinten', *Japanese Journal of Psychosomatic Medicine* 58: 534–41.

Nitobe Inazō (1911), *Shūyō*, Tokyo: Jitsugyō no Nihon Sha.

Nori (2018), 'Kakō ni atta "datsu-supi sōdō" de no hihan to konpon gen'in ni tsuite ima sara boku ga omou koto', *Jinsei to wa moraimono*. https://nori-blog.com/chat/de-spirituality/ (accessed 14 February 2022).

Nose Masashi (2019), *Heisei shuppan dēta bukku*, Tokyo: Minerva-shobō.

Oates, Lori Lee (2020), 'Imperial Occulture: The Theosophical Society and Transnational Cultures of Print', *International History Review* 43 (4): 815–35. doi: 10.1080/07075332.2020.1846588.

Okamoto Ryōsuke (2021), *Shūkyō to Nihonjin*, Tokyo: Chūkō-shinsho.

Okano, Kaori and Motonori Tsuchiya (1999), *Education in Contemporary Japan: Inequality and Diversity*, Cambridge: Cambridge University Press.

Okuyama Terumi (2005), *Zense ryōhō e yōkoso: Jinsei wa itsudemo nandodemo yarinaoseru*, Tokyo: PHP Kenkyūsho.

Ōmi Toshihiro (2020), 'Taishō no kyōyōshugi to seimeishugi', in Nishimura Akira, Ōtani Eichi, Sueki Fumihiko and Shimazono Susumu (eds), *Kindai Nihon shūkyō-shi vol. 3: Kyōyō to seimei*, 39–66, Tokyo: Shunjūsha.

Ó Muireartaigh, Rossa (2012), 'Preaching to the Converted: D. T. Suzuki's Zen Buddhism as a Case Study of a Microsociological Model of Translation', *Translation Studies* 5 (3): 280–95. doi: 10.1080/14781700.2012.701939.

Ó Muireartaigh, Rossa (2015), *Begotten, Not Made: Explorations in the Philosophy and Sociology of Religious Translation*, Dresden: Atropos Press.

Ono Yasuhiro (1995), *Taniguchi Masaharu to sono jidai*, Tokyo: Tōkyōdō-shuppan.

Ōshima Michiko and Makoto Kōno (1963), *Ai to shi o mitsumete*, Tokyo: Daiwa-shobō.

Ōtani Eichi (2020), 'Sōron: Taishō shūkyō-shi no shatei', in Nishimura Akira, Ōtani Eichi, Sueki Fumihiko and Shimazono Susumu (eds), *Kindai Nihon shūkyō-shi 3: Kyōyō to seimei*, 3–38, Tokyo: Shunjūsha.

Owen, Alex (2004), *The Place of Enchantment: British Occultism and the Culture of the Modern*, Chicago: University of Chicago Press.

Ozawa-de Silva, Chikako (2006), *Psychotherapy and Religion in Japan: The Japanese Introspection Practice of Naikan*, London: Routledge.

Patrick, Jeremy (2020), *Faith or Fraud: Fortune-Telling, Spirituality, and the Law*, Vancouver: UBC Press.

Primiano, Leonard Norman (1995), 'Vernacular Religion and the Search for Method in Religious Folklife', *Western Folklore* 54 (1): 37–56. doi: 10.2307/1499910.

Prohl, Inken (2000), *Die 'Spirituellen Intellektuellen' und das New Age in Japan*, Hamburg: Gesellschaft für Natur- und Völkerkunde Ostasiens eV.

Prohl, Inken (2007), 'The Spiritual World: Aspects of New Age in Japan', in Daren Kemp and James R. Lewis (eds), *Handbook of New Age*, 359–74, Leiden: Brill.

Quinlan, Michael (2012), 'The "Pre-Invention" of Precarious Employment: The Changing World of Work in Context', *Economic and Labour Relations Review* 23 (4): 3–24. doi: 10.1177/103530461202300402.

Raku-hapi (2019), *Datsu supirichuaru: Ese supirichuaru ni damasarenai!* https://ameblo.jp/raku-hapi/ (accessed 14 Feburary 2022).

Reader, Ian (2012), 'Secularisation, R.I.P.? Nonsense! The "Rush Hour Away from the Gods" and the Decline of Religion in Contemporary Japan', *Journal of Religion in Japan* 1 (1): 7–36. doi: 10.1163/221183412X628370.

Redden, Guy (2005), 'The New Age: Towards a Market Model', *Journal of Contemporary Religion* 20 (2): 231–46. doi: 10.1080/13537900500067851.

Ritzer, George, and Nathan Jurgenson (2010), 'Production, Consumption, Prosumption: The Nature of Capitalism in the Age of the Digital "Prosumer"', *Journal of Consumer Culture* 10 (1): 13–36. doi: 10.1177/1469540509354673.

Roemer, Michael (2009), 'Religious Affiliation in Contemporary Japan: Untangling the Enigma', *Review of Religious Research* 50 (3): 298–320.

Roof, Wade Clark (1999), *Spiritual Marketplace: Baby Boomers and the Remaking of American Religion*, Princeton, NJ: Princeton University Press.

Roof, Wade Clark (2003), 'Religion and Spirituality: Toward an Integrated Analysis', in Michele Dillon (ed.) *Handbook of the Sociology of Religion*, 137–48, Cambridge University Press.

Rots, Aike P. (2017a), *Shinto, Nature and Ideology in Contemporary Japan: Making Sacred Forests*, London: Bloomsbury Academic.

Rots, Aike P. (2017b), 'Public Shrine Forests? Shinto, Immanence, and Discursive Secularization', *Japan Review* 30: 179–205. doi: 10.15055/00006738.

Rots, Aike P. (2019), 'The Elusive Adjective: Overcoming Methodological Nationalism in Japanese Studies', *Essay Written for the Toshiba International Foundation 30th Anniversary Essay Contest.* https://www.eajs.eu/index.php?id=786 (accessed 18 November 2021).

Sakamoto, Kazue (1999), 'Reading Japanese Women's Magazines: The Construction of New Identities in the 1970s and 1980s', *Media Culture Society* 21: 173–93. doi: 10.1177/016344399021002003.

Sakanaka Masayoshi (2015), 'Nihon ni okeru pāson sentādo apurōchi no hatten: Bunken-shi o chūshin ni', *Academia, Humanities and Natural Sciences: The Journal of the Nanzan Academic Society* (9): 167–76.

Sakurai Yoshihide (2004), 'Kyōdan hatten no senryaku to "karuto" mondai', in Itō Masayuki, Kashio Naoki and Yumiyama Tatsuya (eds), *Supirichuariti no shakaigaku: Gendai sekai no shūkyōsei no tankyū*, 205–24, Tokyo: Sekaishisōsha.

Sakurai Yoshihide (2009a), *Rei to kane: Supirichuaru bijinesu no kōzō*, Tokyo: Shinchōshinsho.

Sakurai Yoshihide (ed.) (2009b), *Karuto to supirichuariti: Gendai Nihon ni okeru 'sukui' to 'iyashi' no yukue*. Tokyo: Minerva-shobō.

Sasaki Kōkan (1995), *Shūkyō jinruigaku*. Tokyo: Kōdansha.

Satō Hatsume (1997), *Omusubi no inori*, Tokyo: PHP Kenkyūsho.

Satō Takehiro (1999), 'Okinawa shāmanizumu to seishinsekai no kōsaku: Yuta to serapisuto no deai kara', *Journal of the Folklore Society of Okinawa* 19: 53–74.

Sawada, Janine Anderson (2004), *Practical Pursuits: Religion, Politics, and Personal Cultivation in Nineteenth-Century Japan*, Honolulu: University of Hawai'i Press.

School Pupils Section, Elementary and Secondary Education Bureau, MEXT (2007), 'Shiryō 6: "Sukūru kaunserā" ni tsuite', *Ministry of Education, Culture, Sports, Science and Technology.* https://www.mext.go.jp/b_menu/shingi/chousa/shotou/066/shiryo/attach/1369883.htm (accessed 18 November 2012).

Schrimpf, Monika (2018), 'Medical Discourses and Practices in Contemporary Japanese Religions', in Dorothea Lüddeckens and Monika Schrimpf (eds), *Medicine – Religion – Spirituality: Global Perspectives on Traditional, Complementary, and Alternative Healing*, 57–89, Bielefeld: Verlag.

Sheldrake, Philip (2012), *Spirituality: A Very Short Introduction*, Oxford: Oxford University Press.

Shimazono Susumu (1989), 'Shūkyō no sōzō: shohyō to shōkai', *Shūkyō kenkyū (Journal of Religious Studies)* 63 (2): 305–9.

Shimazono Susumu (1991), 'Yakusha atogaki', in R. N. Berā hoka (Robert N. Bellah, Richard Madsen, William M. Sullivan, Ann Swidler and Steven M. Tipton) (eds), *Kokoro no shūkan: Amerika kojinshugi no yukue*, 395–401, Tokyo: Misuzu-shobō.

Shimazono Susumu (1992), *Shinshinshūkyō to shūkyō būmu*, Tokyo: Iwanami bukkuretto.

Shimazono Susumu (1993), 'New Age and New Spiritual Movements: The Role of Spiritual Intellectuals', *Syzygy: Journal of Alternative Religion and Culture* 2 (1–2): 9–22.

Shimazono Susumu (1995), 'Minshū shūkyō ka, shin-shūkyō ka: Futatsu no tachiba no tōgō ni mukete', in 'Edo no shisō' henshūiinkai (ed.), *Edo no shisō* 1, 158–69, Tokyo: Perikan-sha.

Shimazono Susumu (1996), *Seishin sekai no yukue: Gendai sekai to shinreisei undō*, Tokyo: Tōkyōdō-shuppan.

Shimazono Susumu (1997), *Gendai shūkyō no kanōsei: Oumu Shinrikyō to bōryoku*, Tokyo: Iwanami-shoten.

Shimazono Susumu (1998), 'The Commercialization of the Sacred: The Structural Evolution of Religious Communities in Japan', *Social Science Japan Journal* 1 (2): 181–98. doi: 10.1093/ssjj/1.2.181.

Shimazono Susumu (1999), ' "New Age Movement" or "New Spirituality Movements and Culture" ', *Social Compass* 46 (2): 121–33. doi: 10.1177/003776899046002002.

Shimazono Susumu (2000), 'Gendai shūkyō to kōkyō kūkan: Nihon no jōkyō o chūshin ni', *Japanese Sociological Review* 50 (4): 541–55.

Shimazono Susumu (2002), 'Serapī bunka no yukue', in Tanabe Shintarō and Shimazono Susumu (eds), *Tsunagari no naka no iyashi - Serapī bunka no tenkai*, 1–33, Tokyo: Senshū University Press.

Shimazono Susumu (2004), *From Salvation to Spirituality: Popular Religious Movements in Modern Japan*, Melbourne: Trans Pacific Press.

Shimazono Susumu (2007), *Supirichuariti no kōryū*, Tokyo: Iwanami.

Shimazono Susumu (2009), ' "Nyūeiji" kara "supirichuariti" e', *Star People* 29: 14–16.

Shimazono Susumu (2012), *Gendai shūkyō to supirichuariti*, Tokyo: Kōbundō.

Shimazono Susumu (2014), ' "Shinka" to chōetsu-kai no jiritsusei: Robāto Berā no shūkyō-ron no tōtatsuten', in Robert N. Bellah, Shimazono Susumu and Okumura

Takashi (eds), *Shūkyō to gurōbaru shiminshakai: Robāto Berā to no taiwa*, 214–26, Tokyo: Iwanami-shoten.

Shimazono Susumu (2019), 'Minshū shūkyō hassei-ron no genzai', in Shimazono Susumu, Yasumaru Yoshio and Isomae Jun'ichi (eds), *Minshū shūkyōron: Shūkyōteki shutaika to wa nani ka*, 367–81, Tokyo: University of Tokyo Press.

Shimazono Susumu (2020), *Shin-shūkyō o tou*, Tokyo: Chikuma-shinsho.

Shimazono Susumu and Tim Graf (2012), 'The Rise of the New Spirituality', in Inken Prohl and John Nelson (eds), *Handbook of Contemporary Japanese Religions*, 459–85, Leiden: Brill.

Shiotsuki Ryōko (2012), *Okinawa shāmanizumu no kindai*, Tokyo: Shinwasha.

Shiozawa Minobu (1985), *Ureba bunka shitagaite kuru*, Tokyo: Nihon Keizai hyōron-sha.

Shiozawa Minobu (1998), *Shuppansha wo yomu*, Tokyo: Shinpū-sha.

Shiozawa Minobu (2003), *Shuppansha Daizen*, Tokyo: Sōgensha.

Shogimen, Takashi (2020), 'Rethinking Heresy as a Category of Analysis', *Journal of the American Academy of Religion* 88 (3): 726–48. doi: 10.1093/jaarel/lfaa039.

Smiles, Samuel ([1859] 1876), *Self-Help; with Illustrations of Conduct and Perseverance*, London: John Murray.

Smith, Jonathan Z. (1990), *Drudgery Divine: On the Comparison of Early Christianities and the Religions of Late Antiquity*, Chicago: University of Chicago Press.

Spanos, Nicholas P. (1996), *Multiple Identities and False Memories: A Socio-Cognitive Perspective*, Washington: American Psychological Association.

Standing, Guy (2011), *The Precariat: The New Dangerous Class*, London: Bloomsbury Academic.

Stein, Justin (2023), *Alternate Currents: Reiki's Circulation in the Twentieth-Century North Pacific*, Honolulu: University of Hawaii Press.

Steinberg, Marc (2019), 'Delivering Media: The Convenience Store as Media Mix Hub', in Daniel Herbert and Derek Johnson (eds), *Point of Sale: Analyzing Media Retail*, 239–55, Brunswick, New Jersey: Rutgers University Press.

Sugimoto, Yoshio (2003), *An Introduction to Japanese Society*, 2nd edn, Cambridge: Cambridge University Press.

Sugimoto, Yoshio (2021), *An Introduction to Japanese Society*, 5th edn, Cambridge: Cambridge University Press.

Sugitani Masayo (1989), 'Nihon ni okeru kaunseringu undō: Sono rekishiteki henyō o saguru', *Journal of Suzuka Junior College* (9): 73–82.

Sullivan, Winnifred Fallers ([2005] 2018), *The Impossibility of Religious Freedom*, 2nd edn, Princeton: Princeton University Press.

Suzuki, Daisetz (1972), *Japanese Spirituality*, trans. Norman Waddell, Tokyo: Japan Society for the Promotion of Science.

Swyngedouw, Jan (1976), 'Secularization in a Japanese context', *Japanese Journal of Religious Studies* 3 (4): 283–306. doi: 10.18874/jjrs.3.4.1976.283-306.

Swyngedouw, Jan (1993), 'Religion in contemporary Japanese society', in Mark Mullins, Shimazono Susumu and Paul L. Swanson (eds), *Religion and Society in Modern Japan: Selected Readings*, 49–72, Nayoga: Nanzan University Press.

Taira, Teemu (2009), 'The Problem of Capitalism in the Scholarship on Contemporary Spirituality', *Scripta Instituti Donneriani Aboensis* 21: 230–44. doi:10.30674/scripta.67353.

Takehisa Yuriko (2018), '"Datsu supi" dōshitemo kyōso ga hoshii kata e no teian', *Parupunte*. https://takehisayuriko.tokyo/2018/02/06/1093/ (accessed 14 February 2022).

Takeuchi Yō (2005), *Risshin shusse-shugi: Kindai Nihon no roman to yokubō*, enlarged and revised edition, Tokyo: Sekaishisōsha.

Takizawa Taihei (2017), 'Datsu supirichuaru', *Tenka Taihei*. http://tenkataihei.xxxblog.jp/archives/51955906.html (accessed 4 August 2019).

Tanabe Shintarō (1989), *Yamai to shakai: Hīringu no tankyū*, Tokyo: Kōbundō.

Tanabe Shintarō, Shimazono Susumu and Yumiyama Tatsuya (eds) (1999), *Iyashi o ikita hitobito: Kindaichi no orutanatibu*, Tokyo: Senshū University Press.

Tanabe Shintarō and Shimazono Susumu (eds) (2002), *Tsunagari no naka no iyashi: Serapī bunka no tenkai*, Tokyo: Senshū University Press.

Tanaka Masakazu (2021), 'Shūkyō kenkyū to Nihon no shūkyō jinruigaku', in Nagatani Chiyoko, Bessho Yūsuke, Kawaguchi Yukihiro and Fujimoto Toko (eds), *Shūkyōsei no jinruigaku*, 33–56, Kyoto: Hōzōkan.

Tanojiri Tetsurō (2019), 'Katsugen undō no rekishi: Noguchi seitai no shiteki henyō', in Kurita Hidehiko, Tsukada Hotaka and Yoshinaga Shin'ichi (eds), *Kingendai Nihon no minkan seishin ryōhō: Fukashina/okaruto enerugii no shosō*, 191–213, Tokyo: Kokushokankōkai.

Taussig, Michael (1992), *The Nervous System*, London: Routledge.

Taves, Ann, and Michael Kinsella (2013), 'Hiding in Plain Sight: The Organizational Forms of "Unorganized Religion"', in Steven J. Sutcliffe and Ingvild Saelind Gilhus (eds) *New Age Spirituality: Rethinking Religion*, 84–98, Sheffield: Equinox.

Terada Yoshirō (2015), "Jisshō-teki shūkyō shakaigaku no kanten kara', *Shūkyō to shakai (Religion and Society)* 21: 121–33.

Thomas, Jolyon B. (2019), *Faking Liberties: Religious Freedom in American-Occupied Japan*, Chicago: University of Chicago Press.

Thompson, John B. (2012), *Merchants of Culture: The Publishing Business in the Twenty-First Century*, 2nd edn, Cambridge: Polity.

Toffler, Alvin ([1980] 2022), *The Third Wave*, New York: Random House.

Tomotomoheaven (2019), 'Datsu supirichuaru joshi! Hontō ni kaiun suru teppan no hōhō wa?' *Dorinku katate ni chotto hitoiki*. https://dricho.com/20181223/ (accessed 4 August 2019).

Tovey, Philip, Gary Easthope and John Adams (eds) (2004), *The Mainstreaming of Complementary and Alternative Medicine: Studies in Social Context*, London: Routledge.

Tsukada Hotaka (2015), 'Hōkoku 1. *Shūkyō to Shakai* zen 19 gō no gairyaku', *Shūkyō to shakai (Religion and Society)* 21: 122–5.
Tsukada Hotaka (2018), 'Shūkyō ga seiji ni kakawaru to iu koto', in Nishimura Akira (ed.), *Ima shūkyō ni mukiau vol. 2: Kakusareru shūkyō, arawareru shūkyō*, 2, 31–48, Tokyo: Iwanami-shoten.
Tsukada Hotaka (2021), 'Naha Kōshi-byō seikyō bunri soshō: Saikō iken hanketsu no imi', *Sekai* 944: 10–14.
Tsushima Michihito (1999), 'Shūkyō to kagaku no hasamade: Gendai Nihon no "shinreikenkyū" undo', in Shūkyōshakaigaku no kai (ed.), *Kamigami yadorishi machi: Sezoku toshi no shūkyōshakaigaku*, 225–53, Osaka: Sōgensha.
Turner, Bryan S. (2004), 'Foreword: The End(s) of Scientific Medicine', in Philip Tovey, Gary Easthope and John Adams (eds), *The Mainstreaming of Complementary and Alternative Medicine: Studies in Social Context*, xiii–xx, London: Routledge.
Tweed, Thomas A. (2002), 'On Moving Across: Translocative Religion and the Interpreter's Position', *Journal of the American Academy of Religion* 70 (2): 253–77. doi: 10.1093/jaar/70.2.253.
Umemura, Maki (2011), *The Japanese Pharmaceutical Industry: Its Evolution and Current Challenges*, Abingdon: Routledge.
Uozumi Akira (2021), *Shuppansha to kenryoku: Kōdansha to Noma-ke no 100 nen*, Tokyo: Kōdansha.
Uritani Yūkō (1983), *Shinsō jiko no hakken*, Tokyo: Tama Shuppan.
Uritani Yūkō (1990), *Mushi no ai yo towa ni*, Tokyo: Tama Shuppan.
Urushibara Naoyuki (2012), *Bijinesu-sho o yondemo dekiru hito ni wa narenai*, Tokyo: Mainabi shinsho.
Ushiyama, Rin (2019), 'Discursive Opportunities and the Transnational Diffusion of Ideas: "Brainwashing" and "Mind Control" in Japan after the Aum Affair', *British Journal of Sociology* 70 (5): 1730–53. doi: 10.1111/1468-4446.12705.
Vaca, Daniel (2019), *Evangelicals Incorporated: Books and the Business of Religion in America*, Cambridge, Mass: Harvard University Press.
Van der Veer, Peter (2014), *The Modern Spirit of Asia: The Spiritual and the Secular in China and India*, Princeton: Princeton University Press.
Van Hove, Hildegard (1999), 'L'Émergence d'un Marché Spirituel', *Social Compass* 46 (2): 161–72. doi: 10.1177/003776899046002005.
Voas, David (2008), 'The Rise and Fall of Fuzzy Fidelity in Europe', *European Sociological Review* 25 (2): 155–68. doi: 10.1093/esr/jcn044.
Von Stuckrad, Kocku (2015), *The Scientification of Religion: An Historical Study of Discursive Change 1800–2000*, Berlin: De Gruyter.
Wada Shigemasa (1982), *Haha no jidai*, Tokyo: Jiyūsha.
Wakao Masaki (2015), 'Josho: Shobutsu, media to shakai', in Shimazono Susumu, Takano Toshihiko, Hayashi Makoto and Wakao Masaki (eds), *Shobutsu, media to shakai (Nihonjin to shūkyō): Kinsei kara Kindai e*, 5, 3–32, Tokyo: Shunjūsha.
Watanabe Mieko (2002), *Kaunseringu shinrigaku*, Tokyo: Nakanishiya.

Watanabe-Muraoka, Agnes Mieko (2007), 'A Perspective on Counseling Psychology in Japan: Toward a Lifespan Approach', *Applied Psychology: An International Review* 56 (1): 97–106. doi: 10.1111/j.1464-0597.2007.00278.x.

Weber, Max (1958), *From Max Weber: Essays in Sociology*, trans. and ed. by Hans Heinrich Gerth and C. Wright Mills, Oxford: Oxford University Press.

Weeks, Kathi (2011), *The Problem with Work: Feminism, Marxism, Anti-Work Politics and Post-Work Imaginaries*, Durham, NC: Duke University Press.

Weiss, Brian L. (1988), *Many Lives, Many Masters: The True Story of a Prominent Psychiatrist, His Young Patient, and the Past-Life Therapy That Changed Both Their Lives*, New York: Fireside.

Wilding, Mark (2021), 'Inside the Spirituality 'Cult' Whose Members Allege Sexual and Financial Exploitation', *Vice*, 24 May. https://www.vice.com/en/article/k78ay3/inside-the-bizarre-cult-whose-members-allege-sexual-and-financial-exploitation (accessed 18 November 2021).

Wood, Matthew (2007), *Possession, Power and the New Age: Ambiguities of Authority in Neoliberal Societies*, Aldershot: Ashgate.

Woodhead, Linda (2007), 'Gender Differences in Religious Practice and Significance', in James Beckford and N. J. Demerath III (eds), *The Sage Handbook of the Sociology of Religion*, 550–70, London: Sage. doi: 10.4135/9781848607965.n28.

Woodhead, Linda (2010), 'Real Religion and Fuzzy Spirituality? Taking Sides in the Sociology of Religion', in Stef Aupers and Dick Houtman (eds), *Religions of Modernity: Relocating the Sacred to the Self and the Digital*, 31–48, Leiden: Brill.

Wright, Stuart A. (2014), 'Disengagement and Apostasy in New Religious Movements', in Lewis R. Rambo and Charles E. Farhadian (eds) *The Oxford Handbook of Religious Conversion*, 706–35, Oxford: Oxford University Press.

Wu, Yu-Chuan (2018), 'Techniques for Nothingness: Debate Over the Comparability of Hypnosis and Zen in Early Twentieth-Century Japan', *History of Science* 56 (4): 470–96. doi: 10.1177/0073275317743120.

Wuthnow, Robert (1989), *Meaning and Moral Order: Explorations in Cultural Analysis*, Berkeley: University of California Press.

Wuthnow, Robert (2015), *Inventing American Religion: Polls, Surveys, and the Tenuous Quest for a Nation's Faith*, Oxford: Oxford University Press.

Yagi, Darryl Takizo (2008), 'Current Developments in School Counseling in Japan', *Asian Journal of Counseling* 15 (2): 141–55.

Yamaguchi Hiroshi (2003), 'Shūkyō toraburu ni torikomu: kihonteki shiten', *Consumer Law News*, September Special Issue: 50–7.

Yamakawa Akiko (2018), *Jibun ni mezameru supirichuaru tabi e*, Tokyo: PHP Kenkyūshō.

Yamakawa Kōya (2009), *Rinne tenshō o shinjiru to jinsei ga kawaru*, Tokyo: Kadokawa.

Yamakawa Kōya and Yamakawa Akiko (2018), *Kamisama ni aisareru saikō no ikikata!* Tokyo: Koyokan.

Yamakawa Kōya, Yamakawa Akiko and Kokusai Un (2015), *Yamakawa-san, Kokusai-san, imasaranagara supirichuaru-tte nandesuka?* Tokyo: Nihonbungeisha.

Yamanaka Hiroshi (2020), 'Joron: Gendai shūkyō to supirichuaru māketto', in Yamanaka Hiroshi (ed.), *Gendai shūkyō to supirichuaru māketto*, 1–23, Tokyo: Kōbundō.

Yasumaru Yoshio (1974), *Nihon no kindaika to mishū shisō*, Tokyo: Aoki Shoten.

Yates, Lindsey B. (2016), 'Emile Coué and His Method (I): The Chemist of Thought and Human Action', *Australian Journal of Clinical Hypnotherapy and Hypnosis* 38 (1): 3–27.

York, Michael (2001), 'New Age Commodification and Appropriation of Spirituality', *Journal of Contemporary Religion* 16: 361–72. doi: 10.1080/13537900120077177.

York, Michael (2009), *The A to Z of New Age Movements*, Plymouth: Scarecrow Press.

Yoshiharu Motoo, Yukawa Keiko, Arai Ichiro, Hisamura Kazuho and Tsutani Kiichiro (2019), 'Use of Complementary and Alternative Medicine in Japan: A Cross-sectional Internet Survey Using the Japanese Version of the International Complementary and Alternative Medicine Questionnaire', *Japan Medical Association Journal* 2 (1): 35–46. doi: 10.31662/jmaj.2018-0044.

Yoshinaga Shin'ichi (1998), 'Zentai tōgi no gaiyō (Wākushoppu (1) "Seishin sekai" no kōzō (1): Gendai shakai to gendaijin no ishiki o rikai suru tegakari toshite)', *Shūkyō to shakai (Religion and Society)* 3 (Suppl.): 35–42.

Yoshinaga Shin'ichi (2010), 'Kindai Nihon ni okeru shinchigaku shisō no rekishi', *Shūkyō kenkyū (Journal of Religious Studies)* 84 (2): 579–601.

Yoshinaga Shin'ichi (2014), 'Suzuki Daisetsu and Swedenborg: A Historical Background', in Hayashi Makoto, Ōtani Eiichi and Paul L. Swanson (eds), *Modern Buddhism in Japan*, 112–43, Nagoya: Nanzan Institute for Religion and Culture.

Yoshinaga Shin'ichi (2021), 'Spiritualism and Occultism', in Erica Baffelli, Andrea Castiglioni and Fabio Rambelli (eds), *The Bloomsbury Handbook of Japanese Religions*, 229–39, London: Bloomsbury.

Yumiyama Tatsuya (1994), 'Purorōgu: Shūkyō fukkō no Kizashi', in Haga Manabu and Yumiyama Tatsuya, *Inoru, fureau, kanjiru: Jibun sagashi no odessē*, 13–34, Tokyo: Inter Press Corporation.

Yumiyama Tatsuya (2000), 'Nyū eiji to kyūsai shūkyō to no aida', *Shūkyō to shakai (Religion and Society)* 6: 156–60.

Yumiyama Tatsuya (2002), 'Subete ni inochi ga', in Kashio Naoki (ed.), *Supirichuariti wo ikiru*, 137–50, Tokyo: Serika-shobō

Yumiyama Tatsuya (2004), 'Kachisōtaishugi e no taiō: Aum Shinrikyō to nyūeiji undo', in Itō Masayuki, Kashio Naoki and Yumiyama Tatsuya (eds), *Supirichuariti no shakaigaku: Gendai sekai no shūkyōsei no tankyū*, 249–68, Tokyo: Sekaishisōsha.

Yumiyama Tatsuya (2015), 'Jiyūtōron no kiroku to shōkatsu', *Shūkyō to shakai (Religion and Society)* 21: 146–48.

Yuzawa, Fumio and Akiro Amano (2019), *Information Media Trends in Japan 2019*, Tokyo: Dentsū Media Innovation Lab.

Zinnbauer, Brian J., Kenneth I. Pargament, Brenda Cole, Mark S. Rye, Eric M. Butter, Timothy G. Belavich, Kathleen M. Hipp, Allie B. Scott and Jill L. Kadar (1997), 'Religion and Spirituality: Unfuzzying the Fuzzy', *Journal for the Scientific Study of Religion* 36 (4): 549–64. doi: 10.2307/1387689.

Zuboff, Shoshana (2019), *The Age of Surveillance Capitalism: The Fight for a Human Future at the New Frontier of Power*, New York: Public Affairs.

Index

agency 14, 53
Alcoholics Anonymous 4, 8, 50, 54, 67
alternativity 12–14, 20–1, 96, 181–9
American
   influence 41–2, 46, 81, 96, 109, 116, 127
   religion / spirituality 5, 28, 47, 49, 60–3, 69, 76, 133–6, 177
answer-seeking 37, 41, 50, 90, 92, 103, 139
anxiety 108, 117, 120, 174
   definitional 70, 169, 175
Araki Michio 57–8
attention, *see also* self-attention
   crisis 128, 130
   regime 185
Aum affair 7, 48, 135, 172, *see also* post-Aum
   and religious studies 10, 18, 44–6, 52–6, 65, 70, 157, 182
aura 6, 47
   photography 1
   reading 27, 108, 139, 141
   reiki 110
   soma 149
authentic
   consumer 178
   essence 10
   religiosity 53, 76, 156, 179
   self 135
   spirituality 25–6, 74, 159–63
authenticity 140, 178
authority
   anti- 27, 60
   religious 5, 42, 112
   scientific 153
   self- 160
   sources of 31–2, 69, 78, 102, 129, 162

Bellah, Robert 60–3, 65, 69
Bender, Courtney 7, 25–6, 153
biography 19, 25–6, 75, 83–4, 90–2, 97, 99, 102
book trade 84–5

Buddhism 15, 62, 71, 81, 172, *see also* Zen
   and hypnosis 127–8
   and publishing 75–6, 87
   and spirituality 55, 60, 62–3

capitalism, *see also under* consumer; spirituality
   bad 163–4
   gendering of 152–3
   late 69, 104, 134–5, 185
   rise 61
   spirit 153
capitalist
   culture 104–5, 185
   ethics 19, 153, 157, 163–4, 178, 179–80
   frame 158
   market 78, 135
   system 12, 20
certification 33, 38, 39, 107, 138, 162, 168
   cost 110, 137
channelling 35, 40, 42, 99, 119–20, 149
   American import 116
   seminar 167, 170
choice 96, 115, 134, 163–4, 178, 186
Christianity 15, 62, 76, 81, 98–9, 178, *see also* Protestant
   post- 24
commodification 47–9, 133–6, 155–8, 160–1, 164, 170
complementary and alternative medicine (CAM) 28, 36–8, 112, 117–18
constructionism 17, 19, 53–4
consumer
   capitalism 152, 158, 180
   choice 115, 134, 164, 177–9
   complaints 166, 174–6, 178
   culture 104, 156
   fraud 155, 161, 175, 181, 185
   market 131, 137, 139
   needs 117
   spiritual 136, 138, 157, 160–1, 177, 186

Consumer Contract Act 167, 175–7, 186
consumer protection 133, 154, 164, 166
   law 20, 155, 171, 179, *see also* Consumer Contract Act
consumerism 15, 74, 128, 160–4
   altruistic 153
   medical 111–12
consumption
   ethical 163, 188
   religion and 156, 160, 164
   strategy 135
counselling 22–5, 38–43
   business 22, 34–5, 108, 143–4, 155
   cosmetics 129, 144
   Ehara model 10–11, 23, 24, 38
   popularity 17, 39, 43, 69, 116, 119, 132, 187
   Rogerian 17–18, 40–2, 183
   spirituality of 38–42
counter-cultural
   legacy 104–5
   movements 58
   narratives 185
   new religions as 53, 59
   spirituality as 25, 32–3, 51, 73, 88–9, 187
Covid-19 165–6
cruel optimism 133, 144
crystal healing 108, 110, 121–2, 129
cult 161
   issue 28, 55–6, 67, 70, 135

depression 19, 103, 106, 115–18, 137, 139
   epidemic 118, 185
didactic literature 19, 37, 74, 87, 92
disenchantment 135, 153
ditching
   religion 90, 183
   the spiritual 20, 155, 158–66, 183
divination 1, 82, 146–7

economic
   crisis (2008) 137, 140, 143
   downturn (1990s) 11, 86, 114, 117, 132, 147, 158–9
Ehara boom 18, 24, 34, 43
Ehara Hiroyuki 2, 148
   phenomenon 8–9
   popularity 22–3, 74–5
   publications 8, 18–19, 82

   spiritual counselling 10–11, 23, 24, 26, 38–9
emotion 107, 122, 129, 140, 163, 173, *see also* anxiety; happiness; hope; stress
   feminine 152, 185
   religious 76
empowerment 96, 99, 104, 144, 146–7
energy work 30, 33, 108, 119, 122, 164–5
essentialism 15–16, 54–71, 80, 96, 179, 181–2
evolutionism 45, 49–50, 60, 63–70

failure 122, 137–9, 142, 149, 153–4, 163, 179–80
   of therapies 42, 102
fairness 162, 164, 174, 177, 179–80, 185
femininity 20, 145–9, 152–3
folk religion 57–8, 60, 65, 66, 68, *see also* popular religion
fortune-telling 6, 110, 136, 138, 149
   court cases 171, 173–4, 177–8
   market 6
   publications 82, 146, 148
fraud 155, 157–8, 161, 163, 166, 185
   court cases 167–79
freedom 42, 58, 132, 148, 163, 153–4, 180
   of choice 178
   concept 128
   expression 19, 130
   of religion 65, 161, 168–9, 170
Fujiwara Satoko 7, 53, 60

Geller, Uri 4, 46
gender
   assumptions 20, 117, 147–50, 152, 185
   discrimination 20, 147–8, 149, 150–1
   and economy 144–8, 185
   regime 185
   roles 144–8, 150, 152
   and spirituality 20, 142–4, 148–54
globalization 70, 104, 127, 134, 184
good
   consumption 163
   religion 54, 156–7, 161, 172
   spirituality 20, 157, 179

Hacking, Ian 11, 127, 184
happiness 80, 96, 121, 159, 164, 186
Hardacre, Helen 7, 146–7

Index

Hashisako Mizuho 146–7, 152, 157
healing, *see iyashi*
healthism 19, 107, 111–15
Heisei era (1989–2019) 11, 146, 159
heresy 161–3, 169
hope 133, 166, 176–7, 185–6, 189
  loss 47
  messages 19, 75, 104, 123, 184
  for renewal 50, 55, 59–60, 62–5, 182–3
Horie Norichika 7, 9, 10, 38, 45, 63–5, 156–7
human potential movement 95, 99
hypnotherapy 106, 107–111, 115, 120, 123–30, 138, 185
  Ericksonian 108–9, 124
  history in Japan 113, 127–8

identity 27, 89, 134–5, 160
  professional 47, 148
  religious 4–6, 27, 68
individualism 15, 25, 57, 61, 68, 96, 133, 159
inochi 88–9
integrity 20, 164, 170, 177, 179
iyashi 10, 29, 63, 84
  boom 112–15, 117, 132
  labour 145
  market 23
  marketing 114, 118, 185

Japan
  making 60–6, 70
  vs West 7, 15–16, 57, 60–2, 69–70
Jiyūsha 73–4, 88–9, 97–8, 100–1, 103, 183

Kadokawa-shoten 83–4, 103
Kashio Naoki 3, 47, 48–50, 54, 67, 73
Kitanaka Junko 114, 116–17, 120, 122, 129, 179
Koch, Gabriele 144–5
Kōdansha 78–80, 81, 97
Krasner, A. M. 109, 126

lawyers 20, 155, 166, 169–71, 176, 179, 185–6
  national network 172
liberation 61, 111, 137, 145, 152, *see also* freedom

lifestyle 129, 150, 159
  alternative 144, 187
  American 116
  healthy 113, 114, 117
  spiritual 46, 54, 110, 133
looping effect 11, 21, 117, 147, 184–6
loser 12, 162–3, 179–80

MacLaine, Shirley 97, 100
  books 83, 93, 154
  Out on a Limb 73, 88, 89, 92, 97–101, 183
macrobiotics 66, 69, 132, 141
massage 1, 35, 36–7, 38, 108
  shiatsu 29, 30, 32
Masuda Masao 88–9, 92, 100
Matsui Takeshi 113–15
Matsushita Kōnosuke 80, 83, 91
mediatized religiosity 9–10, 48–9, 63–4, 70, 156, 159
medicalization, *see* socialising medicalisation
medicine, *see also* complementary and alternative medicine
  integrative 36, 38, 112, 125
  legalized practice 30, 33, 183
  scientific 111–13
meditation 34, 47, 67, 78, 91, 158
Meiji 57, 65, 169
mind-body-spirit fairs 1–2, 137–8, 143–4, 157, *see also* SUPICON; SUPIMA
mindfulness 122, 136
minkan ryōhō 17, 24, 28–9
minshū shūkyō 18, 56–60, 64, 70
modernity
  late 112
  losses 71
  narratives 16, 61, 62, 65
  religion and 135, 178, 180
monetization 20, 133, 154, 186
moral
  act 122, 163
  essence 182
  imperatives 3, 8, 14, 185, 189
  judgment 155, 163–4, 165, 166, 177–9, 185, 188
  literature *see* didactic literature
  order 46, 61, 65, 78, 146
  superiority 15
  value 20, 179, 186

morality 188
  book category 81
  personal 78, 128
  popular 61
moralizing causation 184–6, 189
mushūkyō 5, *see also* non-religious

Nagaoka Takashi 59–60
neoliberal
  economy 131, 186
  game 162
  ideals 20, 21, 154, 163–4
neoliberalism 133–6, 163, 180
New Age, *see also* sacralization of self;
    seishin sekai
  bricolage 15, 25, 32
  and capitalism 133–6
  femininity 152
  literature 19, 32, 73–4, 92–4, 97
  Movement 4, 9, 27, 49, 60, 74, 102, 112
  seminars 52, 87, 97
  vs spirituality 46–50, 60, 104–5, 134
  therapies 116, 129
  translators 19, 77, 83, 89, 92–104, 183
new religions
  attacks on 76
  counter-cultural 53, 59
  and gender 146–7
  legal cases 171–2
  and publishing 75–8
  salvific 57–60, 62
  and spirituality 4, 45, 48–9, 50–2, 68,
    70–1, 90–1, 182
  study of 18, 25, 44–5, 56–60, 62, 65, 67
  therapeutic 62
new spirituality 161
  culture 8–10, 28, 49–50, 51, 57, 61–70,
    73–4, 92
  movements 4, 60
  publications 84, 87
  in the West 69
New Thought 77, 78
Nippon Decimal Classification (NDC) 81–2
Noma Seiji 79–80
non-religious 5, 6–7, 15, 24, 66

occult
  boom 4, 95
  category 88, 91, 189
  fans 51
  literature 32, 46, 75, 77, 99
  publishers 85, 87, 90
  suspicion of 75
occultism 146
Ōmoto 56–7, 58, 59

pain 50, 100, 122
  relief 30, 37, 38
PHP Kenkyūsho 78, 80, 83
pop spirituality 10, 63–4
popular religion 13, 18, 56–60, 64–6,
    70–1, 182
popular therapies, see *minkan ryōhō*
precarity 12, 13, 15, 79, 96–7, 123, 186,
    see also under spiritual business
  gendered 142–5, 147–8
privatization 25, 48, 49, 55, 133, 159
post-Aum
  climate 7, 10, 33, 104
  religion 11, 23–4, 28, 42–3
post-war
  America 76
  psychology 39, 41–2
  publishing 77, 80, 85, 90, 113
  religious studies 18, 45, 56–60, 64,
    70–1, 182
  society 7, 59, 65–6, 89, 159
print culture 51, 75–81, 76, 104
Protestant 42, 61, 69, 71, 178
psychic
  powers 174–8
  readings 93
  therapies 77
psychics 4, 8, 90, 173
psychology 10–11, 38–42, 91, 136
  book category 81
  para- 81, 91
  of religion 59, 63
publishing industry 18–19, 43, 74–92, 104,
    183, 188
  healthist boom 113–15
  and religious groups 75–8, 89–90

reiki 30, 108, 139, 141, 149
  aura- 110
  massage 1
  master 33–5
  vital 121, 129

reinō 171, 173
reinōsha 26–7, 32, 35, 68, 166
reisei 4, 10, 51, 68
religion, *see also* New Age; new religions; popular religion; spirituality
 detraditionalization 10, 24–6, 27, 32, 42
 and economy 20, 133–6, 146–7, 156–8, 164, 179
 and gender 146–7
 privatization 25, 48–9, 55, 133
 psychologization 24–6, 38, 43, 91
 scientification 37
 and state 38, 168–9, 177–8
 sui generis 67–9, 134
Rogers, Carl 40–2

sacralization of self 24, 25, 41, 43, 112, 135, 180
Sakurai Yoshihide 11, 67, 135, 170
salvation religion 5, 62, 68, 70
Satō Hatsume 68–9
Second World War, *see* post-war
secularization 4, 7, 38, 63, 65, 169
 discursive 7, 11, 45
 theories 60, 71
seishin sekai
 book category 8, 73–5, 78, 85
 boom 85
 composition 51–2
 gatekeepers 74, 92, 93, 104
 Japanese New Age 5, 9, 28, 47–9
 literature 19, 37, 73–5, 78, 92–104, 183
 market 74, 78, 81–2, 101–2
 publishers 82–5, 87–92, 97–8, 104
 and self-development 78, 82
seitai 31, 36
self-actualization 8, 63
self-attention 107, 111, 115, 121–3, 160, 185–6, 188
 as ability 19, 123–31
 ubiquity 180
self-cultivation 74, 187, *see also shūyō*
self-development, *see also under* seminars
 book market 81–7, 183
 culture 104
 ideals 13, 37, 75
 literature 71, 75, 78, 92, 103, 139
 and spirituality 4, 75, 78, 87, 95, 131, 183, 186–7

self-esteem 97, 106, 159–61, 179
self-help
 groups 48, 50, 70, 178
 literature 74, 78, 80, 81, 86, 152
 movement 71
self-transformation 12, 54, 57, 61, 68, 71, 153
 and consumption 156, 158
 narratives 43, 71, 95, 99
seminars
 cost 123, 160, 165, 167–8, 173, 208 n.41
 and fraud 164–70
 hypnotherapy 126–7
 profit-orientation 155, 158, 160, 161, 162
 self-development 37, 51–2, 54, 66, 95–6, 97, 87, 100
 training 46, 141, 143, 150, 167
service industry 20, 106, 133, 141, 154, 168, 185
 women in 144
shamanistic 28–9, 58, 68, 110
Shimazono Susumu 4–5, 8–9, 46–50, 56–7, 60–6, 70–1, 73, 156
shin-reisei, *see* new spirituality
Shinto 10, 26, 27, 60, 81, 168
 American 62
 State 57, 60
shūyō 19, 75, 78–80, 91, 92, 183
sincerity 13, 20, 170, 175, 177–80
social networking services (SNS) 18, 34, 64, 128, 130, 139
socializing medicalization 115–18, 120–3, 130, 179
Soka Gakkai 75–6, 147
spiritual (*supirichuaru*)
 entrepreneurship 133, 137–142, 152–3, 154, 188
 fans 34, 51, 103, 139, 158
 heretics 162–3, 166, 180
 label 7, 23, 33–6, 74, 87, 88, 107, 170, 187
 market 6, 8, 134–5, *see also* SUPIMA
 narratives 18, 24–6, 139, *see also* Yamakawas
 powers 26, 31, 35, 171, 172–7
 revolution 3
 sales 20, 155, 157, 166–77, 179, 186

seishinteki 198–9
world, *see seishin sekai*
spiritual boom 2, 159, 187
  end 2–3, 14, 34
  peak 8, 82, 103, 107, 110, 111, 148
  proof 1–2, 8–11, 18
  representatives 23, 75, 94, 102, 184
  therapy culture 118–20
spiritual business
  commercialism 159–60, 164, 166, 170
  competition 131, 133, 134, 140, 154
  gendered 142–5, 148, 154
  growth 11, 118–19, 159
  legality 167–70, 175–9
  precarity 20, 132–3, 136–42, 143–4, 149–50, 154, 185
  professional ethics 20, 140, 154, 166, 177, 186, *see also* consumer protection
spiritual but not religious 5, 6, 8, 18, 28, 42, 104,
spiritual therapies 36–8, 106–11, 118–23
  gendering of 148–53
  market for 117, 135, 139, 185
  marketing 28, 137–40, 141, 148–49, 155, 158, 162, 173
  not medicine 24, 30–3, 107
  prices 1–2, 14, 22, 27, 108, 125, 138, 140–1, 174
  sessions 22, 29–30, 121–2, 123–7
  testimonials 118, 120–22, 126, 129, 132, 140
  ubiquity 173–4
spiritual therapists 16
  clients 29–30, 37, 115–16, 129, 143, 148–52
  counter-cultural discourse 27–8, 32–3
  demographics 20, 142–3
  income 24, 33, 108, 130, 131, 136, 139, 141, 143–4
  life stories 14–15, 33–5, 106–7, 110–11, 115, 132, 136–42, 143–44, 150–1, 155, 164–6
  use of 'spiritual' 13, 17, 23–4, 26–8, 31, 33–8, 42–3
spirituality (*supirichuariti*), *see also* new spirituality; *reisei*; *seishin sekai*
  and alternativity 3–8, 12–15, 181–9

  and capitalism 52, 91, 104–5, 133–6, 156–8, 160–4
  corrupt religion 133, 135–6, 156–8
  definitions 6, 7, 10–11, 25, 33, 48–50, 53–5, 67–8, 159, 181–2
  ditchers (*datsu-supi*) 20, 155, 158–66, 179–80, 183, 185
  fad 2, 23, 33, 88, 181
  grounding function 32–3, 35, 43
  literature 37, 74–5, 81, 87, 94
  novelty 2–3, 8–12, 27–8, 46–50, 63–4, 67–9, 135, 182–3
  relation to religion 3–8, 182–4
  as religious essence 10, 46, 49, 54–5, 64–5, 181–2
  rise 3–9, 13, 18, 46–50, 70, 112, 132, 146, 184–7
  safety device 45, 157, 179
  salvific 46, 61–68, 70–1
  studies 2, 10, 18, 44–56, 63–71, 181–2, 186
  superficiality 25, 34–5, 48, 68, 160
stress 116, 121, 129–30, 143, 152
  life of 153, 185
  reduction 120, 122
success 40, 78–80, 86, 91, 155, 186
  business 10, 91, 138–9, 145
  material 134
  and positive thinking 84, 109
  stories 19, 75, 78, 82, 83–4, 89, 92, 183
  therapeutic 121, 125–6, 129, 177
suffering 111, 115, 117, 121–3, 132
suicide 116, 117, 122
SUPICON (spiritual convention) 1–2, 3, 94
SUPIMA (spiritual market) 2, 139
Suzuki, D.T. 94–5, 197 n.2

Tama Shuppan 85, 87, 90–1, 104, 183
Tanabe Shintarō 29–31, 33
Tenrikyō 56, 58, 68
Theosophical movement 4, 76, 77, 99
Therapy All Guide 118–20
therapy culture 8, 11, 24, 107, 111–15, 130, 178
  American 116
  global 111, 122
  shift in 118–20
Tōhoku earthquake and tsunami 2, 62, 67

translation 10, 73, 78, 92–3, 98–9
translators, *see also* Yamakawas
   Hu, Terry 102
   Matsuo Kazuyuki 97–8
   Nakamura Keiu 78
   Shimazono Susumu 61–2
   Suzuki, D. T. 94
   Tomoda Fujio 41

uranai 146, 171, 173, *see also*
   fortune-telling
Uritani Yūkō 85, 90–2, 104

Weber, Max 61, 111, 153
Weiss, Brian 92, 93, 102, 106, 127
world renewal, *see yonaoshi*

Yamakawa Akiko 153–4, 180, *see also*
   Yamakawas

Yamakawa effect 95
Yamakawa Kōya 89, *see also* Yamakawas
Yamakawas 19, 73–5, 92–104, 106,
   132, 183
Yasumaru Yoshio 58, 59, 61, 62
yoga 25, 67, 138
   commercialization 38, 136
   market 6
   and spirituality 91, 136
yonaoshi 58–9, 62, 71
youth 15, 55, 79–80, 89, 135, 183
   culture 7, 47–8, 96
Yumiyama Tatsuya 44, 49–50, 52, 55–6,
   67–9, 182

Zen 94, 88, 128

www.ingramcontent.com/pod-product-compliance
Lightning Source LLC
Chambersburg PA
CBHW062135300426
44115CB00012BA/1926